KILLING CHARLIE

Wensley Clarkson is an investigative journalist and the author of many other true crime books, including *Killer on the Road*, *Bindon*, *Whatever Mother Says*, *Hit 'Em Hard* and *Moody*. He has also written screenplays and television documentaries, and his books have sold more than a million copies in 17 countries worldwide.

Killing Charlie

The Bloody, Bullet-Riddled Hunt for the
Most Powerful Great Train Robber of All

Wensley Clarkson

MAINSTREAM
PUBLISHING
EDINBURGH AND LONDON

To Andalucia . . . the last frontier

This edition, 2006

First published in Great Britain in 2004 by
MAINSTREAM PUBLISHING COMPANY (EDINBURGH) LTD
7 Albany Street
Edinburgh EH1 3UG

ISBN 1 84596 035 1

A catalogue record for this book is available from the British Library

Typeset in Myriad and Van Djick
Printed and bound in Great Britain by
Cox & Wyman Ltd

Contents

Author's Note

It was inevitable I'd upset a few people by writing a book about Charlie Wilson. One of the chaps I came across on the Costa del Crime told me: 'A lot of people are getting chopped up round here these days. You should be careful doing a book on Charlie. Last bloke who tried it gave up after a few days.'

I've had to trust the judgement and recollections of numerous individuals, many of whom would rather not have their names reproduced in this book. Being dependent on the memories of men and women – fallible, contradictory, touched by pride and capable of gross omission – can be a risky business, but there should be no hidden agendas in this story because Charlie is no longer with us.

The pace and contents of this book rely on a long series of interviews, conversations and recollections supplied, at times unwittingly, by dozens of individuals in all four corners of the globe. Naturally, some important names are missing and that will have frustrated those who were involved in Charlie's world, but I'm sure they'll understand my reasons for anonymous quotes to avoid any 'aggravation'.

Ultimately, I have tried to recreate a life story that twists and turns from the blitzed streets of south London to hostile prison corridors, and from the manic, cocaine-fuelled Costa del Sol in southern Spain to the killing fields of Colombia, ending in what some might call an inevitable fate. It was a bizarre, sometimes risky journey which I hope you will enjoy and relish as much as I have.

Wensley Clarkson
2004

Supporting Cast

BUSTER	Robber whose life took a tragic turn
THE COLONEL	Loyal childhood pal-turned-train robber
FRENCHY	Former war hero who saved Charlie's skin
THE GREY FOX	Workaholic detective who never gave up
KING OF CATFORD	Brinks Mat suspect who got too flashy
JIMMY	Master smuggler who needed a big favour
EL DOCTOR	The twentieth century's richest and most notorious drugs baron
THE LUMP	West London hard man out for revenge
THE MEAN MACHINE	Ex-robber and Krays' henchman
THE MEXICAN	Medellín man with Spain at his fingertips
MAD MICKEY	Short-fused south Londoner on a mission to destroy
THE MILKMAN	Kilburn Irishman with a finger in every pie
LA PATRONA	The Colombians' London sexpot
THE PIMPERNEL	The most artful dodger of all
PORKY	Escaped convict with a lot to lose
THE PREACHER	Cold-blooded Amsterdam kingpin
THE PROFESSOR	Graduate Scotsman with Colombian connections
SCARFACE	Shooter with a death wish
THE TIGRESS	ETA's deadliest brunette
THE WEASEL	Pint-sized train robber whose thoughts turned to gold

I come to lead you to the other shore
Into eternal dark, into fire and ice.

Dante, Inferno

GREAT TRAIN ROBBER SHOT DEAD

Front page, London Evening Standard, 24 April 1990

Great Train Robber Charlie Wilson was murdered at his villa in Marbella last night – by a gunman riding a yellow bicycle.

Spanish detectives believe he was killed by a hit man because of his role in a plot to smuggle massive quantities of drugs into Europe.

He was found choking to death by the side of his swimming pool, the body of his pet dog, an Alsatian-husky, at his side. Wilson, 58, had apparently been hit in the windpipe by a single karate blow.

However, a pathologist later found a small entry wound made by a 9mm bullet in his neck. Police would not confirm that he had been shot. One said: 'There was so much blood around his neck, it's impossible to say whether it came from a nosebleed, the dog or a bullet wound.'

Police believe that Wilson, who worked out regularly, may have fought back but was felled by the karate blow to the neck.

The man rode off into the gathering dusk and Wilson's wife, Patricia, 55, called police. He was still alive when they arrived, but died in an ambulance on the way to a Marbella clinic.

Neighbour Marti Franco told this afternoon how Wilson's wife ran to her for help. She said the couple had been watching television at about 6.45 when the doorbell rang. 'Charles answered the door and Pat heard him talking to someone,' she said. 'They walked around the side of the house to the pool.

'Suddenly, she heard the dog barking and became alarmed because the animal was going mad. Then she heard two shots fired in quick succession. Pat ran out and found Charles face down with their pet by his side. The man who had called was nowhere to be seen.

'She came running to me for help, she was heartbroken and shocked. When I went to look at Charles, I could see he was not actually dead. But what surprised me most was that there seemed to be no bullet wounds and Pat had told me she heard a gun.

'There was a big swelling on the right side of his neck. There was also a small slit on his neck, so tiny that it seemed like it was made by a small blade or scalpel. I saw no blood on the dog, either.'

Today, the £500,000 villa, with mock castle turrets, was being searched by police who removed boxes of papers and plastic bags full of Wilson's belongings.

The house, cheekily named Chequers, was clearly built with security in mind. All the windows are permanently barred and a six-foot stone wall surrounds the property.

One policeman said: 'There are many possible reasons why Mr Wilson might have been killed, and the possibility of his being involved in a drug deal must come near the top of our list.'

Marbella is a major centre for drug running. Police believe Wilson may have financed his lifestyle, like many other British criminals here on the Costa del Sol, with lucrative drug-runs from Morocco or South America to Spain.

Wilson was sentenced to 30 years' imprisonment for armed robbery and conspiracy to rob after the £2,500,000 train robbery in 1963.

Like all the other Great Train Robbers, the former south London bookmaker never revealed his true role in the planning of the raid. But underworld legend has dubbed him 'the Treasurer'.

Fellow Great Train Robber Ronnie Biggs, still on the run after escaping from prison in 1965, spoke about Wilson today from his hideaway in Rio de Janeiro. Biggs, 60, said: 'Charlie was full of fun and had a wild sense of humour. He was very easy to get along with. This is a sad, tragic loss.'

It was a murder that shocked the underworld. Even Charlie Wilson's 'old enemy', the police, were appalled by an act of such cold-blooded violence. But then Charlie never did things by halves.

PART 1

FUELLING THE LEGEND: 1932–64

Train up a child in the way he should go,
And when he is old, he will not depart from it.

Proverbs 22:6

1

More than 500 years ago, along the edge of the River Thames between Lambeth, Southwark and Wandsworth, the Bishops of Rochester and Winchester bought properties, which were later leased out by their successors. During Henry VIII's reign, Rochester's cook, Richard Ross, poisoned the soup at a banquet, and became the sole victim of Henry's new penalty for poisoners when he was boiled alive. Meanwhile, Winchester's Thameside territory became notorious for its brothels and carnival atmosphere, which was enhanced by bear-baiting rings, theatres and the first of the South Bank pleasure gardens. All these attractions encouraged the criminals of the day to head into the crowds and steal from the pockets of the rich visitors, before heading back to their homes in the dreadful slum areas close to the river.

Westwards, numerous leatherworks and candle factories centred on the community of Battersea; the obnoxious odour which drifted across the entire area from the workshops resulted in the atrocious slums becoming the worst examples of urban deprivation in the nation. It was from these South Bank ghettos that the great nineteenth-century cholera epidemics sprang.

With the arrival of the railways, Waterloo Station influenced the banks of the Thames to such a degree that it dragged the residential neighbourhood down even further. The riverside became an increasingly dismal district of filthy, run-down, overcrowded properties dominated by violence and deprivation. The area never properly shook off the stench of real poverty until over 100 years later when the combined efforts of Hitler's bombing raids and the economic realities of life in post-war Britain provided fresh hope for the inhabitants of the Thameside slums. The descendants of those disease-ridden ghetto victims were encouraged to turn their backs on the area's cobbled streets and start afresh in the suburbs of south London. However, many families, like the Wilsons, simply couldn't afford to make such a move.

It was into this environment, just seven years before the world was thrust into the second conflict of the twentieth century, that one of the most notorious outlaws in British criminal history arrived in the world. Charles Frederick Wilson was born on 30 June 1932, just at the beginning of the most Depression-hit decade of the last century. Charlie would grow up amongst dire poverty and misery on the streets around his native area with one priority: survival. The names of big-time criminals like Jack Spot and Billy Hill would dominate his childhood, but Charlie's achievements would outstrip them all.

He was born into a hard-working family caught in a poverty trap from which there seemed no escape. As a small boy, his mother Mabel was the strongest influence in shaping his later attitudes towards life. She found herself cursed with a powerlessness caused primarily by the family's poverty. Despite her obvious wisdom, the fate of her children was completely out of her hands. Her husband Bill Wilson's job as a bus driver barely covered the rent and family food bill.

At first, the Wilsons lived in a low-level tenement flat close to the river in Battersea. Charlie's dad worked long hours on the buses, with plenty of overtime, in order to provide his family with the basics. That pressure would lead to clashes between father and son, caused primarily by Charlie's complete and utter aversion to rules and regulations.

Back then, Battersea was many light years away from the comfortable, tree-lined streets of upwardly mobile professionals it became in the '70s and '80s. In the '30s and '40s, it was a collection of drab, cobbled streets lined with tatty red-brick tenement blocks and workmen's cottages, most of which had been built more than 50 years earlier for the servants who worked in the big houses north of the river. The Wilsons eventually scraped together the princely sum of £250 in order to buy their own house, most of the money coming from a building society loan. The house had electricity, but the only hot water came from a smelly gas boiler in the kitchen. An old tin bath was brought out no more than twice a week and everyone in the Wilson family was expected to share the water to save money.

With unemployment and the Depression sweeping the nation, firms were having to lay off their workforces virtually every week. As queues grew increasingly longer outside labour exchanges, clothes became threadbare and food scarce. Across the Atlantic, the Depression hit even harder and sparked bloody riots in many US cities. In Europe, the sound of Nazi jackboots had sparked a flood of Jewish refugees fleeing from Germany.

With money so scarce, it was hardly surprising that most of Charlie's schoolmates were up to no good from a very early age. Charlie soon grew to appreciate the thrill of grabbing a bar of chocolate from the corner shop counter and dashing out of the door. It was a buzz he'd spend the rest of his life addicted to.

Charlie was still a child when the Second World War broke out. Rationing was in place in London, so few luxuries were available, and, with most men away fighting on two fronts, crime soon increased. The blitzed streets of south London were like one big adventure playground for Charlie and gangs of young tearaways. Unexploded bombs, condemned buildings and lumps of shrapnel were all ample evidence of Hitler's bombers. Chirpy young cockney Charlie adored being out and about in the city, getting up to no good, ducking and diving to his heart's content. Boys like Charlie soon learned to identify the types of German aircraft from the noise they made and they'd often count them in and out as they buzzed loudly up through the breaks in the moonlit clouds. Kids were obsessed by stories of Hitler's evil empire, provided by a weekly diet of comic books devoted entirely to images of 'our boys' thrashing the Germans. Charlie particularly enjoyed impersonating dive-bombing Messerschmitts. The once-familiar skyline was replaced by barrage balloons and pyramids of smouldering rubble, and tall, jagged shells of brickwork that had once been factories. Bomb craters filled with rainwater and burnt-out shells of rows of terraced houses were everywhere. Deep, flooded pits that had claimed the lives of innocent London residents pockmarked the streets in and around where Charlie lived.

Back at home, Bill and Mabel found it difficult to keep tabs on their young son and were relieved when Charlie was evacuated to stay with a family on the south coast of England. He lived there, by the seaside, for a year. Childhood friend Bruce Reynolds recalls spending time with Charlie soon after they'd both returned to south London: 'We used to sit in the Anderson shelter at the back of his garden smoking Woodbines and discussing the mysteries of women.'

The Wilsons' terraced house contained three bedrooms and one reception room. Charlie's bedroom – which he shared with his brother – was at the back, so he'd often slip out of the house by climbing down the drainpipe, then hopping over the back fence and running down the badly lit alleyway behind the terrace. By this time, Bill Wilson was working on the 77 bus route, running from Battersea to Charing Cross. He'd come home at night exhausted from a 12-hour day, flop in front of the open fire and eat some tea before falling asleep. There was little communication between father and son.

During those war years, policemen and local youths were regularly involved in clashes and the long arm of the law knew few restraints when it suited them. The police station at Nine Elms, near the old Covent Garden fruit and vegetable market, was increasingly familiar to both Charlie and Bruce. One night, Reynolds was arrested and the local station sergeant sent a car round to his grandmother's to tell her of the arrest. The policeman didn't bother giving her a ride back to the station three miles away, though; instead, she had to walk.

Charlie had his collar felt for the first time by the local constabulary when he was just ten years old. With a face like thunder, his irate father showed up at the local police station to take his young son home. Charlie knew he was in for a beating; that usually meant the belt followed by a lot of yelling, but no actual tears from the proud Charlie. Afterwards, he'd dust himself down and walk away without a word of remorse. Charlie understood that more often than not he deserved to be punished, but what upset him the most was that his father rarely communicated with him and explained why what he had done was wrong. 'The old belt would just come out and I'd get a lashin', but he never said a word,' explained Charlie many years later. Charlie tried his hardest to please his father, but, by the time he was 12, their relationship had further deteriorated: at meal times, they would barely exchange a word.

At school, Charlie was constantly playing pranks in class and being kept in at the end of the day for detention. Yet, despite his frequent absence from class, Charlie thoroughly enjoyed reading books – he was just lazy about writing up essays describing them afterwards. He was known for being a cocky, strong-willed child and took out the frustrations and violence of his home life on other kids by extorting money from them in exchange for protection from the bullies who dominated the classrooms in those days. Charlie wasn't very popular, but few had the courage to stand up to him. One old childhood friend recalls, 'Even then, he had these piercing blue eyes that used to challenge you. They made Charlie seem a bit mad and scary.'

Charlie wasn't unique in his ability to be thoughtless, unreasonable and even illogical. His mind, like all others, was a creative instrument which veered off in certain directions depending on his surroundings. It's certainly true to say, however, that Charlie did often draw different conclusions from many others in a similar situation and make judgements which were not exactly traditional.

Psychologists say an individual's personality reflects a characteristic set of behaviours, attitudes, interests, motives and feelings about the world. It includes the way people relate to others. Extreme forms of abnormal behaviour are supposed to be easy to recognise, but that doesn't mean they can be instantly rectified. Charlie was undoubtedly narcissistic, which was reflected in his over-generosity towards certain people, his need for admiration and his complete lack of empathy towards those outside his own world. He also had a sprinkling of obsessive-compulsive thrown in for good measure: a preoccupation with orderliness, perfectionism and control. Certainly, Charlie was already developing into what one might call a born leader. A number of attributes, including intelligence, confidence, his heavy build and handsome appearance, must have helped.

Charlie's early friends included two young tearaways called Jimmy Hussey and Tommy Wisbey, who both worked every weekend at Covent Garden fruit and vegetable market with Charlie, where they all humped crates around to earn 'a few extra bob'. The three of them often went to a youth club at the Elephant and Castle on Friday and Saturday nights with another kid called Joey Pyle, who later recalled that Charlie had 'an eye for the main chance' and was 'a strong, hard kid'.

Some nights, Charlie hung out with Joey Pyle and others at a mobile snack bar on the south side of Albert Bridge, next to Battersea Park. During the hotter summer months, hundreds of south London youths would congregate there before police tried to move them on because their presence was causing major traffic problems. Another childhood friend of Charlie's, Nosher Powell, explained: 'Charlie was a right cheeky chappy when he was a teenager – we was that close I knew what his left hand was up to – but he worked hard at the markets and had a real work ethic.'

While desperate poverty still surrounded Charlie's home environment, south London's post-war youths were emerging as a restless, rebellious generation determined to make a mark for themselves in the world. Although Charlie and his mates undoubtedly committed numerous petty crimes, they still retained standards and their behaviour abided by certain codes. Targeting a man walking along the street and stealing his watch was frowned upon, while raiding cigarette wholesalers or shops was totally legit. 'The fat cats were there for the taking, but you didn't rob your own – ever,' explained Joey Pyle.

Every youngster out on the streets back then was fascinated by guns. Most had their own popgun and a few had even managed to find real weapons through fathers or grandfathers fighting in Europe or further afield. Charlie longed to find out what it was really like to fire a gun and kept his eyes and ears peeled for an opportunity to steal one when the moment was right.

By the age of 13, Charlie had little need for any further education. He was a bright, quick-witted teenager with an eye for the main chance and he'd already started earning a crust through crime and by lugging crates around various markets. To adults who employed him, Charlie seemed a humorous, happy-go-lucky kind of character, tall and strong and deeply proud of his Battersea roots.

Most Sunday afternoons, Charlie and his south London pals, including Bruce Reynolds and another gangly kid called Gordon Goody, from nearby Putney, would go to the pictures at Clapham Junction. The majority of teenage boys back then still wore suits and, although Charlie wasn't flush with cash, he somehow managed to afford to buy a smooth mohair suit that greatly impressed the girls. At weekends, Charlie and his friends also went to the Lyceum Ballroom in the West End, the Hammersmith Palais and the Wimbledon Palais for dance nights. Many of the boys, including Charlie, carried blades. He even practised stabbing motions on old cabbages when he was working in the markets. At that time, incidents of 'chivving' (scarring) opponents with knives were numerous amongst petty criminals and racetrack gangs.

Usually, these gangs of youths met at least twice a week in one particular place, either a café or a youth club. Charlie emerged as one of the leaders of a bunch of tearaways who specialised in smash-and-grab raids on phone boxes, as well as stealing handbags from unattended cars. One-time Krays' henchman Freddie Foreman encountered Charlie in south London on numerous occasions back then. He explained: 'Charlie and I had a lot in common. We grew up on the same manor. We were born the same year and the war had a very big influence on our upbringing. Our paths crossed all the time. He stood out as someone special, even back then.'

Another popular venue was a coffee stall in front of the Plough pub on Clapham Common, which still exists today. Charlie, Bruce Reynolds, Gordon Goody and Freddie Foreman all adored the meat-and-onion pies sold at the stall. 'Then we'd go on to the Clapham Manor dance hall because all the town halls back then were turned into dance halls at weekends,' explained Foreman. 'There were some big names performing, like the Stan Kenton Band . . . we'd all be suited and booted, looking the business for a night out.'

Freddie Foreman recalled that youths like him and Charlie needed money to subsidise their lifestyle and were out 'doing whatever [they] could'. In the case of Charlie and his two close pals, Reynolds and Goody, that meant 'a bit of burglary and thieving, and stuff like that'. Foreman specialised in safes in offices and snatching wage deposits. He said: 'I didn't like the idea of entering someone's private property, but it didn't seem to bother Charlie and his mates.'

If they hadn't managed to steal a car for the night, all of them travelled out of south London by Tube. 'Up West' on a Friday night, Charlie and his friends drank heavily and chased girls. Freddie Foreman recalls: 'We even shared certain girls between us. There was one pair of birds known as 'the gobble twins'. They had big high-wedge heels on and we'd take it in turns to have some fun with them.'

During the day on Saturdays, Charlie went shoplifting in the big department stores in affluent areas such as Knightsbridge and Kensington. One favourite shop was men's outfitters Cecil Gee. Bruce Reynolds recalled the time he was buying a couple of shirts for £3 each when a friend of theirs, a stocky character called 'Buster' Edwards, grabbed 10 or 15 ties and ran out of the shop. When Reynolds eventually left the shop, he found Edwards further up the street having already sold the ties for a pound each to a local stallholder.

As Freddie Foreman explained: 'We all wanted to nick from people who had the money in the first place. I'd snatch at cash registers and grab cash from places like Dorothy Perkins, which was one of my favourites. You could get fists full of money out of the cash drop by the changing rooms, then you'd have a taxi waiting for you just round the corner.' Another popular chain for the gang was Stones Electrical Supplies where washing machines and fridges were displayed on the pavement outside shops. One of the gang would go inside and chat to the storekeeper to keep him or her occupied. As Foreman explained, 'You'd just pick 'em up, do a dead lift and walk round the corner and sling 'em in the back of a van.' When Stones finally cottoned on and began chaining up their goods, Charlie and his pals simply nicked themselves a pair of boltcutters.

It was during the summer of 1948, when Heathrow Airport was being developed to replace Croydon as London's main airport, that legendary London criminal Jack Spot masterminded a robbery he believed would confirm his status as one of the 'Kings of the Underworld'. Sammy Josephs, a well-connected Jewish thief, told Spot that a big shipment of valuables was arriving on a certain date and being kept overnight at the airport. Spot's team planned to dope security guards with sedatives in their coffee, after which ten raiders – all wearing nylon stockings over their faces – would follow a single torchlight to the Customs shed where

£300,000 worth of loot was stored. The plan was sabotaged when someone on Spot's team grassed them up. By 11 p.m., all roads leading to the airport were under police surveillance. In the Customs shed, thirteen Flying Squad detectives lay in wait and ten more were hiding in a van around the back. As Spot's team crashed in, a bloody battle ensued. Three of Spot's mob got away, but the rest of the battered robbers were dragged off in waiting black Marias. They were all convicted and received up to 12 years' imprisonment each.

Up-and-coming young south London tearaway Charlie Wilson knew a few of Spot's team. On the underworld grapevine, many were saying that one of Spot's henchmen grassed his mates up because he hadn't been properly paid for a previous robbery. Charlie swore then that he'd 'do' any grass who cost him his liberty. 'They're scum and should be put down,' he told one friend at the time.

Not long after the airport raid, in the winter of 1948, a pair of young tearaways called the Kray twins, aged just 15, were getting lots of local press coverage in the East End. Reggie Kray won the London Schoolboy Boxing Championships after having been champion of Hackney, and the following year he became the South Eastern Divisional Youth Club Champion and the London ATC Champion. His brother Ron also won the Hackney Schoolboy and London Junior Championships, along with a London ATC title.

Ron and Reg had their own gang of young hoodlums and had been barred from most of the cinemas and dance halls in the East End. The twins proudly let it be known they kept choppers, machetes, knives, swords and a variety of other weapons beneath the bed they both slept in at their parents' home in Vallance Road, Bethnal Green (known as Fort Vallance). Ronnie – clearly the more outrageous of the two brothers – liked sharpening his cutlass on oil he spread across the doorstep of Fort Vallance. He'd often swish the blade through the air in an arc, his face contorted with venom and the anticipation of pleasure in combat. Ronnie boasted that he'd purchased his first gun before he'd turned 17 and that he fully expected to shoot someone 'sooner rather than later'. When they slept, the twins always placed newspapers around the floor so that they'd hear the rustle of the papers if an intruder entered their bedroom.

Hearing about the up-and-coming Krays made young tearaways like Charlie flex their muscles. In one dance hall in Brixton, he got caught up in a gang clash involving razors when a couple of young hoods smashed their pint glasses on the bar counter and challenged all-comers to a fight. It was a test of strength 'to see who was boss' and, afterwards, some even shook hands, but it also took four buckets of water to clear the blood off the floor.

Youths like Charlie Wilson and the Krays often visited Ziggy's Café in Cobb Street, just off Petticoat Lane in the East End, on Sunday afternoons after spending money at a record stall which was always filled with dozens of youths from other parts of London. Amongst them were characters with names like Curly King, Checker Berry and Flash Ronnie.

The owner of the café, Ziggy, was a smart-looking middle-aged man with a stout gut and a fat cigar always hanging out of his mouth. His wife served the teas and lunches while Ziggy made sure all his customers knew he had a police truncheon on show behind the bar. Ziggy's other regulars included characters like Sammy Wilde, a boxer from the Gold Coast in Africa. He had tribal markings cut down the side of each cheekbone and always had a knife in a sheath attached to his waistband. Wilde wore a small woollen beret with a coloured tassel on top and some nights made appearances on stage as a fire-eater.

Back home in Battersea, Charlie's self-destructive personality continued to emerge. As a child, he certainly didn't receive the sensory stimulation he required from his family and increasingly found it difficult to establish a boundary between himself and the world beyond his caring mother and siblings. Charlie had quickly become an all-encompassing individual, seeing things from his own perspective and no one else's. Other family members have commented that they noticed how fearless Charlie became in his teens and the selfish way he'd try to manipulate situations to suit himself. He also often seemed incapable of realising when he'd hurt other people's feelings and felt little remorse, and certainly no sympathy, for his victims.

Beneath his bubbling, chatty exterior was an inner sadness because he found it difficult to take part in 'normal' activities. Being a teenager was supposed to have been a pleasurable experience – learning how to be happy and derive happiness from as many situations as possible – but Charlie didn't really seem capable of enjoying things in the normal sense of the word. His development had its own twisted symbology, steeped in terror of some unpleasant memories and fears that were permanently stored in his mind. Charlie had also by this stage promised himself he'd *never* struggle financially in the way his father had done.

Out on the streets of south London, though, Charlie carefully hid his true feelings. His friend Joey Pyle explained: 'Charlie was always laughing, always good for a giggle, if you know what I mean. Charlie was up for anything. It was like he had to have a laugh all the time.' Charlie had become what his mates later described as 'part of the south-west London crowd'. Besides Bruce Reynolds, Joey Pyle, Nosher Powell, Gordon Goody and Buster Edwards, there were also characters such as 'Big Freddie' Gould and Georgie Osborne, whose cousin Patricia had already caught Charlie's eye at a local dance.

Some Sundays, Charlie and his crew organised road trips to Brighton using stolen cars and featuring specialised 'drivers', who were already experts behind the wheel even though they were all only in their teens. They included a small kid called Roy James, later to be known as 'The Weasel' on account of his short stature and propensity for wearing ludicrous fur coats, a cheeky youth from Fulham called Mickey Ball, and a budding racing driver called Ritchie Bristow, who later died racing in Belgium. On one occasion, James and Ball raced each other down to Brighton in two stolen 4.2 litre Mark 2 Jaguars. Charlie and his pals all put heavy bets on who would win before the two high-powered vehicles set off through south London towards the coast, a big statue on the seafront at Brighton being the pre-arranged winning-post. Joey Pyle explained: 'There was no motorway back in them days, just the twisting and turning Brighton Road that ran from Reigate Hill all the way through the Surrey and Sussex countryside. I can't remember exactly how long it took but Roy James won by more than a mile.' Charlie and his mates decided pint-sized James would make a superb getaway driver if they ever started robbing banks and security vans.

Around this time, Charlie began fencing stolen goods when he worked the odd day in a scrap-metal yard near Battersea Bridge. He soon got a reputation for 'finding a home' for all sorts of stolen property. According to Joey Pyle, Charlie was also 'very handy with his fists. He was solid, quite tall, not a bully, not nasty, very fair. He would never take any liberties but he was a right fuckin' hard bastard.' Charlie sometimes boxed at a local club and had a reputation as a ferocious fighter.

At the age of 18, Charlie was called up for National Service, which came as quite a shock since he was earning a decent wedge ducking and diving around the south London streets. The Army taught him the importance of being fit, even though he had a lot of problems obeying orders. It was no surprise that, when Charlie emerged from the Army in 1952, he immediately linked up with his dodgy south London pals again.

Even as a young hoodlum, Charlie knew the rules of the game, as did most of the other young criminals on his manor. Not grassing up your mates was taken for granted. Joey Pyle explained: 'If you went on a job and you got nicked and another fella who was on the job with you didn't grass you up, then he'd just done exactly what he was supposed to have done. I'd never look at someone and think "Oh, he didn't grass me up, what a lovely fella." I wouldn't be with him in the first place if I thought he was gonna turn grass on me. Grassing is a terrible, despicable thing. People like myself and my friends would rather fuckin' die than be a grass.'

Many of Charlie's contemporaries may have been petty thieves, but to become a *real* outlaw you had to do everything *your* way. Nobody and nothing else mattered – apart from your loved ones, of course – and that made you more feared and respected. No one could get away with pulling a fast one on Charlie because beneath that wisecracking exterior lurked a cold, calculating individual capable of making split-second decisions that could mean the difference between life or death to certain individuals. On the streets of south London, some people saw villains like Charlie as budding Robin Hoods, striking blows against the traditional enemy, the police – the filth, the cozzers, along with any other derogatory names they were called. Even back then, some of Charlie's crimes were celebrated and talked about in the pubs because they represented getting one back on the Establishment.

Charlie played up to his growing reputation. When he walked into certain taverns, the place really did go quiet like it does in the movies. Charlie wanted to be more than just a bit of local muscle, though; he saw himself as a leader of men, an artful criminal capable of taking on and beating anyone. Charlie's ascent through the criminal fraternity owed much to the transitional period that Britain was going through during the '40s and '50s. This was a time when spivs were the people to talk to if you wanted a piece of decent meat for tea. Wartime rationing had continued for years after the end of hostilities in Europe so people – especially the poor – were forced to go out and find those little luxuries for themselves. Charlie just reflected an attitude which prevailed at the time. He wanted money and believed that it would create happiness; something his poverty-stricken father had never managed to bring to the table as a lowly paid, overworked bus driver. Charlie was a quick learner and observer. He'd watched his older contemporaries getting out and about, dealing in everything from coffee to nylons. He understood the importance of money and he'd decided that he would be rich, come what may.

2

While Charlie was undoubtedly in some respects a cold-blooded thug, he had a social conscience as well and showed great loyalty to those he liked. He also knew when to help rather than hinder. He was shrewd and arrogant, but wanted wealth so badly that he was prepared to milk his own popularity. He was, in the words of one of his contemporaries, 'a strange combination of hard heart and soft mind: capable of beating a man, but also just as likely to help an old lady cross the street'. Charlie was a genuine creature of circumstance; a complex, contradictory and ultimately very dangerous man, mainly because he did not know where the traditional lines or boundaries in life existed.

By this stage, he was undoubtedly becoming addicted to crime. Nosher Powell explained: 'One day, Charlie was out walkin' with a mate near The Savoy and he said, "Quick, get a fuckin' cab," and then disappeared into a shop. He came rushin' out with a handful of clothes and said, "Where's the fuckin' cab?" This geezer hadn't called one so he had to make a dash for it.' The need to experience this thrill and the ease with which he managed to finance his life from this kind of stunt was becoming second nature to Charlie by this stage.

Charlie and his pals had been burgling and carrying out raids on the nearby docks for some time so it was inevitable they'd graduate to bank robberies, or 'blags' as they were known. Joey Pyle explained: 'When you're on a blag, it's like being part of a football team. Each person has his role and you count on the rest of them to pull their weight. It's a fantastic feeling. We'd get tip-offs about likely targets and the normal percentage for that kind of information is 10 per cent of whatever you get. It's all a game.'

Once Charlie and his gang had picked a day to commit a robbery, they'd work on getting all their tools together plus a stolen car for a fast getaway. A classic blagging for Charlie and his young pals back then would be a man collecting takings from spielers, illegal betting clubs, but they soon graduated to much bigger jobs. Pyle recalls: 'We was even blowin' safes back in them days. We also did smaller things like jumpin' over counters in banks and grabbing a handful of cash. We also hit post offices because their security was rubbish. Some companies left wages in the safe overnight and, of course, there were no cheques or monthly salary slips back then. It was a weekly thing, always with cash.'

Pyle recognised Charlie's abilities even back then. 'Charlie was well known as being a good man to go to work with because he was very sound, game and if you went across the pavement [robbed a bank], Charlie would be the first one out of the car and the first one in to grab the dosh.' Pyle added, 'Charlie's main aim back then was the money. That's what drove him on. Pounds, shillings and pence.'

As a young hood with a few bob in his pocket, Charlie began visiting the clubs, dives, spielers, pubs and hotels of Soho, although he carefully avoided any direct criminal involvement in the lucrative vice trade. Flying Squad chief Bert Wickstead later commented that Charlie and his gang just weren't qualified for that kind of business, it being 'a very specialised form of crime'. He went on: 'You need men who can acquire property in the right places and at the right prices. They have to recruit and organise the girls. You need rent collectors and a small army of frighteners to make sure that the girls and the collectors stay honest.' Charlie did, however, work as an enforcer for some of the violent and unscrupulous characters who ran protection rackets in the West End. Charlie was soon renowned for his relentless pursuit of cash on behalf of those criminal associates. As one West End criminal from back in those days explained: 'Charlie knew the rules of the game. If someone had to be taught a lesson, then so be it, even if that meant waving a knife in his face.'

Soho's favoured tools of the trade at this time also included razors, broken bottles, revolvers, hammers, hatchets, coshes and knuckledusters. Charing Cross Hospital employed a special staff of medical seamsters to deal with the gaping wounds made by many of these weapons. Victims seldom complained, but harboured a grudge to get even with their attacker. Flying Squad chief Wickstead recalled: 'One well-known tearaway who was chivvied had a beautiful curvature of the face that stretched from one ear right round his chin to the other ear. He had to have 99 stitches inserted to draw this gaping wound together.'

Following the war, the West End thrived because people needed to enjoy themselves. The London underworld in those post-war days was an ever-shifting nucleus of people, moving backwards and forwards across the capital. Now drugs, blackmail and classic long-firm tactics could be added to an already potent mix. (Long firms were fake companies set up by villains, who persuaded gullible people and banks to invest in the business then abandoned it, taking the money with them.)

One of the most powerful criminals to emerge after the war was a smooth-talking former smash-'n'-grab merchant called Billy Hill. He was a real West Ender: born in 1911 at Seven Dials on the Holborn side of Leicester Square, which was then a Dickensian-type area filled with poverty and street beggars, just a stone's throw from the vice dens of Soho. In his own words, Hill got out of Borstal at the age of 19 as 'a tough and bitter young thug, ready to do anything except go straight'. During the war, Hill specialised in throwing bricks into jewellery shop windows and grabbing everything in sight. On one occasion, he teamed up with a character called 'John the Tilter' and they pretended to be police detectives in order to relieve a couple of crooks of their haul of stolen parachutes, which they then sold for £500.

Many younger villains had begun to notice that Billy Hill and his archenemy Jack Spot were making a fortune working as bookies at horse-racing meetings across the country, so it was no surprise that small-time crooks, like Charlie Wilson, started working as illegal bookies. Sometimes, Charlie spent entire weekends laying off bets at point-to-point races, which were not so well policed. Charlie went whenever there was a meeting and stood on a couple of boxes beside a post with a bookie's name on it and a board to write the odds on. This was known as a bookmaker's 'joint'. Although it could be put up in seconds, villains still had to pay other spivs for the privilege, plus the chalk and even the water to wipe the board clean between races.

Charlie also attended illegal bare-knuckle boxing bouts in fields well away from the prying eyes of police and race officials. Carloads of crooks would turn up in fields close to tracks such as Epsom with their favourite bruiser to take on an opponent. One Derby Day, renowned racetrack hard man Albert Dimes oversaw a fight to the death between one of his boys and a pikey (gypsy) at the Epsom Downs camp close to the racecourse. The two fighters smashed each other to pieces for a £100 prize. More than ten times that amount changed hands in bets. In the early 1950s, Charlie, who was proud of his fitness and fighting skills, entered at least half a dozen such contests, eventually retiring unbeaten having made a small fortune betting on himself.

Charlie was well known at a fairground in Barnet, north London, where he often fenced stolen goods for the gypsies who ran the site. One friend explained: 'Charlie was always flogging lots of tom [jewellery] he'd got up at Barnet. He told me he knew the gypsies wouldn't grass him up. He obviously felt in safe hands with them.'

Charlie's criminal activities didn't end there; he also became an expert at getting what were called dockers' tickets or books, which he would then sell on for a fee. The charges depended on the wealth of the 'client'. The dockers' books enabled anyone to work as a docker at the quayside, loading boats and barges. Back then, they were paid vast wages compared with most jobs, even though the working hours were very short, so Charlie could make quite a lot of money from them. He had developed into a very smart, supposedly independent entrepreneur of crime.

One of his regular haunts at the time was an old snooker hall in the Elephant and Castle, renowned as a place to buy stolen goods. It was used by many in the local criminal fraternity and, as Nosher Powell joked, 'we called it Fortnum & Masons because you could buy anything in there you wanted'.

Charlie was also discovering the importance of 'greasing palms'. Nosher recalls: 'Back then, in the 1950s, I was working the door at a club up West and we had to pay backhanders to all the big coppers at West End Central at that time. Tenners here, fivers there. They'd earn four times what they earned in salary out of bungs from the clubs. It was just accepted.'

That type of bribery and corruption coloured Charlie's attitude towards the police for the rest of his life. His argument was simple: 'How can you trust a copper if most of them want a backhander? They're the enemy, but most of them are less honest than we are.' From an early age, Charlie had decided that he'd always hate the police.

Charlie also teamed up with old friend and Elephant and Castle regular Buster Edwards and the two men regularly went 'hoisting' (shoplifting) in London's West End for new clothes. Charlie took real pride in his appearance because he felt it was important to show other people that he was on the rise.

Charlie had a penchant for stealing flash cars like Jaguars and Rovers, although he told one friend he preferred the Rover 3.5 coupé to the Jaguar Mark 2 because they had more legroom for his tall frame: 'Fuckin' Jags are for midgets. Great motor, but just not right for me, unless we're on a blaggin', of course.' As Joey Pyle commented: 'Charlie did well out of thieving in the '50s. He always looked pristine in a suit and tie. He always drove the right motor. He had style.'

Charlie Wilson didn't recognise anyone in authority – apart from perhaps the occasional underworld name – as he climbed the criminal ladder on the streets of south London. He regarded the status of policemen, Judges and Home Office officials as meaningless.

When Charlie had a violent clash with a south London villain called Tony Routger, brother of a feared character called Peter Routger, it seemed a big risk considering Charlie was still a relative upstart at the time. Pyle recalls: 'The Routgers were two flash bastards, but Charlie laid into Tony at a pub on Camberwell Green. They went out back and had a scrap. A few minutes later Charlie walked back in and Routger was never seen again. That incident made people realise just how strong a character Charlie was.'

Charlie Wilson was six-foot tall and well-built with a fresh complexion. He had dark-brown, well-greased hair, blue eyes and a scar on the knuckle of the first finger of his left hand. Naturally, he also spoke with a strong cockney accent and used to break into entire sentences of cockney rhyming slang at the drop of a hat. Nosher Powell explained: 'Charlie was a bit of an outsider, a loner in many ways, because he spent a lot of those early days in places like Peckham, away from his manor in Battersea. But you looked to people like that to watch yer back and you knew they'd look after yer missus and kids if you got put away.'

Charlie was a regular at a pub in Lambeth Walk, often filled with characters such as the powerful Richardson family. Nosher recalls: 'A press photographer was in there one time and I saw Charlie disappear into the toilet because he definitely didn't want his photo taken. It was the type of place where you went to meet the chaps.' Being described as one of 'the chaps' meant a villain had well and truly arrived in terms of criminal status.

There were other venues Up West such as the Jack of Clubs in Rupert Street, Soho, where Charlie sometimes popped in for a pint before slipping into an illegal drinking club round the corner in Walker's Court. Nosher recalls how Charlie would spend time in those drinking establishments when they were filled with faces like the Nashes and the Krays. Powell said: 'He'd sit there very quietly, observing them all. He'd come up to me working in the cloakrooms for a chat or send me a drink and give a nod in my direction. That was typical Charlie.'

In the middle of all this frenzied criminal activity, Charlie still found time for romance. He had a soft spot for Patricia Osborne, the pretty blonde cousin of his friend Georgie Osborne. Once he'd been demobbed from the Army, Charlie had started courting her and the couple eventually married in 1955. He was 23 and Pat was 21. At first, they moved into a small flat, but Charlie promised Pat he'd soon buy them a proper house. Within a year, the couple's first child, Cheryl, was born.

Charlie Wilson definitely wasn't afraid of hard work. Throughout this period, Charlie not only made money from crime, but also helped run his new in-laws' fruit and vegetable business in Penge. Pat also earned an additional £15 a week working from home as a dressmaker. Charlie was up at four each morning to go to Spitalfields Market to buy fruit for the shop. He often also did the buying for other shopkeepers, who trusted him implicitly and relied on his good judgement. Pat later insisted she had no idea Charlie was still involved in criminal activity. She explained: 'Charlie was always cheery, with quick-witted jokes tumbling from his lips. People in our road used to say they could set their clocks by him, he was so punctual, getting home for his 7 p.m. supper. Charlie was proud of that side of his character.'

'Never keep anyone waiting in life,' he'd say to Pat in a cheery voice. 'Not only is it bad manners, but it shows bad management on your own part.'

It was only when Charlie got into trouble with the police again that Pat realised her husband was still up to no good. It was a minor offence concerning a car and he was given a conditional discharge, but she admits she was upset by it. Pat says she begged Charlie to give up his underworld friends, but Charlie insisted his friends were his friends and told her not to interfere. She was often afraid of the men her husband brought home, although she insists that they never did or said anything to upset her, but that 'it was obvious what they were'.

Charlie was soon able to afford to buy the family a comfortable £10,000 three-bedroom house in Crescent Lane, Clapham, just around the corner from a bookmaking business he ran with Pat's cousin Georgie Osborne. Their new home was a grey-brick Victorian terraced property with a yellow front door, plus a neatly trimmed hedge at the front. Pat – who'd been brought up in a tiny house in the East End – was delighted.

Charlie's second brush with the law came shortly after Pat, Charlie and baby Cheryl moved into that house in Clapham. Pat and their daughter had been away for the weekend, staying with relatives, and returned to find the whole place a shambles after a police raid. All Charlie would say from his police cell, though, was: 'Don't worry, love. Everything will be all right.'

Then, to make matters even worse, Cheryl was taken to hospital seriously ill with tonsillitis and doctors discovered she had a hole-in-the-heart condition. When Charlie, who was still in custody, eventually appeared at the Old Bailey accused of receiving stolen cars and other property, his defence counsel Mr Colin Nichol told the judge that his daughter was 'fretting for her father'. However, Charlie had his application for bail refused after prosecutor Maxwell Turner and Detective Sergeant William Gay poured scorn on his lawyer's claims about Cheryl's medical problems. Charlie was incensed by their attitude and saw it as yet further confirmation that the police were 'scum'. He was eventually locked up for eight months of a one-year sentence. The couple's second child, Tracey, was born five weeks after Charlie was imprisoned. Cheryl, to their relief, survived her illness.

Not long after his release from prison, Charlie was locked up again, this time in Maidstone Prison, for handling a small amount of explosives which had been found during yet another raid on his home. Police alleged the explosives were to be used for safe-cracking. In prison, Charlie befriended a likeable young rogue from Bermondsey called Jimmy Rose. They got talking about how their fathers hadn't handed down jobs to them and that they'd just had to go out and earn money by whatever means possible. Both men had what some might call an unhealthy obsession with money and keeping fit. As one friend later explained: 'These two were so focused on making money that they never talked about anything else, so it was no surprise they became such good mates.' Later, that friendship between Wilson and Rose would be put to the ultimate test.

Far from discouraging his criminal activities, prison reinforced Charlie's desire to get active again. While in jail with Jimmy Rose, the two men discussed numerous new crimes they intended to commit on their release.

In 1960, Charlie – who by now had a share in at least two bookies businesses with Georgie Osborne – got involved with Joey Pyle in running a gambling club called The Charterhouse in the old Smithfield Market area. The club was owned by master criminal Billy Hill and a well-known car dealer called Johnny Matthews. Pyle explained: 'It was open only for traders from the market, not the overalls who wanted early lunches.' Besides food and alcohol, there were facilities for gambling. 'A licensed bookmaker called Charlie Monk used to take bets,' added Pyle. 'It was a very busy place, full of chaps.' There was also a casino on the premises and Charlie got his jailhouse pal Jimmy Rose a job as a croupier on the roulette table, as well as employing an up-and-coming wisecracking Kilburn Irish teenager called Brian Wright. Pyle later explained that after initially running the dining table, Billy Hill allowed them to take over the downstairs and all their own people came in at weekends and in the evenings.

A few months later, a young gangster was gunned down and murdered in a highly publicised incident at the Pen Club in east London, at which

Joey Pyle was present. Finally, Scotland Yard woke up to the fact they needed to know much more about 'the enemy'. As a result, the Criminal Intelligence Branch was formed to coordinate information about organised crime. Up until then, the police had little or no idea who they were up against. Young, ambitious gangsters like Charlie Wilson were already giving them a run for their money.

3

In 1960, Charlie teamed up again with his childhood pal Bruce Reynolds, who'd just been released from prison after serving time for robbing shops in south London. Charlie was already working with Buster Edwards and Gordon Goody, whom they called 'Footpad' because he often wore a long check coat that gave him, with his height, the appearance of a street mugger. Charlie, Reynolds, Edwards and Goody saw themselves as professional criminals or 'high-class jewel thieves' as Reynolds liked to say. They nicknamed Reynolds 'The Colonel' because he liked to think he was in charge of the gang.

Robberies on banks and armoured vans carrying wages were booming at the time. Even the latest technology, which was supposed to tighten security, could be turned to the criminal's advantage. A classic example was the argon arc gun, a highly powered electric torch that could cut its way through metal. The guns weren't available in shops and had to be ordered (which was supposed to make it easier for the police to trace them back to their owners), but Charlie and his friends eventually discovered a factory in Staines which stored the guns, and broke in and stole six of them.

Equipped with these state-of-the-art weapons, Charlie, Edwards, Goody and Reynolds met up with a character called Bill Jennings, who told them about a prime robbery target: railwaymen's wages paid out from an office to all the sidings and marshalling-yard workers of the Western Region Railway. The cash was delivered by security van to a single-storey office next to some sidings. The clerical staff always bolted themselves in while they sorted the money into wage packets and then paid it out at a small window. So, late on the night before the next delivery, Buster Edwards and Gordon Goody let themselves into the deserted office with a skeleton key. They examined the bolt and saw that it ran through the jamb of the door into the concrete of the wall. They unscrewed it from the door, cut the screws short and snapped off the end of the bolt so that it only just went into the clasp, then put everything back into place.

The following day, a five-man team, including Charlie, waited in a stolen van in the street outside the entrance until they saw the security van leave. The gang then pulled down their stocking masks, drew out their coshes and Goody drove up to the office. One kick smashed the door open to reveal five men and one woman; the men dived straight to the floor, but the woman came flying at the blaggers. Buster Edwards grabbed the screaming woman and they fell to the floor where she was knocked unconscious while the other robbers began packing bundles of banknotes into a holdall. The gang locked the door behind them and broke the key in the lock deliberately. As the blaggers scrambled into their getaway car, Gordon Goody ripped off his stocking mask. Charlie turned to him and yelled, 'Put it back on, you ugly bastard!' Goody laughed at Charlie's wisecrack, although there were other times when his non-stop quips could also be irritating. 'Charlie had a joke for everything and sometimes that could really get on your nerves,' one old friend later explained. Back at their safe house, the team counted the money, which amounted to £26,000.

Next came the audacious hijacking of an armoured van after one of the drivers provided inside information that at least £70,000 in cash was on offer. This time, joker Charlie was told beforehand to 'keep it buttoned'. The Colonel was particularly keen for the team to remain quiet and thoroughly professional throughout the operation. The gang pulled in front of the armoured van before turning around to ram it head on. The terrified guards flung open the doors and were immediately hauled out of the van and coshed by the group of masked men, although Reynolds later insisted that they were 'only glancing blows, designed to mark, not injure them'. Charlie then jumped in the back of the van and ripped open the wages compartment before the blaggers formed a chain and began slinging boxes from hand to hand into the boot of their getaway car. Within a few minutes, they'd already quit the scene and swapped their first vehicle for another, half a mile away. This time, their haul was more than £60,000 in cash and the London underworld was starting to sit up and take notice of this young, fearless band of robbers.

Of course, there were failures along the way, as well. The team's next job – the burglary of a millionaire's mansion – had to be abandoned after a policeman on a bicycle saw the gang's stolen Jag parked on the street outside with the keys in the ignition (in case they had to make a quick getaway). The gang's lookout watched from a distance as the copper stopped, examined the Jag and took the keys out. The gang called off the job and retreated on foot.

A few weeks later, the team were meeting to discuss the hijacking of yet another security van when Bruce Reynolds mentioned that legendary London gangster Billy Hill always told his boys 'trains are the thing'. In fact, Hill had even sent his gang out to check on the movements of certain trains that carried 'bundles of readies', but nothing ever came of it. Not long after that meeting, Buster Edwards came up with a job to test that theory.

In the middle of 1962, Edwards was tipped off about boxes carrying wages for railway workers in Swindon, Wiltshire, which were loaded under tight security onto the Irish Mail Train each week at London's Paddington Station. Charlie and the rest of the gang jumped the train shortly after it pulled out of Paddington and got to the boxes, but never managed to open them. They eventually leapt off the carriage after the alarm was raised. Only Gordon Goody managed to keep one of the boxes, which contained just £700.

Next, the gang hatched a plan to rob a train carrying gold bullion, shipped each week from South Africa by the Union-Castle Line to Southampton. It was then transported by rail to Waterloo and met by an assortment of police, Bank of England officials and security guards before being escorted to the Bank's vaults. Plans were abandoned after Charlie pointed out that security was so excessive, the gang's chances of pulling off the job were virtually zero. The plan had whetted the gang's appetite about the vulnerability of trains, though. Surely, there had to be a 'Big One' out there, waiting to be robbed.

4

The two different sides of Charlie Wilson's character were already clearly defined by this stage. If you saw him out with his wife and daughters on Clapham Common on a sunny Sunday afternoon, you'd never guess he was a ruthless criminal already responsible for many robberies across the capital. Nosher Powell recalls: 'I bumped into Charlie out with his wife and kids at London Zoo one afternoon. His daughters were on the donkey ride and he looked like any other proud dad. We nodded at each other and then carried on our separate ways. Charlie wasn't a villain that day, he was a happy, smiling family man.'

A few weeks later, Nosher was at a pub in Camberwell Green, southeast London, when he bumped into Charlie again. 'This time he offered me a lift home in his brand new Cortina. Never said a word during the whole drive, but then he never did say a lot – although I do remember Charlie was wearing a hand-tailored, mohair suit. He always had the best gear on.' By this time, Charlie's suits were being made at an East End tailors called Levys or at Johnny Nortons in the West End. They cost more than £30 each and Charlie usually rounded things off with a £15 shirt from Adams in Coventry Street.

Nosher says that, on both those occasions, there was a constant hint of the 'other side' in Charlie's face: 'Charlie's eyes were close together and they'd scan ahead, always on the lookout for trouble. This was a fella who didn't miss a trick.'

Not long after that ride home, Nosher spotted Charlie in the world-famous Foyle's Bookshop on the Tottenham Court Road: '. . . there he was, going through a load of maps. I asked him what he was up to and he said, "Just browsing." Next time I looked, he'd disappeared in a puff of smoke. Typical Charlie, always keeping a low profile.'

To this day, Nosher is full of admiration for Charlie: '[He] was a very, very clever fella. He always had money in his pocket, but he wasn't flash. No jewellery, just a pricey watch. That was typical Charlie. [He] would have made a great spy because he didn't trust no one and he was always taking everything in around him. I think the only person he ever truly trusted was his missus, Pat.' Nosher later reflected that although Charlie was well known in his line of business, he wasn't really known by anyone.

Charlie was also renowned as 'a man with a plan'. One of his oldest south London friends reflected that Charlie enjoyed the planning stages of a job, mapping things out very carefully and often coming up with something a little unusual to catch people off guard. A classic example of this was when, on 14 August 1962, a team, including Charlie and Gordon Goody, used a fake blind man as look-out while they robbed a bank.

Witnesses at the National Provincial Bank in Clapham High Street, less than a mile from Charlie's family home, later said there was a man outside the bank with a white stick, but that he was not there by the time police arrived after the robbers had struck. The raiders – described as 3 men in their 20s by police – calmly walked into the bank where one of them leapt over the counter and struck a cashier, 21-year-old Ronald Powell, with a pickaxe handle. Charlie jumped in and grabbed a tin box containing £9,150 lying at the cashier's feet and threw it across to one of the other two before all three raiders ran out of the bank and clambered into a stolen blue Ford Zodiac. Neighbouring shopkeepers thought the bank siren was a jammed car horn until they saw the men run out of the bank and drive away. The getaway car was later found abandoned in nearby Northbourne Road, Clapham Common.

The police considered the raid fairly unique because everything had happened with such incredible speed and precision – none of the people inside or outside the bank had had time to lift a finger to stop the robbers. This implied that some careful planning had gone into the job. Cashier Powell was only slightly bruised and declined to go to hospital. He later visited Scotland Yard with a female clerk to look through photographs in the police's 'rogues gallery' album of known criminals. And there, police later claimed, the cashier hesitatingly identified Charlie as one of the robbers. Less than three hours later, Charlie was arrested, even though no one else had fingered him for the job. Naturally, Charlie protested his innocence, but was charged with robbery.

On 13 December 1962, at South Western Magistrates' Court, the same bank clerk pointed at Charlie in the dock and told the court: 'I think that is one of them, but I am not at all certain.' Charlie's defence counsel, Mr John Mathew, pointed out that the only relevant evidence against Charlie was from the cashier who wasn't even certain Charlie was one of the robbers. The charges were dismissed. Charlie was immediately discharged and granted £40 costs. Had somebody leaned on Powell? As one of Charlie's oldest south London friends later said: 'Either the Old Bill tried to fit Charlie up [frame him] or some of Charlie's people leaned on that bank clerk.'

After his acquittal on the Clapham job, Charlie arrived home and persuaded Pat – now expecting their third child – to join him on a holiday to celebrate his release. The couple flew, with their two daughters, to Jersey, where they stayed in a five-star hotel and spent money like water. Charlie's dual personality was in its element: he was the loving, doting husband and father, never happier than when helping his daughters dress their dolls or making them toys with his own fretwork set, whilst simultaneously craving excitement and danger, and the sort of huge profits that big-time crime could provide. Pat had her suspicions, but she chose not to deal with the issues most of the time. When groups of heavy-looking men called round at the house, Charlie told Pat they were just part of a betting syndicate and assured her there was nothing illegal going on. No matter how hard she tried, Pat could not draw out Charlie completely. His loyalty to his 'associates' was almost as strong as his devotion to his wife and children.

When keep-fit fanatic Charlie turned the garden shed into a mini gym, complete with weights, chest expanders and a punch bag so he could be in prime condition, Pat would joke about him training for the next Olympics. He'd respond with 'just keeping fit for my job', or something similar. It was a different job, however, from the one Pat wished he'd been referring to. Charlie's obsession with exercise had started in his teens and had been fuelled by those early terms in prison. He had a genuine belief that a healthy body led to a healthy, clear mind, which meant he was much less likely to make any costly mistakes when he was out robbing and thieving.

5

Charlie's growing reputation as a 'pro' led to a meeting with a man who worked in BOAC Airlines' administrative offices based at Comet House, Heathrow Airport. It was the largest building on the south side of the airport and was separated from the passenger terminals by the airport's two main runways. The A4 road from London to the south-west ran right along the other side. The two men met to discuss the movements of wages for the entire airline staff. Charlie's informant told him that a security van left a nearby bank and arrived outside Comet House every Tuesday morning with two guards, who unloaded a box that contained between £300,000 and £400,000 in wages. Charlie's contact recommended lifting the money from the vault in the bank before it got to Comet House.

The first full meeting to discuss the airport job was held at Buster

Edwards' flat in St Margaret's Road, Twickenham. During an early reconnaissance trip, Charlie and Bruce Reynolds quickly realised they'd have to grab the money after it was taken out of the bank and inside Comet House to stand any chance of getting away safely. Charlie's offbeat, creative contribution was to suggest the entire gang disguise themselves as City gents, in suits and bowler hats, so they would arouse less suspicion. At least three gang members would enter the building and hide in the third-floor men's lavatories, where they'd watch for the security van on its way from the nearby bank. Skilled drivers Roy James and Mickey Ball were recruited for the gang's getaway vehicles.

It was during the early planning stages of the airport raid that Charlie met a man known as 'Frenchy', who would eventually play a pivotal role in Charlie's life. He had a resonant, well-educated voice with a very slight French accent and a penchant for wearing black berets. He rapidly came up with some much-needed extra financial backing for the airport job through a group of old-time London criminals. Charlie's wife later recalled: 'Often I'd hear [Frenchy] talk about his love of horse racing and, on many occasions, he'd recount stories of how he had been associated with the French Resistance Movement during the war, but, apart from that, no one knew much about him.'

Frenchy claimed he'd been awarded high honours for his work with the Resistance and had been thanked personally by Winston Churchill. His speciality during the war had allegedly been coordinating daring raids to destroy German ammunition and troop trains in occupied France. He also helped organise the escapes of Resistance members being held by the Germans.

Pat held a slight grudge against Frenchy, however, for encouraging Charlie to become a reckless player of *chemin de fer* and baccarat at some of the leading gambling clubs in London's West End during the early 1960s. Charlie was a skilful and, sometimes, lucky player. On occasions, he'd arrive home, toss a huge roll of £5 notes on the table and jokingly make Pat guess where he had got it from. Pat would go completely pale and he'd put an arm around her, exclaiming with a laugh: 'It's straight money, love. I won it gambling.' Whenever it was Pat's or one of their daughter's birthdays, Charlie would play a bit of roulette and put a £100 chip on the date.

Around this time, Pat also noticed that Charlie spent much more time using his weights in the shed at the bottom of the garden and there were more conferences with groups of those heavy-looking characters at the house. Pat – content to make out she thought they were discussing betting – even commented to Charlie: 'All the horses will be dead before you make your betting coup.' Charlie often just laughed back and quipped: 'D'you want a bet, love?'

Behind the smiles, Pat has said she was irritated that the family home in Clapham was once again being invaded by a bunch of hoods. 'Don't worry, love,' Charlie told her one day, after she'd had a moan at him. 'They won't hurt you. Neither will I.'

Pat rolled her eyes because it was the only way she could deal with it. Charlie was the man she loved and adored more than life itself. He was a caring father and husband who made sure they were never short of money and showed a great deal of affection towards Pat and their daughters whenever he was at home. She found it difficult to challenge him, especially when he clearly had work on his mind.

During one meeting about the airport job, Charlie came up with the ingenious idea of lining the bowler hats the gang would wear with steel so they didn't have to carry coshes. Specially made umbrellas were also ordered, which didn't keep out the rain because they were also made of solid steel. Later, the metal bowler idea was used to great effect by James Bond's archenemy Oddjob in the 007 movie *Thunderball*.

In the two weeks before the Heathrow robbery, Charlie and three members of the gang continued to target the men's toilets on the third floor of the Comet building where they had a perfect view, 50 feet above street level, of the security van driving up to the door to deliver the wages. Charlie and his pals built up a split-second time schedule washing their hands and faces while they peered through the windows above the sinks.

* * *

At 9 a.m. on Tuesday, 17 November 1962, a group of men dressed in natty City suits, wearing bowler hats and false moustaches, and carrying neatly furled umbrellas took up their various positions. The bowler hats concealed the stocking masks they had on their heads. One witness said he noticed the group of men, but thought they were solicitors. Two other members of the gang were positioned by a nearby bus stop.

Most of the gang had decided to carry extra armoury in addition to their steel-lined headgear and brollies: Buster Edwards had a foot-long piece of pipe-spring, filled with lead and bound with tape ('Buster was a fuckin' liability,' one of Charlie's associates said later. 'He was the one who usually lashed out, went a bit OTT, if you know what I mean.'); Charlie had a length of cable down his trousers; and Goody carried a truncheon he'd bought in Madrid from a member of the *Guardia Civil*.

At 9.45 a.m., on the third floor of Comet House, five smartly dressed men separately entered the room marked: 'CL31 – Gentlemen'. Attendant Bert Turner noticed the new arrivals all wore bowler hats except for one, who had on a Robin Hood trilby. It seemed a bit odd, but Turner didn't linger on it. Two of the strangers were gazing out of the window by the basins while two were initially inside the cubicles; Buster Edwards stood by a urinal.

Goody, Charlie and another member of the team called Harry Booth continued washing their hands, combing their hair and straightening out their ties to distract the elderly attendant, who was intrigued by Edwards, standing at the urinal for so long. Then Edwards spotted the security men coming out of Barclays up the street, zipped up his trousers and winked at another team member who slipped out of the Gents to call the lift.

A big, black box containing a fortune in cash wages was being loaded into the armoured security van 100 yards down the street. The van moved off, escorted by a security officer in a car in front and another behind, and headed towards the BOAC building.

At 9.59 a.m., the five men from the third-floor Gents waited by the lift. On the floor below, three other smartly dressed men – all in bowlers with one carrying a dispatch case – began to head towards the stairs. No one had paid much attention to them up until then. They had been standing near a door marked 'Staff Vacancies', as if waiting their turn for an interview. The one with the dispatch case had spent most of his time looking out of the window.

Outside Comet House, the wages convoy drew up. Brian Howe, a security officer with BOAC, who'd travelled with the convoy, unlocked the rear of the armoured van. Arthur Smith, the security officer from the car in front of the van, stood guard as Ronald Grey and his assistant loaded the box onto a trolley, which they began wheeling across the pavement. On the third floor, Charlie and the other team members scrambled into the lift. As the doors shut, they pulled down their masks.

The security men had pushed the trolley into the entrance hall of Comet House and were approaching the lift. Grey pressed the elevator button and noticed from the indicator light that the lift was already starting its descent from the third floor.

At precisely 10 a.m., the lift passed the second floor on its sixteen-second journey to ground level. A few yards away, three of the smartly dressed men who'd been on that same floor were now running down four flights of stairs – fifty-five steps in all.

Back on the ground floor, the security men waited patiently.

The three men reached the ground floor on foot at the same moment the lift with their five associates came to a halt. At sixteen seconds past 10 a.m., the lift doors opened and all five leapt out with stocking masks over their faces and bowler hats still on their heads. They pulled coshes, iron bars and sawn-down pickaxe handles out from under their suit jackets and stormed towards the security guards yelling like warriors.

The heavy padlock from the van was still in Brian Howe's hands and he was turning to hand it to his colleague Smith. 'That's when I heard shouting and the sound of running feet,' he later recalled.

Just then, the blaggers from the second floor also dived towards the pay clerks. Howe explained: 'I turned round and saw just one big mêlée going on. One man attacked me and hit me over the head with what I think was a sawn-off pickaxe handle.' Howe got his truncheon out and managed to hit one robber when another came tearing into his side and knocked him flying. He was then hit hard on the head.

'In the course of that struggle, I was carried out of the foyer, through the swing doors and onto the pavement outside,' recalled Howe. 'They used their coshes viciously. I'm not quite sure what happened after that because I was so dazed by the second blow across my head.' The other security guard, Smith, was also hit at least twice as he tried to get his truncheon out and fight back against the robbers. Staff members Grey and Harris were also hit by blows to the head and body.

At 10.03 a.m., as two stolen Mark 2 Jags were being reversed towards the front doors of Comet House by the team's drivers, disguised as chauffeurs, Charlie and one other, carrying the wages box, came running out. The rest of the team followed still brandishing their weapons. The money was thrown in the back seat of the first Jag while Charlie headed for the second. Moments later, the vehicles screeched off at high speed and headed across the grass embankment towards an emergency gate locked with a chain and padlock on the perimeter road of the airport. The raiders had cut it earlier with giant bolt-cutters. Buster Edwards leapt out of one of the Jags and pulled at the gates, which fell open with ease. By taking this route, the gang got off the airport compound within just 250 yards of Comet House. Once again, expert planning had proved vital to the robbery.

Mickey Ball's Jag was the first one out onto the main A4 Great West Road, but he hesitated when he spotted a little Austin A40 in his rear-view mirror, trying to reverse to block off the other getaway vehicle driven by Roy James, who just swerved to avoid it and squeezed through the gap in the entrance. Moments later, James accelerated past Ball. Both drivers were still disguised as chauffeurs. To avoid suspicion at a possible roadblock, the men had replaced the back seat of one of the Jaguars with the wages box and covered it with a grey rug. Three of the blaggers then sat on that 'seat'.

The Jags continued at high speed to their changeover point: a garage in Hounslow, two miles from the scene of the robbery. There, they transferred the money into a minivan, which Mickey Ball was to drive to a flophouse – organised by Bruce Reynolds – in the south London suburb of Norbury. The others were to make their way to the flophouse independently. Driver James had a getaway motorbike standing by, but it would not start, so his intended passenger, Gordon Goody, gave up waiting and headed to the nearest Underground station. Buster Edwards took a bus to Vauxhall. Charlie just wandered off in a southerly direction. All of them knew the most important thing was to split up before the police spotted them.

Afterwards, three of the security staff had to be treated in hospital for their injuries. Bert Turner, the lavatory attendant, who'd earlier seen those five men, realised he was a very lucky man. He told reporters: 'There was I in the presence of a vicious cosh gang without knowing it. I shudder to think what might have happened if I'd rumbled what they were up to. I'd only walked a few yards after seeing them go down in the lift when I was told there was a raid.'

The gang's stolen Jags – identical metallic-blue Mark 2s – were later found by police, discarded chauffeur's uniforms in the boot of both cars. A pair of bolt-cutters were also discovered in each vehicle, plus three blue balaclava masks. It later emerged that one of the stolen cars belonged to a famous TV star called Craig Stevens, known throughout America at the time as TV detective Peter Gunn. The car had been stolen the previous month from outside Stevens' home in Eaton Square, Belgravia. The 'City Gents Gang', as Fleet Street was about to dub them, had just pulled off one of the most dramatic robberies of all time.

However, at their Norbury flophouse later that day, the gang were bitterly disappointed to discover they'd only managed to steal £62,500. Each man was given £4,000 to tide him over until the next big job, while the remaining £22,500 was kept in reserve to finance any new projects and provide retainers for new recruits. It had already been agreed that everyone should get the same share, no matter what his role, so there'd be no temptation to 'grass up' the others to the police. It was in Norbury that Bruce 'The Colonel' Reynolds mentioned for the first time a night train from Glasgow to London that 'might be worth a tug'. He didn't elaborate any further.

Charlie Wilson later told a close friend that the airport heist had provided him with 'the ultimate fuckin' buzz'. He and the other blaggers had proved beyond doubt they had the bottle to carry out spectacular jobs in broad daylight. The only disappointment was the money, which fell hundreds of thousands of pounds short of their expectations. They had no control over how much money was on offer, however, so their reputations as master robbers remained intact.

Pat Wilson later described first hearing about the airport raid: 'I was sitting at home watching television when it came on the news. I'll never forget how my heart sank. I knew immediately that Charlie had deceived me with that betting coup story.' A voice inside Pat's head kept saying over and over again that Charlie and Frenchy must have masterminded it.

When Charlie finally arrived home, later the same day of the robbery, Pat plucked up the courage to confront him. Charlie didn't blink an eye or show any sign of surprise when she mentioned the robbery. He flashed Pat one of his brightest smiles and said casually: 'Good luck to 'em – such planning deserves every success.'

Charlie admitted to Pat that everyone was talking about the job and even told her the gangsters believed they were going to get £200,000 not a mere £62,000. 'It was hardly worth the trouble for the risk involved,' he said before turning to Pat and telling her: 'D'you know, I hear the actual bowler hats those robbers used at the airport were lined with steel.'

Pat was infuriated with Charlie for so blatantly ignoring her initial questions, so she asked him outright if he was involved in the robbery. Charlie took a deep breath and replied very quietly: 'Darling, don't worry. I won't let you down. Just don't ask questions.'

Pat later said that Charlie had an extremely happy-go-lucky and even-tempered character *most* of the time, but when he did lose his temper – which was about twice a year – sparks would fly. On those occasions, Pat admitted she would 'dissolve into tears under the weight of his verbal lashings'. In other words, she knew better than to ask him awkward questions about his criminal activities.

The Heathrow raid sparked a blaze of publicity because of the daring – and bizarre – nature of the robbery. As one detective said at the time: 'These blaggers were utter professionals: cold, calculating and very well organised. The moment we got down to the scene, we knew we were dealing with a ruthless band of pros.'

Police quickly established that the well-dressed villains had taken it in turns over several weeks to recce the location of the robbery. Finger smudges were uncovered on the window sills in the gentlemen's toilet where the gang had watched the money being delivered in the security van. A reward of £6,500 was immediately offered for information leading to the arrest of the gang, but few expected it to bring any results.

Charlie's only real concern after the raid was a story in the *Sunday People* newspaper claiming that Scotland Yard had received an early tip-off about the robbery from an inside source and that was why the security guards were carrying far less cash than was expected. This meant someone inside the gang might be a police informant, 'a grass'. Charlie told another gang member that if he found out who it was, he'd 'wring his fuckin' neck'. And he meant it. Charlie still firmly believed informants were 'Judases who should be drowned at birth'.

The police soon came knocking at Charlie's front door in Crescent Lane, Clapham, enquiring about his movements on the day of the airport robbery. Charlie was so confident they had no evidence he agreed to go down to Cannon Row Police Station on three occasions to clear up any misunderstandings. Mickey Ball and Gordon Goody were also pulled in. The police seemed to have more evidence against them.

On each occasion Charlie visited the station at Cannon Row, he and the others were asked to appear in identity parades. The first time, Charlie agreed to wear a City suit, bowler hat and false moustache. None of the security guards brought in for that first parade recognised any of the three suspected robbers. Then, as everyone was breaking up, one guard saw Gordon Goody in profile and put the finger on him. At a second parade, all the suspects were put up without make-up or a special style of dress and all 38 supposed witnesses failed to pick out Charlie. Much to the amusement of Fleet Street, Scotland Yard then recruited real City gents from Whitehall to take part in a third parade. Charlie and his airport heist mates found it hard to keep straight faces. On that third parade, Charlie, Gordon Goody and Mickey Ball were once again made to wear moustaches, dark suits and bowler hats. It was only then that all three were positively fingered. Later, while being interrogated, one of the gang even asked a detective what he would do when the really big one took place. The officer involved thought the comment was just a sarcastic joke. It wasn't until many months later they realised they'd stumbled on a clue that the gang might be planning a much bigger crime.

On 17 December 1962, Charlie (by now 30), Gordon Goody and Mickey Ball were charged at Harlington Police Station with robbery with violence and stealing £62,500 at Heathrow Airport a month earlier, on 17 November. Typically, none of the men confessed to police, even after they'd been charged. Charlie later alleged that 'once a few bob had been thrown in the right direction', the suspects would be given bail, despite the serious nature of the robbery. The police pulled in other members of the gang, but failed to make any charges stick. The following morning, at Uxbridge Magistrates' Court, all three were given a total of £30,000 bail after Detective Superintendent Maurice Osborn told the court: 'They have on three occasions voluntarily come to the police station to attend identity parades and under these circumstances we don't think they would abscond.'

At their Uxbridge Crown Court trial two months later, the jury was told that make-up, false moustaches and chauffeur's hats were found at Gordon Goody's home in Putney, west London. The court heard he had told police they were bought for a Christmas fancy dress party. The court was also told of a similar find, including chauffeur's caps, greasepaint, false moustaches and sideboards, at Ball's home in Lambrook Terrace, Fulham, south-west London. Charlie later insisted they'd all been planted by police desperate to prove the prosecution case.

One witness told the court he'd seen men in bowler hats and dark overcoats, wearing spectacles and false moustaches, walking on the road near Comet House. Shopkeeper Edward Murray said that they were 'definitely out of place' and that 'their moustaches appeared to be out of character with their features, you might say'.

Two other witnesses swore in court they'd seen Charlie, but in different places at the same time, which weakened a prosecution case which seemed to be based entirely on circumstantial evidence. At the end of the trial, the judge, Sir Anthony Hawke, directed the jury to acquit Charlie on the grounds that the evidence against him was 'of such a doubtful character that it did not justify proceeding against him further'. The jury couldn't decide whether Gordon Goody was innocent or guilty, so he was ordered to face a retrial.

Just before Goody's new trial, Charlie later claimed he 'persuaded' a bent copper to swap a checked cap Goody had worn during the robbery – and now in the possession of the police – for one three sizes bigger. When Goody was handed it to wear in the dock, he put it on his head and it fell over his ears and eyes. Gang member Buster Edwards also approached a juror who agreed to bring in a verdict of 'not guilty', so the judge was eventually left with no choice but to free Goody as well.

On 26 March 1963, driver Mickey Ball was found guilty after prosecuting counsel Mr Michael Corkrey told the court: 'The raid was a masterpiece of criminal planning. Meetings happened at people's homes, in bars and clubs. This was a highly professional operation.' Charlie later said he liked that description very much.

Charlie was so delighted to get off the airport robbery charges he bought himself a well-cut black suit, a bowler hat and an expensive silk umbrella. He'd wanted to take Pat off on another fancy holiday, but she wasn't keen on going abroad. So instead, he set off alone on a tour of Europe's best hotels and casinos. A few weeks later, Charlie returned home, bronzed and fit, and ready to buckle back down to work. He knew Pat was fed up with all his criminal activity and, to placate her, he started getting up again at four every morning to get fruit and vegetables from the market for her family's shop. She prayed he'd keep out of trouble this time, hoping two major acquittals would have taught him a lesson.

Charlie also bought himself a gleaming new maroon four-door Rover 3.5 coupé, which became his pride and joy. He spent two hours each weekend polishing it and refused to allow Pat to get into it without taking off her shoes first. Yet despite his new-found riches, Charlie continued to worry about providing for their children's futures. Charlie's financial insecurities kept driving him forward to find fresh criminal challenges. He was overly generous with his family and close friends, and needed to keep re-financing that extravagant lifestyle. His only personal regret at this time was his relationship with his father, which had got increasingly worse since he was imprisoned in the late '50s.

It was no real surprise that within weeks of getting back from his European tour, Charlie's interest in the fruit and vegetable business started to wane. Then, for the first time in his married life, Charlie began staying out for two or three nights a week, which provoked some uncharacteristically angry words from Pat. She later explained that the trouble was he never lied or gave her excuses, he just simply refused to say anything. The truth was that Charlie was hard at work planning new heists, gambling in all-night speilers and occasionally getting involved with a few 'ladies of the night' in Soho.

Charlie continued to split those two distinct sides of his life down the middle. As Nosher Powell explains: 'Charlie was essentially a loner and, although a lot of people knew him as the opposite, Charlie rarely got too close to people. It's a funny thing to say, but he was a great family man who didn't like or trust many other people. As he once said to me after a spell inside, "The bird [sentence] was easy, but the absence of the wife and kids was sometimes too much to take.'"

Charlie thrived on the security of a stable home to return to after days and nights of partying and thieving. He knew he couldn't survive in the real, hard world if he didn't hold onto part of the good world as well. The birth of Charlie and Pat's third daughter Leander in 1963 summed this up perfectly. There was no question of Charlie going off the rails, getting a divorce and going downhill. He liked his life the way it was and had no intention of changing it. His only disappointment might have been that he hadn't yet fathered a boy. In other ways, he was relieved Pat had only had girls because he didn't want to end up repeating history. Charlie's poor relationship with his father had had a far-reaching effect on his life, leaving him deeply suspicious of most men and unwilling to trust them.

6

An immense cancer had grown inside the detective force of the Metropolitan Police by the early '60s. Bribery and the planting of false evidence was endemic. Many villains, including Charlie, believed that bail and adjusting evidence to suit them could always be bought for a price. Charlie himself alleged he paid a policeman £10,000 to drop evidence from the Heathrow robbery which could have resulted in his imprisonment. Villains like Charlie claimed they used a middleman, often a figure well known to the police, to hand over such bribes. No one knows if Charlie was telling the truth or just trying to smear hardworking detectives, but a deep vein of suspicion between the police and criminals undoubtedly existed.

There were three main forms of corruption at the time: charging for bail, suppressing previous convictions and dropping more serious charges. These offences often involved more senior officers investigating crimes such as bank robbery, drugs and obscene publications. There were also officers who believed the system of justice was weighted against them and felt justified in bending the rules. The underworld had a more down-to-earth classification: bent for yourself (taking bribes) or bent for the job (fitting people up who were believed to be guilty to gain a conviction).

Judge Sir Frederick Lawton, who later jailed gang boss Charlie Richardson, believed that the rot set in because of wartime regulations, which exposed the police to bribery when businessmen and industrialists were able to buy themselves out of trouble if they'd broken the law. Charlie and his criminal associates simply assumed they could also buy themselves out of jail. As one of Charlie's oldest pals said recently: 'There was hundreds of ways to bribe a copper back then and that was part and parcel of your business, and you accepted that. You even built it into your finances.' In one story, when Charlie was arrested in the early 1960s, he complimented a detective on the high quality of his handmade suit. The officer responded by mentioning that he hadn't yet made it to Church's, an expensive West End shoe shop.

It was the practice of 'verbaling' – police altering words in suspects' statements – that Charlie and many others claimed was frequently used against them to secure arrests. Charlie said: 'Once they had our names as suspects from a grass, we knew we was in trouble because they'd falsify the evidence to secure convictions without hesitation.'

The practice of verbaling had been commonplace since the late '40s. Judge Sir Frederick Lawton recalled there was one notorious Met police sergeant who'd always claim suspects had, on arrest, said: 'Blimey, who's grassed me up this time?' It was a classic verbal because the law would immediately infer that the suspect was a criminal because of his use of the slang word 'grass'. One suspect even made a full 'confession', complete with cockney rhyming slang and Yiddish expressions, to the same sergeant – oddly enough, he later turned out to be a well-educated Pole.

Throughout the 1950s, Scotland Yard continued to ignore suggestions of corruption within their force. When Superintendent Bert Hannam produced a report in 1955 outlining the sort of trickery used by the police, it barely got a mention in the media. By the early '60s, payments to detectives by criminals were virtually routine, particularly in specialised areas where the profits were high. One detective later even referred to the actions of bent coppers as those of individuals working in a 'firm within a firm' (a firm is generally held to mean a group of robbers). It wasn't until almost 20 years later that Scotland Yard finally started to tackle the entire question of police corruption properly.

In the early '60s – when Charlie Wilson and his pals were robbing and thieving their way through London – there were three types of officers at the Yard: those who were corrupt, those who were honest but did nothing and those who were too stupid to realise that there was any corruption in the first place. One judge later made what was to become a famous speech when sentencing officers for corruption. He told them: 'You poisoned the wells of criminal justice and set about it deliberately. What is equally bad is that you have betrayed your comrades in the Metropolitan Police Force which enjoys the respect of the civilised world – what remains of it – and not the least grave aspect of what you have done is to provide material for the crooks, cranks and do-gooders who unite to attack the police whenever the opportunity occurs.'

★ ★ ★

One night in the spring of 1963, as Pat and Charlie were watching television at home, there was a knock on the door. It was Frenchy. Pat recalled how her heart sank because she knew this meant another job was on the horizon. Pat was irritated that her husband was up to his old tricks. Their business was prospering. They didn't need any more money with a joint income in excess of £3,000 a year. Why was he doing this?

Frenchy's visit heralded the start of plans for the Big One – the job which Charlie believed would send him into lucrative retirement. Soon Frenchy was calling round three times a week, often with as many as four other burly men. Then they'd sit closeted with Charlie in the front room for hours, as thick clouds of cigarette and cigar smoke wafted through the rest of the house. Whenever Pat was at home, Charlie would simply tell her they were 'discussing business' and ask her not to disturb them.

Pat recalls: 'Those words sent a shiver down my spine. But what could I do? In our home, Charlie's word was law. Whatever he ordered, the children and I obeyed. He was a fair man – but had to be obeyed.'

After each meeting broke up, Charlie left the house with the other men and sometimes didn't return home for days. Every ashtray was full to the brim and there would also be three or four empty bottles of Scotch left on the table in the front room. One time, Pat begged Charlie to tell her what they were planning. She later explained how she even threatened to leave him unless she got a reasonable reply. But Charlie simply looked at his wife and said softly: 'Wait and see, love. What you don't know can't harm you. If this business deal comes off, I will be set up for life.' Then he paused for a moment and added: 'I know you'd never let me down, love.' Of course, Charlie was right. Pat never had any intention of deserting him and, despite all her misgivings about his activities, she knew that the only people he truly cared about were her and the girls. It was them against the world.

In fact, Charlie and the other men had been discussing the Glasgow to Euston Travelling Post Office which was known as the Up Special or the Up Postal amongst rail staff. It left Glasgow at 6.50 p.m. every evening and was scheduled to arrive at London's Euston Station at 3.59 a.m. the following morning. The Travelling Post Office consisted of a diesel engine and 12 coaches. It also housed 77 Post Office employees and, every night, was packed with hundreds of thousands of pounds.

The core of what would become the Great Train Robbery gang was an utterly loyal clique known as the 'Fulham Team'. They consisted of Charlie, Bruce Reynolds, Ronald Arthur Biggs, Douglas Gordon Goody, James Hussey, Roy John James, Robert Welch, Thomas William Wisbey, Brian Arthur Field, Leonard Dennis Field, Roger John Cordrey and John Denby Wheater. They also hand-picked another man known only as 'Stan', who'd worked on the railway and was commissioned to create a blueprint to beat the complicated railway signalling system and teach the others how to un-couple carriages when it came to the actual robbery. Dressed in railwaymen's clothing, supplied by their 'consultant', Charlie and seven others ventured down to the New Cross Goods Yard in south-east London to practise. In the run-up to the train robbery, Charlie and the rest of the gang were promised £100 a week providing they did not undertake any other work; they later insisted they were never told the source of the money.

One day, Charlie and Frenchy called a team meeting on Wimbledon Common because Charlie knew that the chaps constantly arriving at his house were irritating Pat. Ten burly men tried to kick a ball around convincingly, near a well-known tourist spot called The Windmill, as gang member Bruce 'The Colonel' Reynolds reiterated to them that they mustn't tell a soul about their plans. There was an overriding fear of informants and everyone knew that loose words sank ships. Yet the team created for the Great Train Robbery were so untrusting of one another, most of them were armed at such meetings. Charlie was one of those who preferred packing a piece, although none of them would ever admit it to the others.

One well-known criminal who was approached to work on the train robbery was former Krays' henchman Freddie 'The Mean Machine'

Foreman. He'd just carried out a gold robbery in London which had netted a cool £250,000. Foreman explained: '. . . that meant I was in demand, but because I'd already had that great touch with the gold, I told 'em my firm was havin' a rest and wouldn't want to get involved'. There were four or five heavyweight teams of robbers working in London at that time and they all knew one another, according to Foreman: 'We could tell which firm was behind every robbery reported in the papers. Each one had its own trademark, or modus operandi.'

One afternoon, when Charlie and the chaps were meeting in the front room of his house yet again, he asked Pat to take them in a tray of tea. She was amazed to find the group of five men had drawn the curtains and were sitting in pitch black. The character Pat knew as Frenchy was at the table fiddling with a small film projector. As Pat put the tray down, the machine suddenly whirred into life and on a portable screen a few feet in front of the men was a countryside scene that seemed innocent enough at first. Pat later recalled that the film showed a train coming down a railway line which Frenchy tried to pass off as a scene 'just outside Paris'. 'It's on the same line where we blew up a German train,' he said.

Charlie made a point of telling Pat afterwards: 'Frenchy's wartime experiences are very interesting. He had plenty of exciting times.' It was only later that Pat realised the film showed where the Great Train Robbery was to take place.

Frenchy and a cameraman friend had been down at least half a dozen times to the spot near Cheddington, in the Buckinghamshire countryside, 40 miles north of London, where they intended to hold up the train. When a couple of people asked Frenchy what he was doing with the camera, he claimed to be a trainspotter. On each visit, they spent several hours filming every aspect of the crossing area before coming back and showing the films to the rest of the gang. This research was key to establishing the lighting system and the time it took for the train to gather speed again after it slowed down at that signal. Frenchy timed the entire process to perfection. Undercover trips during both night and day to Cheddington followed, with gang members disguised as anglers sometimes spending an entire weekend on reconnaissance. Charlie was equally obsessed with the planning of the job, which was turning into a military-style operation.

Charlie, Goody, Wisbey and Hussey were considered the heavies of the team and were briefed to take 'any measures' required if there were problems during the job. None of them admitted whether this included violence towards the Post Office staff and train crew. Charlie even helped to mark up an Ordnance Survey map of the surrounding countryside for the possible routes they could take when leaving the area following the robbery. Charlie armed himself with the same length of copper cable he'd used for the Heathrow Airport job because he considered it a 'lucky mascot'. Balaclavas or stockings would be used as masks.

Leatherslade Farm, an isolated smallholding near Cheddington, was to be the gang's base and safe house after the robbery. It was just a couple of miles from the heist location, which was a railway bridge called, somewhat confusingly, Bridego Bridge, and was set in a hollow on rising ground which could not be seen from nearby roads. The farm had been purchased for cash through the gang's legal representatives Brian Field and John Wheater. Charlie and Roy James even bought Parachute Regiment uniforms, badges and berets from Army surplus stores after the gang decided to wear uniforms because they knew locals would not be suspicious of an Army convoy parked under Bridego Bridge in the early hours (there was an Army base nearby). They purchased square, coloured stickers normally used to decorate and identify Army vehicles, and had special number plates made up with the military placing of numbers and letters. The team also planned to 'arrest' any nosey policemen who came asking awkward questions. Charlie even provided a box of fruit and a sack of potatoes from his father-in-law's grocery shop to be taken to Leatherslade Farm for the 'troops'.

On the first Saturday of August 1963, Charlie and four of the team went out for a casual drive in the countryside near Bridego Bridge. They eventually rolled up for a pint of beer and a sandwich at a pub in the nearby village of Brill. The landlord later said he remembered the men because they were all strangers, travelling in a posh car and had arrived saying they were all 'bloody starving'. They refused to accept any change when they paid up. A few days later, Charlie and the rest of the team held a full dress rehearsal on a stretch of line near Cheddington. They stopped a train by changing the signals, but then allowed it to go on unhampered, the drivers none the wiser as to the role they had played in the upcoming heist.

On 6 August, alibis carefully established, Charlie and the rest of the gang finally gathered at Leatherslade Farm for the Big One. All the next day, they sat around trying to stay calm by playing board games and drinking incessant cups of tea. Each team member was given a colour as a nickname to ensure no one could identify them later. Then, at midnight, a short-wave radio crackled into life and they heard the coded message: 'It's tonight.'

On the early morning of 8 August 1963, as village clocks chimed 1.30 a.m., a convoy consisting of a three-ton lorry and two Land-Rovers moved down moonlit B-roads watching the shrubs and hedgerows flashing past in their headlights. Radios were tuned into the police frequency, but there was no activity. The team eventually pulled up at Bridego Bridge just after 2.00 a.m., having deliberately taken a long route round. They disembarked and huddled in groups by the side of the track while walkie-talkies were given one final check. Just before 2.30 a.m., they walked up the track to a point known as 'Sears Crossing' to go over the plan one last time.

Typically, Charlie even had time for a few quips with his old friend Gordon Goody, who suggested he would buy a 'new motor' if he could afford it, to which Charlie replied, 'You can afford a Bentley Continental now.'

'I wish I could. I'm fuckin' skint at the moment,' responded Goody, his caution with money already legendary.

Charlie looked at Goody for a beat or two, then, using the teams' nicknames, said: 'For fuck's sake, Blue, put your mask on. You're so ugly.'

Laughing, Goody pulled his stocking mask down to cover his face. By 3 a.m., they were in position. It was time to go to work.

7

Minutes later, two gang members rigged the signal to appear red at the isolated crossing just before the bridge. They didn't disturb electronic 'fail-safe' gadgets, but covered the green signal with a glove and used flashlights to shine the light through the red panel of the signal. The train – which was exactly on time – halted precisely where they wanted it to. So far so good.

As train driver Jack Mills and his engineer David Whitby stepped down to see what was wrong with the signals, they were seized by the bandits, now wearing silk stockings and balaclavas over their heads. At the same time, another group of the robbers uncoupled the first two coaches, while postal workers in the remaining cars continued with their routine, unaware of the drama up front. Mills hesitated about taking the train down the track to Bridego Bridge, where the gang's lorry was waiting, so an infuriated Buster Edwards bludgeoned him with his cosh. Charlie eventually stepped between Edwards and the train driver, and, with his bright blue eyes gleaming through the holes in his balaclava, told the driver not to worry, that no one was going to hurt him. Only then did Mills, just able to stand properly, agree to steer the train down the line.

After arriving at Bridego Bridge, one of the gang shouted, 'Get the guns,' to frighten the Post Office sorters. Charlie was then lifted up by another team member to a level high enough to use his cosh to smash the window of the carriage. Once in, Charlie ran at the men piling sacks against the door with his cosh raised. They turned and dashed past him, down the coach to where another gang member whipped them across the shoulders and told them all to lie face down. One of the robbers then used an axe to smash the padlock to the door containing the mail sacks.

Back up front, robber Bobby Welch was now attending to the injured driver, who'd slumped onto the floor next to his colleague. Charlie then reappeared and got them each a cigarette. Crouching down beside the terrified Mills, Charlie started wiping the blood off his face with a rag, a result of the earlier attack by Edwards. Bruce Reynolds later explained how Charlie had made Mills comfortable, patching him up as they sat on the grass verge beside the tracks. 'I think you're a real gentleman,' the driver told Charlie.

Charlie asked if he wanted any money, offering to leave it on the grass verge for him, but Mills shook his head just as the gang formed a human chain to carefully begin sweeping 120 mail sacks containing cash and diamonds into the awaiting lorry. Reynolds counted down three minutes on his stopwatch, then announced: 'That's it, chaps.'

Charlie chipped in, 'But there's only a few left.'

'Sod 'em,' said Reynolds. 'Time's up, let's get on the road.'

The gang quickly took off in the two identical Land-Rovers and the lorry. The entire operation had taken just 15 minutes.

As the robbers drove steadily through the Buckinghamshire countryside in the early hours, Charlie fiddled with the radio to try and check on police movements. Suddenly, over the airwaves, came the voice of American crooner Tony Bennett singing 'The Good Life'. It was the perfect song. The others began laughing and all slapped one another on the back for the umpteenth time. As fellow robber Tommy Wisbey later recalled: 'We'd got the big prize. It was a feeling of elation. I think it would have been harder taking sweets off a baby.'

Back at Sears Crossing, a Post Office assistant inspector and another colleague scrambled out of the smashed-up coach and headed back along the tracks where the remainder of the train was stranded. On the way, they met a guard and told him what had happened, and together they raised the alarm.

At 3.40 a.m., Charlie and the rest of the team pulled up in front of Leatherslade Farm. At that moment, their short-wave radio crackled into life: 'You won't believe this,' said one policeman over the airwaves, 'but someone's just stolen a train.'

The mailbags were quickly unloaded and stacked along the living-room walls and in the hallway of the farmhouse. Each bag was carefully checked for homing devices, then some of the group started ripping open the bags and stacking banknotes in small piles. Soon, spread out inside Leatherslade Farm, was approximately £1,200,000 in £5 notes and over £1,300,000 in £1 and 10 shilling notes, making a grand total of around £2,500,000. There was a long pause as all of them looked at the extraordinary sight – money literally piled high in front of their eyes. Charlie jumped up and punched the air in delight.

Bruce Reynolds then wished Ronnie Biggs happy birthday and went to each man and shook his hand in thanks. Charlie laughed out loud as he pointed to a bag of money saying, 'Look at that. There's eighty grand in that pile.' Then Charlie started singing 'I Like It', a recent hit record for Gerry and The Pacemakers, as he stared manically at the piles of cash. Some of the others joined in the singing, even grabbing a few old pound notes and using them to light their cigarettes.

> *I like it, I like it,*
> *I like the way you run your fingers through my hair . . .*

The amount stolen by Charlie and the gang would be worth more than £40 million in today's terms. The average salary at the time was £20 a week and Charlie's share of £150,000 was the equivalent of a huge win on the National Lottery. Before the big share-out could go ahead, newsflashes on the radio began sending ripples of anxiety through the gang:

Cheddington, England – A well-drilled gang of about 30 masked bandits ambushed a mail train on Thursday and escaped with loot estimated at millions of pounds in perhaps the biggest

robbery of all time. The job was executed at 3.15 a.m., 40 miles
north of London, with precision and teamwork that pointed to
the strategy of an underworld mastermind who has met with
success in previous train and bullion robberies.

Charlie already knew he'd probably have to go on the run because he
was so well known to the police. He told Buster Edwards at the farm:
'I'll have to go on me toes.'

The initial plan to lie low had to be changed and it was decided to
share the money out immediately. They all knew they had to go their
separate ways quickly, but naturally they all wanted their own share in
their own hands.

The gang knew how important it was to keep the money
successfully (and separately) hidden from police. No traces of it would
ever turn up at the homes of the various suspects. Charlie believed it
was a matter of each man for himself. Many years later, he was credited
with being 'the Treasurer' after the robbery, and was said to be the
only man who knew where the majority of the money was hidden and
the actual size of each cut. Whatever the full extent of his power and
influence over the other gang members, Charlie revelled in his image as
one of the main organisers of the robbery. He wanted to prove that
crime really did pay.

Many believe there was a master plan to dispose of a large part of
the haul which involved pooling a number of individual shares into one
place. Intriguingly, many of the rest of the gang seemed to trust
Charlie implicitly, with the result that much of the Great Train
Robbery cash would be left with Charlie's associates or in lock-ups to
which only he had access. It's long been rumoured that Charlie and
Buster Edwards held back £500,000 of the £1 million fee that was
allegedly to be paid to the so-called 'financiers' and later hid it after
dreaming up all sorts of people whom they claimed were backers, but
who never really existed.

Besides the cash, there was also the question of how the farm would
be 'cleaned' of any clues that might give away the gang's identity if
and when the police discovered their hideaway. In the middle of all
this, Charlie even managed a light-hearted dig at his old friend Bruce
Reynolds, who made no secret of his obsession with the 'cleaning'
operation, saying, 'Why don't you open a fuckin' office cleaning
business? You'd be good at that.'

Reynolds laughed and said, 'Get on with it – you don't want to leave
any dabs, do you?'

'Fuckin' dabs,' said Charlie. 'There won't be any fuckin' surface left in a minute, let alone fingerprints.'

'That'll suit me fine, Chas,' said Reynolds, as he looked at the line of men behind him, each with a damp cloth in their hands, wiping everything in sight.

Charlie was so hungry that morning at Leatherslade Farm that he ate two salt-beef sandwiches, over which he poured a generous covering of salt from a Saxo container, unintentionally leaving a thumbprint on its side. Charlie then changed into his normal working clothes before setting off for London at high speed in a stolen Jaguar E-type. The clothes he had worn during the robbery were left at the farm to be destroyed, along with those worn by other members of the gang.

Charlie, a fast but safe driver, reached London at around 5.30 a.m. and left the E-type at a pre-arranged spot before getting into his more sedate Rover, deliberately parked in Spitalfields Market so that he had an alibi. At the same time, 50 miles away, Frenchy took off in a private plane for northern France with two large grip bags containing at least £400,000.

At Leatherslade Farm, two of the gang were supposed to finish off cleaning everything for possible fingerprints before setting fire to the building, but they left before completing the job. Charlie never forgave them for failing in their duty.

A few hours after the raid, Scotland Yard's Detective Superintendent Gerald McArthur and Sergeant Jack Pritchard, his ex-commando assistant, arrived at Cheddington to assist local chief of police, Detective Superintendent Malcolm Fewtrell, head of Buckinghamshire CID. As Detective Inspector Frank Cater (later commander of the Flying Squad) put it: 'With the Great Train Robbery, it seemed to us that the world of crime detection had changed overnight. A new elite of organised crime had grown up, syndicates of men, not necessarily with criminal records, who specialised. They considered themselves to be in business and, like any other successful businessmen, they insisted on their enterprises being properly supplied with advance finance – equipment and, in particular, information had to be bought.'

Back in Clapham, Pat hadn't been particularly worried by Charlie's absence the previous night, as this had long since become a regular feature of their marriage. He finally turned up at lunchtime the following day, nine or ten hours after the train had been held up.

Within minutes of walking through the front door, Pat heard a bulletin on the transistor radio in the kitchen. Before she could open her mouth, Charlie told her he went straight to work in the market that morning at five o'clock and that there were fifty people who could confirm he was there.

Pat didn't respond at first; her heart was fluttering with fear and disappointment. She asked Charlie on three separate occasions over the following couple of hours if he was involved in the robbery and each time, Charlie replied: 'Don't ask questions. I've told you I was at work at 5.30 a.m. So don't ever ask me that question again.'

That evening, Charlie travelled with Roy James in his Mini Cooper to a lock-up garage in the East End, where Charlie intended to hide his share of the loot. Charlie and James naturally discussed the robbery and how to avoid arrest. Charlie had already been linked with him in past crimes and James admitted to Charlie he'd not worn gloves all the time at Leatherslade Farm. The following day, that same lock-up was used by two of the other robbers to deposit their share of the train robbery loot.

Charlie knew immediately when he saw the newspapers the day after the robbery that the police were going to move mountains to get them and none of the gang were safe. Charlie believed the weak link in the chain was Brian Field, who'd acted as one of the gang's legal representatives. He was not a professional criminal and was therefore more likely to crack under police pressure.

Two nights after the Great Train Robbery, Charlie walked into a pub in Earlsfield, south-west London, owned and run by his old friend Nosher Powell. He later explained: 'Charlie came in, ordered a drink and sat quietly in the corner, minding his own business as he always did. Charlie only ever talked to people he already knew. But he seemed a bit low that night, so I went over and had a chat.'

Charlie told his old friend: 'I fuckin' told 'em. The lot of 'em were unreliable. Too many of 'em.' Powell knew immediately what his childhood pal was talking about. Charlie continued: 'We had too many on that fuckin' job. I told 'em it was too many. We had 15 and we could have done it with half that amount.'

Nosher sensibly didn't ask Charlie to elaborate and hasn't ever revealed this conversation to anyone before. 'Charlie wasn't a big mouth, so I knew he was being deadly serious when he said that. Here was a geezer with the biggest payday anyone could ever dream of and he was miserable and worried. It was a disturbing sight to see him so unhappy.'

The following morning, Charlie rang Brian Field at his office and asked him cryptically: 'Has the dustman been?', a reference to Leatherslade Farm being 'cleaned'. Field assured him that everything had been taken care of, but Charlie wasn't happy and started ringing around the rest of the gang to arrange a meeting. Eventually, Charlie, Reynolds, Edwards and Roy James met at Clapham Common Underground station. Charlie said he didn't trust the men who were supposed to have cleaned the farm after their departure. He wanted them to go back and do it themselves, but no one else agreed so he didn't pursue the matter.

Next morning, Charlie and the others held a second meeting, this time with Field, outside Holland Park Underground station in west London. Field was quivering with fear and Charlie was so irritated by his nervousness that he had to be restrained by the others from trying to hit him. The lawyer assured the gang he hadn't let them down and even told them: 'If I get pulled, I swear I'll never say anything. I'll never make a statement. I'll never put any of you in it. All I ask in return is that you look after my wife.'

But Charlie, Reynolds, James and Edwards were far from happy once Field had left. After stopping at a café, Charlie once again brought up the subject of going back to the farm to destroy any evidence. Charlie wanted to wait until dark and then sneak back in and burn it down as had originally been planned. 'Mad bastard,' one of the other robbers said years later. 'But that was typical Charlie. He had more bottle than the rest of us.'

In his autobiography, Reynolds reflected: 'We presented an incongruous quartet in that transport café – Buster and I immaculately suited and booted, Chas and Roy in smart casuals.' Sitting around a bare wooden table, the group nursed steaming hot cups of tea and discussed the farm problem. Eventually, they agreed with Charlie's suggestion to go back to the farm that night and clear out all the mailbags, the only clue linking the property to the robbery. They decided against burning it down as it might cause too much attention. The gang were halfway through their second cup of tea when Buster Edwards popped out to get the afternoon newspaper. When he returned, he slapped the paper down on the table without saying a word. 'HIDE-OUT DISCOVERED' read the headline on the front page of the *London Evening News*. The article said that two Land-Rovers bearing identical number plates had been found at the farm along with a lorry with an ingenious secret drawer in the middle of the floor, big enough to take a large suitcase. It was empty.

Charlie felt the whole robbery was doomed from that moment onwards, telling an old friend years later: 'I'd always known we were gonna get nicked. Now it was just a matter of time.' Back in that café, however, Charlie tried to sound upbeat.

'Let's go down there anyway – we can cop for whoever's there and clear out the place,' he said, peering over his cup of tea. Bruce Reynolds later explained that Charlie meant it: '. . . with him it was never bravado. But it made no sense. There would be more Old Bill down there than the passing-out parade at Hendon Police College'.

The big question no one wanted to ask that afternoon was whether any of them were already police suspects. Certainly, Charlie had no idea that he'd left a thumbprint back at the farm on that salt container, even though he thought a 'pull' was inevitable.

After reading some more, Roy James interrupted all their trains of thought by exclaiming, 'Look at this! Fuckin' Tommy Butler's now in charge of the London end.'

Born in Shepherd's Bush, Butler had joined the Met in 1934. Four years later, he'd become a detective and climbed steadily through the ranks, enjoying three spells on the Flying Squad before becoming a detective chief superintendent in July 1963. His nickname – 'The Grey Fox' – was based on his tenacious efforts at bringing justice to such legendary figures as Jack Spot and Billy Hill, one of Charlie's heroes.

Not even Charlie could come up with a quip to counter the shock they all felt about Tommy Butler's involvement. The report said that an informant in prison had told Butler that the gang behind the robbery were all from London, which had prompted his appointment as head of the investigation. This 50-year-old bachelor, with receding hair, dark eyebrows and a thin, pointed nose like Mr Punch, still lived with his mother and adored westerns, but he was a relentless pursuer of villains. As the gang shook hands at the end of the gathering, they knew it might be the last time they ever met together in the outside world.

Charlie abandoned all plans to return to the farm. Later that day, Roy James was driving Charlie home when another report about the police discovery of Leatherslade Farm came on the radio. Afterwards, Roy turned to Charlie and said, 'That's it then, we're nicked.'

Fleet Street saw the robbery as a brilliant circulation spinner. One of the first front-page headlines read: '£1,000,000 BIGGEST MAIL ROBBERY EVER' (although that estimate proved to be way under what was really on the train). The headlines then developed into 'WORLD'S BIGGEST TRAIN HIJACK', but still the true value of the haul was not revealed to the world. It wasn't until a few days later that the *Daily Herald* front page read: 'UP TO £2 MILLION', after the embarrassed Postmaster General, Reginald Bevins, finally got closer to admitting how much was really on the train. When Buckinghamshire

Constabulary put up a £10,000 reward for information to help track down the robbers, it seemed laughable.

One cartoon in the *Daily Express* at the time caught Charlie's eye and always made him smile. It showed a dozen robbers sharing out the money with a caption: '. . . two million, four 'undred thousand, nine 'undred an' ninety-nine. That's British justice for yer, one short . . .' Another cartoon showed the head of Buckinghamshire CID, Detective Superintendent Malcolm Fewtrell, in animated guise with a magnifying glass following a trail of banknotes left by a runaway robber with a sack on his back. It was a farcical image showing how the robbers were already perceived to have humiliated the Establishment in dramatic fashion.

In prisons across the country, the Great Train Robbery was the talk of the landings because it epitomised every villain's dream of one day getting lucky. The train robbery gang had the respect of the entire underworld immediately.

The cash had weighed one and three quarter tonnes, yet it had disappeared without trace. How could it have been got rid of without attracting attention? The banks were only able to give the police numbers for 15,000 £5 notes. The police were still embarrassed by the £250,000 of unmarked banknotes which had been stolen from a mail van in the 1952 Eastcastle Street Mailbag Robbery and disappeared into thin air. Tommy Butler ordered a careful re-examination of that robbery plus two more of the best-organised blaggings in the history of British crime – a £250,000 bullion theft in Finsbury in 1960 and the £62,000 payroll snatch at Heathrow Airport the previous year, which had starred Charlie and most of the gang.

Across the country, alleged 'sightings' of the gang started flooding in. In Warwickshire, police were trying to trace a couple, aged between 20 and 30, who ran away from a hired car which crashed into a garden wall at Berkswell, near Coventry. The couple had offered £5 notes for a quick lift to Birmingham, 18 miles away. Squads of detectives had raided two adjoining houses in Stavordale Road, Highbury, north London. An Irishman from one of the houses commented that, 'They were looking for fivers. They searched the house from top to bottom, but went away empty-handed.' Detectives at Prince's Pier, Greenock, Scotland, screened 260 passengers bound for Montreal on the Cunard liner *Carinthia*, having heard that two of the mail-train gang were Canadians and might have tried to get aboard. Meanwhile, Lancashire County Police were desperately trying to trace the owner of a Ford Consul with the registration 986 RO. The car, with two men inside, was seen in Newton-le-Willows, loaded with luggage. Was some of it from the Great Train Robbery?

Over at Leatherslade Farm, Detective Superintendent Maurice Ray, 54 years old and looking like a not-particularly-prosperous bank clerk, was directing the minute, inch-by-inch search of the farm. He eventually found a number of fingerprints, which were sent to a police laboratory for analysis.

On 16 August, Fleet Street claimed police were hunting for a retired Army officer who was the brains behind the robbery. The *News of the World* said the man was known as 'the Major', but that his nickname should not be confused with a well-known small-time London fence who used the same nickname. (It was later surmised this must have been a reference to Bruce Reynolds, who many thought was an ex-British Army officer, known as 'The Colonel'.) Another popular rumour was that one-time king of the London underworld Billy Hill had bankrolled the entire robbery from his retirement villa in the south of France. Hill told one reporter who knocked on his door in the Côte D'Azur that he knew nothing about it: 'Ring up Scotland Yard yourself. Now, if you like. Book plane tickets for both of us back to London, if you care to do so. I am so flicking mad about all this publicity without the money to go with it.' Behind Hill's irritation was a tinge of jealousy. As he later admitted to another criminal, 'What a masterpiece of a job. If only I could have laid on something like that. Brilliant!'

So, Charlie and the rest of the train robbers had already written their place in the history books. The Great Train Robbery, as it was known by then across the world, would dominate the media for many months, even years, to come as the police, under the command of the tenacious Tommy Butler, began to unravel the crime.

Also on 16 August, two motorcyclists spotted a couple of suitcases in woodland in the Surrey hills, just south of London. The cases contained more than £140,000 in cash from the robbery. In one leather case was a hotel bill made out in the name of Brian Field, the gang's 'weakest link' as far as Charlie was concerned. Hours later, an inch-by-inch examination of a caravan site in Box Hill, Surrey, uncovered £30,000 hidden in the wall lining of a trailer owned by robber Tommy Wisbey.

Then the results of the fingerprint tests taken at Leatherslade Farm came back from the Scotland Yard lab. In particular, they showed that convicted robber Charles Frederick Wilson had handled the Saxo salt container at the farm and two other known criminals – Bruce Reynolds and Jimmy White – had been there as well. Tommy Butler was delighted, although some Scotland Yard officers were already muttering that milk-drinking Butler was trying to turn the investigation into a one-man show. His bosses didn't care, just so long as he got results.

At 1.15 p.m. on 22 August 1963 – just 14 days after the 'crime of the century' had been committed – Scotland Yard issued descriptions of the three men wanted in connection with the Great Train Robbery and top of their list was Charlie Wilson. His photo was splashed across every newspaper in the land. 'YARD SEEK 3 MEN' appeared in the *London Evening Standard* at the time; the media, by then, no longer even referring to the train robbery in the headline. It was already *that* famous.

Less than two hours after that story first appeared, four Flying Squad cars turned up at Charlie's home in Crescent Lane, Clapham, while he was having lunch with his family. As Charlie was taken away in handcuffs, Pat and his three daughters watched from the front window. The search for Reynolds and White continued.

Charlie arrived at Cannon Row Police Station in a Ford Zephyr squad car just before 3.30 p.m. on 22 August to be greeted by Tommy Butler. He was told they were making inquiries into the train robbery to which Charlie responded: 'You obviously know a lot. I've made a ricket [balls up] somewhere, but I'll have to take my chances.' Charlie seemed confident, though, the police wouldn't be able to 'make it stick without the poppy [evidence]' and that they wouldn't find any.

During Charlie's interview, Butler asked Wilson where he had been on the morning of 8 August 1963. Naturally, Charlie replied that he was in Spitalfields Market and had left home about 5.30 a.m. Butler then asked him if he had any receipts or proof of business from that morning, to which Charlie replied: 'No, they don't give receipts. I saw a few friends, though.'

Racing driver Roy James heard about Charlie's arrest on a car radio as he was driving back from motor-racing practice at Goodwood, Sussex. He was sure the cops would connect him to Charlie. When he stopped the car and bought a newspaper, which had photos of the three Great Train Robbery suspects splashed across its front page, James phoned his mother. She told him the police had just been to see her.

Back in Clapham, Pat greeted three more teams of detectives at her yellow front door. They searched the property thoroughly and took a pair of Charlie's shoes from the house for forensic examination. That evening, Charlie was driven from London to Aylesbury in the back of a Jaguar squad car. Two and a half hours later he was charged with carrying out the biggest robbery the world had ever known.

The following day, Charlie was escorted into the court in Linsdale, Buckinghamshire, with a blanket over his head, to make his first appearance in the dock. In the tiny, crowded courtroom, Pat Wilson heard how her husband was accused of being concerned, together with other persons as yet unknown and armed with instruments, in robbing Frank Dewhurst, the General Post Office (GPO) official in charge of the train, of £2,631,784, the property of the postmaster general, at Mentmore, Bucks, on 8 August.

Charlie – who denied all the charges – looked over in the direction of Pat and winked. His legal counsel insisted to the court that, despite police claims to the contrary, Charlie had been at his home the entire time and had made no attempt to avoid arrest. Charlie's barrister noted that it was 'in the highest degree unfortunate that at a time when this man was being questioned by officers, the national press should have been plastered with photographs suggesting he was a missing man. It may well appear that at all times this man was available for questioning'.

Charlie was remanded in custody until the following day. Butler and his train robbery team had rounded up five members of the gang remarkably quickly. They were Roger Cordrey, Charlie, Ronnie Biggs, Jimmy Hussey and Tommy Wisbey, and they had a call out for five other alleged robbers: Bruce Reynolds, John Daly, Buster Edwards, Roy James and Jimmy White. Four others were also on their list of suspects.

Pat Wilson never forgot the appalling intrusion into her life caused by Charlie's dramatic, headline-hitting arrest in connection with the Great Train Robbery. A classic example came in the now defunct *Daily Sketch*, which featured a huge photo of Pat being led into the court in Linsdale with a headscarf and newspaper hiding her face. The headline read 'THE HOODED ONES (CONTD)'. She later said she was deeply distressed by the experience.

8

Charlie's attitude – and that of all the other arrested robbers – was to admit to nothing since they might yet be found not guilty at the eventual trial. When Ronnie Biggs was told by a prison officer inside Bedford Prison that they had one of his mates, Charlie Wilson, inside, he responded with, 'Charlie who? Never heard of him.' Charlie and Biggs later completely ignored one another in the exercise yard. Charlie said in a loud voice, so all the screws would hear, 'Aren't you the bloke who's been charged with the train robbery?'

'Yeah,' replied Biggs, 'but I had nothin' to do with it.'

'Incredible,' said Charlie. 'I've been charged with that too. Bloody liberty.'

On 4 September 1963, Gordon Goody became so worried that Charlie might think he was a grass after being arrested and then released on bail by robbery detectives, he made a secret visit to Bedford Prison, under the false name of Joey Gray, to see his old south London friend. Charlie cut such a menacing figure that Goody believed he could be under threat from Charlie's 'associates'. Goody arrived with Pat and immediately begged Charlie not to draw any conclusions from his freedom.

'Fuck off out of it,' barked Charlie. 'What you talkin' about?'

'I only wanted to reassure you, mate,' said Gordon, 'because if I was you, the same thoughts would have gone through my head.'

'Don't be fuckin' stupid,' replied Charlie. 'I ain't worried about any of our firm.'

Charlie was much more concerned about the gang's elderly railway consultant 'Stan'. Charlie told Goody he had better 'do something about him', believing he'd shop them all if he fell into Butler's hands. Goody returned to London that night and, during a meeting with Buster Edwards, concluded that Stan should get the chop. But there was one problem – Stan had disappeared into thin air.

It wasn't until a few weeks later, following their move to Aylesbury

Prison, that Charlie and Ronnie Biggs made real contact with each other. Both men initially talked secretly in the prison yard and then sent messages to each other through trusted intermediaries. Both concluded that if they were found guilty, they'd get very long jail sentences and that escaping from prison might be the best option open to them.

Charlie was working in the kitchen of Aylesbury's hospital wing, preparing snacks and hot drinks for prison staff. He told Biggs that the two night guards on their wing could be drugged, which would give them enough time to get out of the prison before the alarm could be raised, but that escape plan was quickly abandoned when Charlie, Biggs and the other incarcerated train robbery gang members found out they could get an extra 14 years if caught.

As remand prisoners who were not yet proven guilty, Charlie and the rest of the gang were allowed their own choice of food and drink in prison. Pat made regular trips to Aylesbury to visit Charlie, bringing him clean clothes and some of his favourite food, including boiling ham which Charlie, who considered himself a half-decent chef, was allowed to cook in the prison kitchen with a selection of fresh vegetables and potatoes.

The robbers' wives soon began to form a close bond, although Pat and some of the others were irritated by Ronnie Biggs's wife Charmian, who they all thought spent too much money on clothes. 'We didn't want anyone to think we had loads of money because then they'd think it had come from the train robbery,' explained one wife many years later. The gang members were mindful that other criminals could think their wives and girlfriends had access to the robbery loot.

One afternoon in November 1963, a middle-aged man knocked on the Wilsons' front door in Clapham and told Pat he had something very important to discuss with her. Once inside the house, he said that for £5,000 he'd 'nobble' at least one member of the jury at Charlie's coming trial. Pat was gobsmacked and politely asked the man to leave. The following day, she visited Charlie in prison and he went berserk. 'That's crossin' the fuckin' line and I won't have it!' he told Pat. Charlie immediately sent word to his friends in south London that he wanted this character 'sorted out'. Pat was told to telephone the man and tell him she was willing to pay the money and that he could come round the following day to get it.

When he arrived, a couple of Charlie's pals appeared with a mallet and some six-inch nails. They grabbed the man and dragged him across the street onto Clapham Common where they planned to nail him to a tree. The man broke free and ran down the road into a shop, screaming for help. Charlie's pals followed him, caught him at the rear of the premises and left him bleeding and unconscious in a nearby alleyway. Charlie Wilson had confirmed his reputation as someone not to be messed with.

On 3 December 1963, Charlie tried to 'negotiate' his way out of prison by offering one senior detective a £50,000 bribe to lose the evidence police had against him. He claimed he was framed for the Great Train Robbery by corrupt cops who'd taken his fingerprint samples and ensured they were then conveniently 'found' on that drum of Saxo salt. He therefore believed that offering another officer a bribe was nothing particularly out of the ordinary. Charlie arranged for £50,000 in cash to be left in a telephone box in Great Dover Street, just south of the river in Southwark, but the policeman offered the bribe had already told his superiors about Charlie's offer. The banknotes, which could be traced back to the Great Train Robbery, were so mouldy that most of them were stuck together. One of his oldest friends explained that 'Charlie was pretty low after that little caper' and believed he was heading for a very long stretch in prison.

Charlie's most feasible chance of freedom lay with his legal team at his coming trial. Charlie had hoped to be defended by Jeremy Hutchinson, a lawyer with a fine reputation amongst professional criminals, but in the event he proved unavailable so he hired barrister John Mathew, who'd already successfully defended him in previous cases and later went on to represent notorious criminals such as Brinks Mat gold bullion handler Kenneth Noye.

Just before the trial got under way, the wife of robbery gang member Brian Field claimed to police that an unnamed man had suggested to her that six of the jurors should be paid £500 each in order to influence the verdict at the trial. These sorts of incidents did nothing to help the robbers' case as it made them look even more criminally inclined. Naturally, they all insisted that such attempts to influence the jury were nothing to do with them.

PART 2

INSIDE AND OUTSIDE: 1964–78

Between the acting of a dreadful thing
And the first motion, all the interim is
Like a phantasma or a hideous dream.
William Shakespeare, *Julius Caesar*

1

The Great Train Robbery trial began at the Old Bailey on 20 January 1964. The jury were ordered to be locked away each evening at a secret location to prevent any more attempts at jury nobbling. Prosecuting barrister Howard Sabin summed up the Establishment's view of the train robbery when he told the court the robbery was 'a crime that strikes at the root of civilised society'. The moment Charlie heard that phrase, he rolled his eyes; he knew it meant none of them stood a chance.

When the injured train driver Jack Mills delivered his testimony to a hushed courtroom in a quiet, shaky voice, Charlie whispered to Bobby Welch that Mills was 'a right fuckin' actor'. Charlie knew it looked bad for them. For the following two months, he sat in the dock without uttering a word, resigned to a guilty verdict and constantly thinking about his next move.

At 10.32 a.m. on Thursday, 27 March 1964, the jury returned to give their verdict after being out for a record 66 hours and 56 minutes. The voice of the foreman shattered the silence in the Old Bailey court with one word: 'Guilty'. Over the next ten minutes, he repeated it eighteen times as the ten accused gang members were dealt with. The tension mounted as each prisoner in turn, a warder at his side, stood up to hear the verdict. They left the dock at the rate of one a minute.

When it came to Charlie's turn the judge, Mr Justice Edmund Davies, told him: 'You have been convicted of conspiracy to rob a mail train and of armed robbery. No one has said less than you throughout this long trial. Indeed, I doubt if you have spoken half a dozen words. Certainly no word of repentance has been expressed by you. If you, or any of the other accused, had assisted justice, that would have told strongly in your favour. The consequence of this outrageous crime is that the vast booty of something like £2,500,000 still remains almost entirely unrecovered. It would be an affront to the public if any one of you should be at liberty in anything like the near future to enjoy those ill-gotten gains.'

One young rookie police officer called Ken Rogers travelled with Tommy Butler to the train robbers' trial on a number of occasions. Butler even insisted that Rogers be present on the day of the convictions. As the robbers were being taken away, Butler turned to Rogers and said 'Take a good look at them as they will be over the wall soon.'

Charlie and the gang were then taken back to the hospital wing of Aylesbury to wait for Ronnie Biggs's separate trial, after which they'd be sentenced by the judge. All of them were resigned to their fate except for two of the accused – Bill Boal and Lennie Field – who insisted they took no part in the actual robbery. The only alleged gang member to be acquitted was John Daly.

Charlie and Gordon Goody knew they were facing extremely long sentences and believed an immediate escape was the only option as the hospital wing at Aylesbury was far less secure than an actual prison. Charlie and the other gang members slept in cells that could only be locked from the outside and, at night, there was just one prison officer on duty in the corridor, plus another one sleeping on the floor below. Goody's job cleaning the officers' quarters meant it was possible to get into the loft of the prison from a cupboard in one of the officers' rooms. Once in the loft, they could walk under the roof to the end of the entire building, remove some tiles and climb down onto the street below.

Goody had key-blanks, files, a chisel and money smuggled in. He carefully studied the keys hanging on the warder's chains and then at night would file away at the part he'd memorised. After just one week the key was ready. It fitted the cell, but could not be used at night when it was locked from the outside. Goody carefully rehearsed with Charlie how they'd tie up the nightwatch warder before fleeing. They then agreed on a date to escape and Charlie got a message out to some of his boys to make sure they would be at the prison with transport on the night in question.

When the date arrived, Goody and Charlie waited in their cells fully dressed for Bill Boal, who was in a less secure cell, to use the specially made key to release them. Boal changed his mind though, after deciding that his appeal against his conviction would stand even less chance of succeeding if he was caught aiding the escape. Charlie and Goody remained locked in their cells spitting blood. Charlie was already angry with some of the other gang members for not wanting to join in the escape bid in the first place.

Next morning, prison officers went straight to the crevices beneath the sinks in the washrooms where Goody had hidden the keys; someone had grassed them up. Bill Boal was naturally the chief suspect.

Charlie was further infuriated before his sentence when some newspapers alleged that he and the rest of the gang had offered to tell police where all the train robbery money was in exchange for reduced sentences. That could not have been further from the truth. As one of Charlie's oldest friends said many years later: 'No one, least of all Charlie, would give the police the time of day, let alone the key to all that cash. In any case, Charlie had big plans for the future.'

On Wednesday, 15 April 1964, Charlie and all the convicted gang members were brought to the Old Buckinghamshire Assizes Court to be sentenced. It was a sombre building with dark panelling and an enormous coat of arms above the judge's throne. Mr Justice Edmund Davies, wearing the wig and robes of the Law, was flanked by the sheriff of the county, also dressed in ceremonial attire. The barristers were wearing robes and wigs and the policemen were in their uniforms. Of the principal players, only Charlie and the other robbers were in contemporary clothing. Charlie later told a friend that it summed things up, really: 'Them against us.'

Before sentencing, Judge Davies told the gang members: 'Let us clear out of the way any romantic notions of daredevilry. This is nothing more than a sordid crime of violence inspired by vast greed. All who have seen that nerve-shattered engine driver can have no doubt of the terrifying effect on law-abiding citizens of a concerted assault of armed robbers. To deal with this case leniently would be a positively evil thing. Potential criminals who might be dazzled by the enormity of the prize must be taught that the punishment they risk will be proportionately greater.' Charlie was then handed down a 30-year sentence.

There was barely a flicker of emotion from Charlie's eyes in response to the judge's words. This was Charlie Wilson at his most defiant. He certainly wasn't going to give the cozzers and that judge the satisfaction of seeing any shock in his face. And as for the judge's barbed comments about how he had not helped police with their inquiries, Charlie would never grass anyone up. Never in a million years.

The train robbers' sentences were at the time the longest handed out to such a group of criminals in British history:

Ronald Arthur Biggs: conspiracy to rob mail, 25 years; armed robbery, 30 years

Douglas Gordon Goody: conspiracy to rob mail, 25 years; armed robbery, 30 years

James Hussey: conspiracy to rob mail, 25 years; armed robbery, 30 years

Roy John James: conspiracy to rob mail, 25 years; armed robbery, 30 years

Robert Welch: conspiracy to rob mail, 25 years; armed robbery, 30 years

Charles Frederick Wilson: conspiracy to rob mail, 25 years; armed robbery, 30 years

Thomas William Wisbey: conspiracy to rob mail, 25 years; armed robbery, 30 years

Brian Arthur Field: conspiracy to rob mail, 25 years; conspiracy to obstruct the course of justice, 5 years

Leonard Dennis Field: conspiracy to rob mail, 25 years; conspiracy to obstruct the course of justice, 5 years

William Boal: conspiracy to rob mail, 21 years; armed robbery, 24 years (reduced to 14 years on appeal)

Roger John Cordrey: conspiracy to rob mail, 20 years; receiving stolen money, 20 years (reduced to 14 years on appeal)

John Denby Wheater: conspiracy to obstruct the course of justice, 3 years

The gang were sentenced to a total of 533 years. As they were all to run concurrently, they were actually to serve sentences that amounted to 307 years. The only outburst came from Leonard Field's elderly mother after he was sentenced to 25 years on conspiracy charges. From the public gallery she shouted: 'He's innocent, sir.' And as a policemen ushered the old lady out of the court she added: 'I'm his mother. He's innocent.'

Just as Charlie was being taken down from the dock, Field shouted: 'Don't worry, Mum, I'm still young.' Charlie looked up and smiled when he heard this. He was followed to the cells by Ronnie Biggs, Tommy Wisbey, Bob Welch, Jim Hussey, Roy James, Gordon Goody and the rest of the robbers. Their reactions to the sentences varied enormously, but Charlie was determined not to show any emotion.

'How d'you get on, Bob?' Charlie asked Bob Welch as Welch arrived back at the cells beneath the courtroom.

'Twelve years,' said Welch, winking.

'Oh, terrific,' said Charlie, winking back. 'I got nine.'

Alongside Welch, Brian Field, tears in his eyes, was asked by Charlie what his sentence was. 'Twenty-five years,' he replied.

'Twenty-five? He made a fuckin' mistake. You must be jokin',' said Charlie. 'Bob here got twelve and I got fuckin' nine.'

Just then, the warder interrupted Charlie. 'What a wicked old man,' he said. 'Don't worry, boys. You won't do that bird.'

The ever-loyal Pat, dressed head to toe in funereal black, managed to get to the exit gates that day as the black Maria carrying her husband off to jail drove out. She caught Charlie's eye through the tiny window and the photo that appeared in some of the following day's newspapers showed the back of Pat, waving a black, leather-gloved hand towards Charlie, who was the second in from the left-hand window. Charlie later said that seeing Pat that day almost broke his heart. Again, it was the absence from his family that would hurt him more than the sentence.

All the train robbers were to be put on a very special Order 44, which meant heavy restrictions on their movements inside prison. It was all part of a specific Home Office policy to separate the gang in order to ensure they didn't team up together to organise escapes. Charlie and the others saw it as more evidence that the powers that be were further punishing them. Charlie knew his sentence was way over the top, but he'd always been a man with a plan and this situation was no different from any other in that respect. No one would keep him locked up like a caged animal for long.

Former blagger Eric Mason explained: 'In the old days, you had this thing, you don't do post offices, banks and trains because they're Establishment. Then, in the '60s, people began to realise that anything was fair game. People realised that politicians, people we looked up to, were just as bent and people lost respect. People began to realise it was all a big con.'

The opening paragraph of one report following Charlie's sentencing summed up the mood of the nation:

THE GOLDEN FLEECE
They played for high stakes – a cool £2,600,031. And the Great Train Robbers earned the nation's grudging applause. But they lost. Now they must face the censure of the nation's laws.

Flying Squad chief Tommy Butler admitted privately that he felt great sympathy for the families of the train robbers, who were going to have to manage on their own for a very long period of time. Butler was a strange animal by all accounts; he'd come into the top job at the Flying Squad with the officers' memories still full of the legendary Reginald Spooner, who'd chalked up a phenomenal number of arrests while in the Flying Squad. Butler was the opposite of the flamboyant, chain-smoking Spooner and was known, perhaps unfairly, as cold and unemotional by his men. They complained that because he was unmarried, he often failed to appreciate the domestic problems of his men, whom he worked long and hard. Butler himself spent countless hours in his small office on every minute piece of paperwork and even charted the clever police traps which helped catch some of the gang. But Butler was also one of the old school, prepared to meet underworld informants at any time of the day or night. And it was Butler who was always there at the final arrest.

Charlie's previous spells inside prison hadn't been so much a punishment as a further education. He'd met a lot of villains, learned a few new tricks and made important contacts for his future in crime. This time he already knew the rules of the game and the thought of rotting away in a prison cell for a third of his life just wasn't acceptable. It was time to make some alternative arrangements.

2

Winson Green Prison is located about two miles from Birmingham city centre in an area of old and crowded streets. It was built in the 1840s for 350 prisoners; by the time Charlie arrived, it was holding nearly 800, with almost half those inmates sleeping 3 to a cell. From a distance, the prison looks like a little toy fort perched on a hilltop overlooking England's second biggest city. Its hopeless-looking drab grey walls are broken only by a pair of massive iron-studded wooden gates. Inside, the atmosphere is grim; that was why it was picked as the perfect jail for the notorious train robber Charlie Wilson. This medieval, high-walled encampment was, like its new star inmate, infamous for its silence. Winson Green had, until a couple of years earlier, been the scene of hangings when the death penalty was still part of the law of the land. At least Charlie's special treatment as a

Great Train Robber had one advantage: he was given a cell on his own.

Charlie's first cell was right in the central hub from which the prison's four main corridors branched off. The use of pastel shades of paint (doors were yellow and brick walls turquoise and white) did little to relieve the omnipresent gloom. There were times when Charlie wished a bulldozer would just come along and demolish the whole fucking place.

The cell blocks were hushed and even the warders seemed to creep around silently. Pictures of country life, painted by a prison artist, decorated some of the bleakest walls and, for some bizarre reason, the fire alarm bell was painted vivid pink. This was a prison badly in need of modernisation and it wasn't helped by a dire staff shortage caused, in part, by a starting salary of just £12 5s a week (rising to £17 9s after ten years' service).

To the right of the prison were the dirty, green, oily waters of a canal, choked with weeds on every bank. On the left, the prison walls, ranging from 10- to 25-feet high, looked out across desolate wasteland. The only activity seemed to come from the corner with the main road where there was a builder's yard run by a company called The Greaves Organisation. Beyond that, the local lunatic asylum.

So when the gates of Winson Green shut behind Charlie in the late spring of 1964, he must have felt the oppression hit him like a wall of stone. He was alone in Cell Block B; the only other celebrity inmate was hated Russian spy Gordon Lonsdale. As a maximum security prisoner, Charlie had four white patches stitched to his navy blue inmates' battledress. He was only allowed occasional contact with other prisoners and earned three shillings a week sewing mailbags during his work periods, much to the amusement of inmates and staff, in light of his famous crime. Charlie kept up his keep-fit regime by exercising at least three times a week in the small prison gym.

Charlie was initially regarded as a quiet prisoner, who kept his head down, even though he was incarcerated under one of the most secure and restrictive systems that a British prison could provide. His single cell was continually lit, both night and day. That would be called sleep deprivation today; back then, it was considered an acceptable punishment for any potentially problematic inmates. Charlie was continually moved about the prison, not only from cell to cell, but also from block to block. At night, the block he was in was controlled by a warder sitting in a central circular room while two colleagues patrolled the four landings, checking locks and peeping through the 'Judas' hole in each cell door every 12–15 minutes. Outside, another officer patrolled the block perimeter, but he did not carry the keys to gain entry to the block itself. They were kept with the principal officer on night duty.

Within a few weeks, some members of the prison staff had decided to make Charlie's life extra-specially unpleasant. 'They'd go in his cell two-handed because Charlie could handle himself and then the bastards would fuckin' lay into him,' one former Winson Green inmate later recalled. Charlie resisted the temptation to fight back because he knew that was what they wanted. If he was going to beat the system, he needed to remain cool and calm in the face of adversity.

As a special 'A'-class inmate, Charlie's bed was 12 inches from the wall and he'd always lie with his head to the door so that the guard who regularly peered through the Judas hole could see him clearly. He had to lie with his hands on top of the blanket, otherwise the guard would kick his door until he moved them. Charlie later joked about the difficulties of masturbating under such awkward circumstances.

During the day, Charlie was rarely out of sight of a warder. As he moved about the prison, one officer handed him over to another. And wherever he was in the jail, those four white patches on his uniform ensured that he could be picked out easily.

Charlie didn't suffer fools gladly. Not long after arriving at Winson Green, he had a confrontation with another inmate: 'It kicked off all of a sudden as Charlie was talkin' to this fella. The screws left 'em to it and the geezer ended up in a crumpled heap on the ground,' one former Winson Green inmate recalled. Within seconds, Charlie had brushed down his immaculately clean prison uniform and returned to his cell as if nothing had happened.

Easily the most pleasant area of the prison was the chapel, which also doubled up as a cinema on Saturday afternoons. Charlie particularly liked *On The Waterfront*, starring Marlon Brando, and watched it at least three times, but westerns starring actors like John Wayne were the most popular flicks with inmates. Winson Green didn't have television, unlike most prisons at this time. Charlie spent most evenings reading either a daily paper or studying Shakespeare and poetry, which he'd first learned to appreciate during an earlier spell in prison. His typical daily routine went as follows:

7.00 a.m. cell doors unlocked followed by a slop out
7.30 a.m. breakfast
8.00 a.m. back to cell while staff have breakfast
9.00 a.m. cells unlocked again

9.10 a.m. work or exercise

11.30 a.m. lunch in dining hall, then back to cells

1.30 p.m. cells unlocked, slop out and back to work

4.45 p.m. dinner taken to cells

7.30 p.m. cocoa to cells; all cells locked and occupants checked

That was it. The potential for boredom is plain to see. No wonder inmates called prisons like Winson Green 'thinking factories'. Charlie couldn't help scheming away because he had little else to do. He was also determined to turn this appalling predicament to his own advantage.

Inside prison, Charlie came across inmates serving less than ten years for crimes he considered much more serious than robbing a train. One man who had killed a barmaid by putting cyanide in her beer because she did not serve him quickly enough had been sentenced to just five years. Then there was the night porter who set fire to a hotel to get rid of some people sitting up late and caused the death of seven of them. He also got just five years. The *Daily Sketch* summed up the mood of the nation in the wake of the train robbers' sentencing: '30 YEARS – ALL BRITAIN ARGUES, IS THIS TOO HARSH?'

Not long after Charlie's sentencing, Pat and the children moved out of the family home in Crescent Lane, Clapham, and into her mother's home in the East End. The house sale was handled by one of Charlie's bookmaking pals and the new owner later explained that Pat never returned to the house, not even when the furniture was taken away to be put into storage. Pat didn't bother leaving her mother's address with neighbours and told few people where she was actually going.

Pat visited Charlie at Winson Green three times in July and early August 1964. He also had frequent visits from lawyers and their associates in connection with his appeal against his sentence (all of the train robbers had decided to appeal even though Charlie and many others were pessimistic about their chances of getting their sentences reduced). Eventually, Charlie told his lawyers he didn't think there was any point in attending the appeal court hearing.

Lurking in the back of Charlie's mind all along had been an escape plan. Soon after arriving at Winson Green, he'd begun stealing sugar from the prison canteen and scattering it outside his cell so, at night, when the prison was silent, he could hear a faint scrunch as the screw came to look at him through the hole in the door and could time the rounds. Charlie also noted that at weekends the older officers were replaced by younger, more vigorous screws, who might prove a problem during a breakout. Charlie also smuggled some of the black grease used in the workshop to waterproof mailbag straps into his cell. He used it to blacken his cell light because the round-the-clock light rule was destroying his ability to sleep properly.

Charlie remained under a constant 24-hour watch and other prisoners were even threatened with disciplinary action if they socialised with him. Charlie kept his head down and bided his time, but he enjoyed the loyalty shown to him by the majority of inmates, who bestowed hero status on him for his role in the robbery. He also believed the screws couldn't keep up their regime forever.

Charlie was eventually allowed to exercise in the prison yard at the same time as other inmates. A few days later, a long-term prisoner slid alongside Charlie and said just five words: 'Frenchy is working on it.' The inmate was gone in a split second, but Charlie's spirits had been boosted for the first time since he'd been arrested. Pat said later that, apart from Bruce Reynolds and Gordon Goody, Frenchy was the only man Charlie trusted 100 per cent.

Frenchy had already begun assembling a team of experts to help spring Charlie from Winson Green. They included a master locksmith, a Belgian light-aircraft pilot, an expert wireless engineer to monitor police broadcasts and two huge bodyguards, who were experienced mountaineers, capable of scaling virtually any wall in the land. The team eventually held a full dress rehearsal at a derelict monastery in northern France, where they perfected their plan before heading for England.

Frenchy photographed a small section of an Ordnance Survey map of the area around the prison with a 35mm camera and blew it up to nearly two-foot square to use during meetings and two friendly inmates passed on the warder's timekeeping records. One sunny Tuesday in early August, the escape team discreetly circled the prison and made a note of heights and certain distances. Charlie's latest cell, in C Block, was pinpointed, then they got key moulds through other inmates. It was agreed that the breakout should happen just after the appeal court hearing, which Charlie expected to lose.

Twenty-five police and prison officers escorted Ronnie Biggs and Roy James from Brixton Prison to the law courts in the Strand for their appeal hearing. Charlie told his legal team he couldn't be bothered leaving Winson Green. His lawyers warned him it was madness not to appear in person, but Charlie was adamant.

In court, Charlie's counsel, Jeremy Hutchinson, QC, said: 'The court has to set its sights on the year 1994 when Wilson's children – one of whom has a hole in the heart – will be in their middle 30s. Many of us in this court will no longer be upon the scene. If the court does endorse this sentence, then the system will obviously have to be changed. No country is going to stand for having individuals in prison for such long periods.' Victor Durand, QC, made an even more heartfelt appeal on behalf of his client: 'I ask you to come down on the side of humanity and have regard for the life of another, otherwise one will be in a state of destroying a fellow being.'

The attitude of appeal court judge, Mr Justice Lawton, however, summed up the Establishment's attitude towards the train robbers: 'The point is whether some shorter sentence will give some prospect of enjoying the proceeds of the crime. How many men, who spend their lives working honestly, might think "Hmmm, 15 years in jail for £150,000, I don't mind taking the chance. And even if I am caught, my wife and children can live in Bermuda in comfort. In ten years, I will be out and able to join them."' He added: 'These were wholly exceptional sentences for a wholly exceptional crime and, in our view, they were not wrong in principle, or excessive.' That decision meant Charlie and the rest of the gang members had taken their last glimpse of the outside world for possibly 20 years – and that took into account the one-third remission they could expect for good conduct.

Back at Winson Green, Charlie greeted the decision with a shrug of his shoulders, just as he was paying two weeks in advance for his daily and Sunday newspapers to be delivered to his cell. In the second week of August, 1964, The Beatles were top of the hit parade with 'A Hard Day's Night' followed by Manfred Mann singing 'Do Wah Diddy, Diddy' and then came the Rolling Stones with 'It's All Over Now'. On Wednesday, 12 August 1964, Ian Fleming, creator of James Bond, died of a heart attack aged 56. That day also happened to be a soggy, cloudy one in Birmingham and the grey stonework of Winson Green Prison looked hauntingly Gothic. At 5 p.m., Charlie, who spoke to few people, looked mightily pleased with himself as he was escorted back to his cell from the tailor shop where he'd been sewing those mailbags.

3

That evening, a little after 5 p.m., Charlie was given a supper of bread and cheese and soup. At 8 p.m., he drained his nightcap of cocoa and toasted 'the outside world'. He then settled down to read a book on ancient history, his latest favourite subject, which he'd borrowed from the prison library. At 9.30 p.m., it was lights out and Charlie climbed into his bed. He immediately closed his eyes, but as he later explained: 'For the next few hours, my ears became my eyes.' He didn't know exactly what time they'd come for him, just that it was going to be that night.

The escape team were already in the vicinity. Frenchy, in a Ford Zodiac, was on stand-by along with a converted petrol tanker, which was to be Charlie's temporary home.

Elsewhere in C Block, other prisoners were lying awake, including one with a tiny transistor radio, modified so that it would transmit rather than receive. Its range was only about 400 yards, but it was enough. Just then, a third vehicle, a fake taxi, fitted with a radio receiver, arrived in the street overlooked by the prison. The driver and one passenger registered a faint message from the radio: 'Screws been to Wilson's cell.' That information would be reported back each time the guard visited Charlie's cell throughout the night.

Outside, Frenchy's blue Zodiac, carrying two other men and a woman, stopped by the corner of the prison overlooking the canal. They parked right opposite the home of mother-of-six Mrs Rose Gredden. She later said she noticed a blonde woman with a wide-brimmed beige hat, pulled down to one side, sitting in the back seat. A few minutes later, she noticed three men talking on the prison side of the canal towpath. 'They were respectably dressed. Two were rather tall,' Mrs Gredden recalled. 'Some prison officers must have seen them. Their social club's only a few yards from where the men were standing and I heard officers leaving the club around that time.'

Around the corner, two men in the petrol tanker pulled up one block from the prison. Three of the team – armed with a set of duplicated keys – headed towards the prison wall, but on the way encountered members of the public. One man spoke to the gang, because they were blocking the pavement, as he tried to get home after a late shift at a local factory. The group parted to let the man through and he got a good look at them by the light of a street lamp as they all called out 'Goodnight.'

The other witness was 44-year-old Mrs Rose Gredden, whose backyard had a perfect view of the prison wall. At 2.35 a.m., Mrs Gredden's baby daughter started crying so she got up to get her some water from the kitchen. As she switched on the main light, she heard a light tap at her back door. Mrs Gredden later explained: 'I called out, "Who is it?" I wasn't going to open the door at that time of the morning. My husband was on night work at a bakery.'

A woman's voice responded: 'Can you tell me the time?' Mrs Gredden told her it was 2.45. She later explained: 'My clock was ten minutes fast, but I'd forgotten that. I heard her going away. She had a London accent, I think. I would know that voice again. She must have been watching the prison from near my backyard.'

Back inside his cell, Charlie Wilson couldn't do anything to prepare for his escape in case it was noticed by the warden carrying out his regular checks. At about half past two, one of the two officers on duty in Charlie's C Block went to put the breakfast porridge on in the kitchen, leaving the prison open to a serious breach of security because the five night-staff patrolling the wings were locked in and carried no keys.

At 3 a.m., Frenchy whispered his final instructions to his two mountain men, and they and the locksmith slipped off into the dark. They wore dark-blue raincoats, black plimsolls and black trousers, making them almost invisible. Their raincoats were all oversized to hide the bulkiness of the ropes and climbing equipment they were carrying. They headed for a spot favoured by escaping prisoners – a corner of the wall where the prison met the canal and the grounds of the nearby mental hospital. It was 3.02 a.m.

The three men dumped their equipment on the ground, then pulled black-stocking masks over their heads with cut-out holes for their eyes. A grappling hook was flung skywards against the outer wall. After climbing over, the three men dropped into the exercise yard outside B Block. There were no prison patrols and no dogs barking, so they hugged the shadow of a long, grey prison wall and headed for C Block.

En route, they even stole a 15-foot-long plank from an equipment box by simply lifting a gate off its hinge, thinking it might be useful for climbing from one roof to another during the escape. Sneaking along the side walls, they reached the 20-foot internal wall of the prison. Then, using a rope ladder – almost certainly fitted with grappling irons – the gang scaled the wall and padded softly through to the cell block where they knew Charlie was under virtually constant supervision.

Less than a minute later, the mountain men knocked night security officer William Nicholls unconscious with a cosh. They tied him up with nylon rope, but knew that by the time he came round they'd all be long gone. Then they used Nicholls' Key One to open the outside door to C Block. This was followed by Key Two to open the steel grille door behind it. Dodging other prison staff, they made straight for Landing No. 2. At 3.08 a.m., the raiders used a key specially cut for the job to open Charlie's cell so quietly that the next-door inmate heard nothing. As the door swung open, the three men crept in.

'Let's go,' whispered the first one, throwing a bundle of clothes in Charlie's direction.

Charlie pulled on a roll-necked black sweater, a pair of dark trousers, plimsolls and a balaclava, then he followed them out of the cell. They went past the trussed-up warder towards the centre of the prison before cutting back through A Wing and past the prison bathhouse then down some stairs. The locksmith stayed an extra two minutes to re-lock all the doors. The full moon meant they had to keep to the shadows of the buildings as they headed for the 25-foot perimeter wall. There were no patrols and they easily scaled the wall with the rope ladder.

An inmate called Leslie Marsden, who was serving 14 weeks for motoring offences, later claimed he had heard it all. He explained: 'I thought the noise was just a prisoner banging his cell door for a warder. Then I heard a man on the bottom landing banging about. Suddenly someone, I thought it was a warder, but it could have been Wilson, shouted, "Hurry up with those keys."'

Charlie and his jailbreak team got out of the prison in under three minutes. Half a minute later they were carrying equipment along the canal towpath towards a bridge that led to the asylum's perimeter wall. That's when Charlie first spotted the petrol tanker parked on the next corner. A flap had been cut in the main tank. Charlie was handed a flashlight and crawled inside. There, he found three mattresses, pillows and blankets. The two expert climbers clambered in behind him. Frenchy closed the hinged flap with the words: 'Next time I see you we'll be drinking champagne, not petrol fumes.'

The tanker immediately trundled off into the night heading for a deserted landing strip. Charlie later described the ride as surprisingly comfortable. At the airstrip, Charlie was highly emotional. As Pat later explained: 'Charlie, in spite of his record, is really a very kind-hearted and emotional man . . . when he was recounting the airstrip parting to me, he said: "You know what I'm like, Pat – sort of soft inside. I embraced all those tough men in the true French tradition when I thanked them. I was really crying with gratitude."' A small plane then took Charlie to a barren landing strip in northern France.

At 3.20 a.m., William Nicholls, the guard who'd been knocked unconscious and bound and gagged by Charlie's escape team, came to and managed to free himself. He immediately reported the incident to the night orderly officer who for 30 more minutes remained locked in his room because he was afraid to emerge in case the intruders attacked him and his staff. The police only received a message at 3.50 a.m. on an ordinary phone line, not the 999 system. A group of police and prison officers eventually assembled at the prison gates at about 4 a.m., but could not enter the prison until the chief officer appeared with the keys.

That delay gave Charlie and his escape team valuable extra time. It would be several hours before the nation's police had even been properly alerted and, by the time the streets of Birmingham had been sealed off and identity checks made, Charlie was already in France.

One of the first people to be told about Charlie's escape was Tommy Butler, still head of the Yard's Flying Squad. Under him, 300 men continued investigating the Great Train Robbery and were looking for Buster Edwards and his wife June, plus the other suspected robber on the run, Bruce Reynolds. Butler was not in the least bit surprised by Charlie's prison break. He'd been predicting such an escape since the end of their trial.

In Birmingham, Detective Chief Superintendent Gerald Baumber, head of the city's CID, was relieved of all other duties to lead a hand-picked team of detectives to hunt for Charlie. Police initially suspected Charlie might be heading for the Republic of Ireland, a popular 'holiday' destination for convicts on the run. A special watch was immediately mounted at Dublin, Cork and Shannon airports. Baumber's squad of 30 officers then visited the prison and began interviewing all 120 warders, governor Mr Rundle Harris, his civilian staff and some of the 800 or so inmates. Detectives also tested the prison's six keys for traces of soap and talked to some ex-prisoners, including 30-year-old Peter Marshall of Hyde Road, Ladywood, Birmingham, well known in the underworld as a 'key man'. He later told reporters: 'The police came to me for my expert opinion. I had nothing to do with Wilson's escape but I have been in Winson Green several times. The Winson Green master cell key is a real precision job. Wax impressions would be no good to copy. The gang must have had the key for some hours. If any part was even a thousandth of an inch out, it wouldn't work.'

Within twelve hours of the breakout, the Home Office had issued warnings to the eight prisons holding the other train robbers that more escapes might be planned. The day after Charlie's breakout from Winson Green, his photo and story were splashed all over the front pages of the nation's newspapers, including the *Daily Sketch* delivered to Charlie's cell that morning despite his absence. Many of the inmates found that highly amusing. Charlie's escape was hailed as more daring than the train robbery itself and there were rumours that a syndicate of specialists, called the 'Freedom Fixers', who organised jailbreaks, were being paid to liberate more members of the gang.

Fleet Street milked Charlie's dramatic escape for all it was worth and came up with some fairly inaccurate theories. The *Daily Telegraph* reported:

> There is ample support for the theory that Wilson never attempted to leave the Birmingham area. There is no reason why he should not remain comfortably undercover for months, waiting for the hue and cry to subside, before attempting to get away. One sound reason for supposing he did not flee the country immediately is money. A man of his taciturn and cautious nature is not likely to have revealed its hiding place in advance to fellow criminals, expecting them to meet him with it at the prison gates. Far more reasonable is the supposition that he will go for the money when the chase quietens, complete the payments undoubtedly promised to his confederates and then, with some of the remainder, buy his way out of the country.

Meanwhile, the inevitable inquests had already begun. Fred Castell of the Prison Officers Association insisted that security was good enough in Britain's prisons, despite Charlie's escape. Although he did concede: 'There has been understaffing at Winson Green, especially during the day. But this prison, and others, are locked and master-locked and are equal to any normal situation. This was an abnormal situation. The truth of this matter is that these boys have beaten the system and they have done it by getting hold of a master key.' There was almost a tone of deference in Mr Castell's voice towards Charlie and his boys!

Charlie's escape undoubtedly further elevated his status in underworld folklore, but there were some less likely characters now singing his praises. The *Daily Express*, a traditionally right-wing Fleet Street newspaper, described Charlie as '. . . gentle, soft-spoken and witty . . . a home-lover, deeply attached to his wife and children . . . a man who wouldn't hurt a fly'. Then in waded the distinguished novelist Graham Greene, who openly admired the robber's skill and courage. Even the most ardent supporters of crime and punishment were appalled by the prison conditions Charlie and the rest of the train robbers faced in captivity. Reports of solitary confinement, all-night lighting and the intrusion of warders banging on their cell doors every 15 minutes, along with the 'ban' on their hands being under their blankets led one commentator to describe the conditions as 'medieval barbarism'.

Charlie believed this reaction was further proof that he was right to break out of prison. As one of his oldest friends later explained: 'Charlie saw it as his duty to escape; a bit like a POW during the last war. Nothing was going to stop him. It didn't matter what they threw at him. It was impossible to break Charlie's spirit.'

And as the hours turned into days following his escape, it was the mighty Establishment who were being increasingly blamed for it. One article in the *Sunday Chronicle* began:

> One hundred hours have passed and Charles Frederick Wilson, the mail robber, who waltzed out of the dour 'maximum security' Winson Green Jail at 3.15 last Wednesday morning, is still free. Police, who hoped they'd be on his trail as he led confederates to the £2,000,000 mail-train loot, have been foiled.

Charlie later told friends the *Chronicle* article lifted his spirits because it had made an all-out attack on the forces of law and order. The paper stated that men serving 30-year sentences when more than £2 million was waiting for them outside were bound to try and escape from prison.

It did seem extraordinary that a car with the escape gang could hang around near the prison late at night and not be noticed by authorities. As one newspaper pointed out: 'The plotters had time to wait. Time to lift a gate off its hinges. Time to cover 500 yards. And who was there to stand in their path? Just one man – a fifty-year-old retired warder.'

Winson Green Prison authorities even admitted they didn't know the identity of everyone who'd been in to see Charlie over the previous few months. It was suggested that some of the individuals who came in under the description of 'legal advisors' to help him with his appeal were part of his escape team.

On 12 September 1964, the *Daily Sketch* claimed Charlie was already in hiding in Mexico City. The paper insisted he'd left Britain on a Spanish ship, landed on the northern coast of Spain and was then driven to Madrid where he was provided with a false passport and flown across the Atlantic. The *Daily Herald* claimed in an exclusive that Charlie had missed being rearrested by minutes just two days after his escape. In a front-page article headlined 'ONE JUMP AHEAD OF THE POLICE', reporter Robert Traini wrote that detectives had burst into a ground-floor flat in west London after a tip-off that Charlie had been taken there by his three-man escape team. The police denied that any such incident ever took place.

Charlie later said he had had a right laugh reading some of the newspaper reports about his escape, but he was even more amused when a bookmaker in Northumberland laid odds on his recapture. A notice propped up against the horse-racing results chart in Alan Dawson's betting shop in Victoria Terrace, Whitley Bay, announced: 'Wilson's recapture: We are laying the following odds on the period of Wilson's freedom. First week, evens; second week 2–1; third week 3–1; fourth week 5–1. Any stipulated weeks, 8–1.' No odds were offered on Charlie remaining at liberty. A spokesman for betting giants Ladbrokes in London responded rather pompously: 'Frankly, this is rather overstepping the mark. Betting on a serious social problem that is facing the country is the sort of thing that brings betting into disrepute.'

Thousands of uniformed police and detectives were now involved in the hunt for Charlie. At an airfield in the West Midlands, officers checked out the sighting of an unidentified two-seater aircraft seen in the vicinity on the day of the escape. Local owners of light aircraft were questioned, but none were able to help investigators. Meanwhile, houses, farms, caravans and bungalows which could have been bought or rented by the escape team were being checked across the country. Police also visited clubs and pubs near the jail used by young warders in case the gang had approached anyone. Detectives believed that a recently released inmate must have provided the escape team with much of their inside knowledge.

Reporters door-stepping the Wilsons' old house in Clapham were told by neighbours there had been no sign of Pat and the couple's three children since Charlie's sentencing. Cheryl and Tracey had attended nearby King's Acre Primary School until the end of the previous summer term. The youngest daughter, Leander, was just 18 months of age and not yet attending school. Reporters initially implied that Pat was 'missing' and probably on her way to meet Charlie at some secret location, while she was actually living openly at her mother's home in the East End. Pat was so angry about the constant round of accusations that she'd 'disappeared', she asked her solicitors Sampson and Co., of St Bride Street, London, to issue and serve a writ on one paper, the *Daily Mail*, alleging libel in respect of an article in the newspaper.

Pat then noticed she was shadowed by two men whenever she left her mother's house. For the following two weeks they stuck to her like glue then, just as suddenly, they disappeared. Pat never found out if they were police, journalists or criminals.

The notion of bringing up three daughters alone was daunting enough, but she was also lying awake for hours each night worrying about the fate of her fugitive husband.

4

Halfway across the globe in Mexico City, one of the two train robbers who hadn't yet been arrested – Bruce Reynolds – was leaning back on a park bench with his feet in the sun when he opened his three-day-old English newspaper to find the headline: 'JAIL BUSTERS FREE TRAIN ROBBER – THEY KNOCK OUT GUARD, OPEN CELL, GIVE PRISONER NEW SUIT.' As Reynolds recalled many years later: 'I just thought to myself, "Nice one, Charlie!" His success filled me with pride. We'd finessed the Establishment yet again.'

In prisons across the nation, all the other train robbers were under surveillance for 24 hours a day. Charlie later told Nosher Powell that the prison guards would give every one of them a going over just because he was free. Nosher explained: 'Charlie knew full well that if he ever got banged up again the screws would go in mob-handed to give him a seeing to for daring to escape in the first place, but he thought they was completely out of order to take it out on his mates.'

Amongst the inmates of Britain's prisons, Charlie was a folk hero. Not only had he been part of a team who'd stuck two fingers up at the the powers that be, but now he'd broken out of one of England's supposedly most secure prisons.

One popular yarn doing the rounds following Charlie's escape was that he was being held captive by other criminals determined to get their hands on the Great Train Robbery £2.6 million. One newspaper even suggested that an inmate involved in the conspiracy in another prison had been stabbed to death, although this was never substantiated. Then a Winson Green inmate was released a few days after Charlie was sprung and told reporters that it was 'no secret' that certain people wanted Charlie out because they were after the train robbery cash.

Flying Squad chief Tommy Butler believed Charlie's associates were planting these stories with the press and the police because they wanted the world to think Charlie was dead so the hunt for him would be scaled down. One of Charlie's oldest criminal friends told one newspaper that Charlie's escape team were waiting for the perfect moment 'to carve him up and nick all the money'. The same source later gave police the names of the group of men he said were responsible. One of them had been acquitted of murder. Others had served sentences for grievous bodily harm, armed robbery and possessing dangerous weapons, such as firearms and iron bars. The newspaper's informant claimed Charlie had already been 'chivvied' by the same people and had a razor scar on his face to prove it. Tommy Butler reckoned it was all a smokescreen to keep the heat off Charlie. Then a man referred to in the papers only as 'Mr X' was arrested in the seaside resort of Brighton after it was claimed he was involved in masterminding the plot to spring Charlie. However, Mr X was eventually released without charge.

Another even more sinister rumour flying around was that Charlie had been freed in order to be killed by the brains behind the Great Train Robbery itself, who suspected Charlie was a 'grass'. Charlie – by now sipping champagne at his French hideaway – was outraged that anyone could dare accuse him of being a police informant.

Joey Pyle knew some of the people who helped spring him and believes to this day that Charlie did not pay out any of his own money to the escape team. Pyle explained: 'I know who got him out, but it wasn't about money. Charlie just wanted out. None of us knew where he was after he went on his toes. We didn't want to know where he was. We didn't want that kind of responsibility.' Former Krays' henchman Tony Lambrianou later claimed one of the men on the Wilson escape team was notorious East End villain Jack 'The Hat' McVitie, whose murder a couple of years later ended in life sentences for the Kray twins. Charlie's wife Pat claimed in an interview that the breakout had cost £50,000 with the locksmith getting £10,000. The other team members shared the rest equally, but Frenchy took no reward because he saw Charlie as an important long-term investment.

A couple of weeks after the Winson Green breakout, Charlie moved from the countryside to an apartment in Paris. When Interpol joined in the hunt for him, he decided he needed a disguise. Charlie didn't leave the Paris flat for the following fortnight while he grew out his prison crop before dying his brown hair jet black (he later grew a beard and a moustache and these were also dyed to match his hair). Frenchy even suggested Charlie should have two front teeth extracted and replaced with false ones because his own were slightly prominent and formed a distinctive V-shape, but Charlie refused on the basis he'd never get used to wearing dentures.

★ ★ ★

The Great Train Robbery had already persuaded many citizens that the nation's policemen were not so wonderful. Now Charlie's 'Great Jailbreak' seemed to confirm that a lot of criminals were sharper operators than the cozzers. Many were pointing at some pretty outrageous details about Charlie's escape plans and asking why no one in power had realised what he was up to. Charlie's decision not to personally attend his appeal hearings should have alerted someone, surely? Then there was the way in which the gang had broken *into* a prison for the first time in British criminal history, an idea not inspired by even the most far-fetched war films of the time. But the biggest question of all was how Charlie's escape team got hold of those master keys? Which trusted prisoner – or warder – borrowed and duplicated them? Did he pinch them from the governor, the head warder or even from the chaplain? Then there was the question of how the gang's plans were relayed ahead to Charlie inside Winson Green. Charlie's escape was a dramatic, enthralling true-crime mystery and for most members of the public, there was an insatiable appetite for the next exciting instalment.

Many in Fleet Street were baying for the blood of long-suffering

Tory Home Secretary Henry 'Babbling' Brooke. One newspaper, the *Sunday Citizen*, wrote: 'Will he resign? To this one question alone, the *Citizen* already sadly knows the answer. No.' It was plainly obvious to most members of the public that Charlie's escape had been aided by inside help. It wasn't until many weeks after Charlie went on the run that a statement from the Home Office reluctantly admitted this was the case: 'The possibility of the corruption of a member of the prison staff cannot be excluded at this stage.' Deputy leader of the Labour Party George Brown demanded to be shown a copy of the report into the escape commissioned by Home Secretary Brooke. Brown told reporters: 'I am writing to Mr Brooke to say the report should be published unless it is of an extremely confidential nature involving security, but this is hardly likely in view of the fact the escape has been made.'

Across the country, prison authorities began moving Great Train Robbery gang members to different jails to try and foil any more escape attempts. The Home Office referred to these moves as 'further security measures'. The *Daily Express*'s veteran crime reporter Percy Hoskins came up with some interesting theories on Charlie's escape in a piece headlined 'WHERE IS HE?', alongside a cartoon drawing of Brooke looking ridiculous in a police uniform. Hoskins warned that Charlie's breakout team would have had 'an equally well-planned escape route to a safe hideout'. He commented: 'I cannot see the planners of this exploit doing anything else but whisking their prize out of the country as soon as possible.' Hoskins believed that Charlie and his pals were floating around on a gin palace somewhere in the Mediterranean. He wrote: 'Bearing in mind that at least one member of the train robbery gang previously owned a motor-cruiser, it would be a perfect hiding place. A streamlined, luxury floating home. Anywhere from St Tropez to the Greek islands.'

In London, Tommy Butler and his detectives had begun tracking down Charlie's old pals when they discovered that two of them had gone missing a few days before his escape. Both men were known to have connections in Ireland, which seemed to back up what they'd earlier suspected about Charlie heading for the Emerald Isle. Across the nation, twitchy police officers were breaking down people's front doors after tips about Charlie. In south-east London, the home of one man was raided at midnight while he and his wife were asleep. He later told pressmen: 'It was all so sudden, I didn't know what had happened. They turned the house upside down searching every nook and cranny. They went into my married son's bedroom and tore the bedclothes from his face so that they could see him properly.' Police hunting Charlie even sped to Lyon's coffee shop on the corner of Oxford Street in the heart of London's West End after a 999 caller told Scotland Yard that Charlie was in the restaurant and had a gun. When police got to the scene they found no one even vaguely resembling Charlie.

At one stage, the hunt for Charlie switched to the English Channel after a powerful motor-cruiser called *Fiducia* vanished from its mooring on the Hamble River in Hampshire. Within hours, the navy and coastguard were scouring the seas for any sight of the vessel. A message was then flashed from Scotland Yard to Interpol headquarters in Paris requesting them to inform all French police forces on the northern and western coast to look out for the 35-foot yacht. Like so many of the incidents in the aftermath of Charlie's escape, it proved completely irrelevant, but it did show the sheer scale of the alert.

Detectives even raided the luxury liner the *Queen Elizabeth* before she sailed from Southampton to New York. After a couple of hours, the search was called off when no sign could be found of the elusive train robber. In Italy, police received reports that Charlie was in Florence and Venice. On a remote stretch of Dutch coastline, Charlie was said to have been one of two men seen landing at night and then driving off in a waiting van. In North Wales, a Royal Navy ship and surveillance aircraft joined the search when police got a tip that Charlie and his gang had stolen another yacht from its moorings. RAF Shackletons from Cornwall and Northern Ireland and a Gnat jet trainer from Anglesey were airborne. HMS *Russell*, a 1,650-tonne anti-submarine frigate, was sent under speed from Clyde. When the yacht was eventually stopped off the coast of Dublin, two teenagers were found to have stolen it. Another fanciful theory doing the rounds was that Charlie had slipped out of Birmingham in a horsebox, travelling as a groom with two thoroughbreds.

By the end of September 1964, sources at the Yard were telling reporters they were convinced the escape was masterminded by gangsters running protection rackets in London's West End. Detectives believed an eight-man team was used to spring Charlie and that they were all employed by a self-styled king of the underworld. However, Charlie's favourite newspaper, the *News of the World*, remained convinced that Charlie was the mastermind behind his own escape. Their special investigation team wrote: 'The silent man of the Great Train Robbery, who said barely six words through all that long trial, planned this escape himself, first in outline, then in detail.' The paper claimed a group of breakout experts they christened 'the

Pimpernels' carried out the escape from Winson Green. 'They volunteered and named their price. The approach was made through visitors to the prison who passed it on.' The *News of the World* claimed the Pimpernels met at various secret locations in London in preparation for the escape, but never in the same place twice. They met in Tube stations, on park benches, in a pale-blue Zephyr parked outside a cinema or at cricket matches. They even used a mock-up model of the prison to practise their plans.

More than six weeks after first arriving in France, Charlie and Frenchy left the Paris apartment and headed south to the French Riviera, where they easily blended in with the wealthy jet set at nightclubs and casinos all along the coast. Charlie adored it so much in southern France that he asked Frenchy to find a house for him and get Pat and the girls. Frenchy said he'd have to travel much further afield and advised Charlie to visit every potential place before making a decision. Charlie amused Frenchy by rolling off a multitude of places he'd never been to in his life: Mexico City, Rio, Tokyo, San Francisco. But Charlie was desperate to see his family. He hadn't dared contact Pat in case she led police to him. Charlie presumed detectives would be watching her mother's home, intercepting all mail and perhaps even monitoring all her telephone calls.

After 47 days on the lam, Fleet Street and the nation were growing mightily impatient. 'JUST HOW MUCH LONGER CAN THIS MAN STAY FREE?' asked the *Sunday Mirror*. A government report on the escape was branded a complete whitewash because it failed to address the three most important questions behind the breakout: 1) How did the escape gang get the prison master key? 2) Why, after the escape, did it take 25 minutes to raise the alarm? 3) How far had Wilson travelled before road blocks were set up?

Questions were even asked about the quality of Charlie's mugshots, which were supposed to help people recognise him while he was on the run. The *Sunday Mirror* pulled out a much more recent shot of Charlie and pointed out few people would recognise him from his older, 'official' wanted photo, which had not been updated since the late 1950s. On the run in Europe, Charlie Wilson read about the problems with relish. Sure, he was a professional criminal, but he also loved poking two fingers up at the 'beaks' who ran his country.

From Charlie's point of view, the worst aspect of his escape was that it brought the public spotlight firmly back onto the whereabouts of the Great Train Robbery millions. Scotland Yard believed the money was dispersed soon after the crime was committed and reckoned the rank-and-file gang members each took away £150,000, but that left at least £1 million for the 'principals'. Was Charlie one of them?

It was now a year since the robbery had taken place, but public pressure was immense to locate the missing cash. With Charlie on the run, the police were convinced that he'd eventually show up wherever his share was to be found. Was the money buried, walled up or stashed in some secret location? Could it be hidden in a house bought specially for the purpose, before the robbery was committed? Had it all been smuggled out of the country under diplomatic immunity? So the theories continued.

Despite an intensive hunt, Charlie was still on his toes and Scotland Yard openly admitted they didn't have a clue where he was. Police suspected he'd altered his appearance and was using some of his share of the stolen loot to finance a new life on the run. It was certainly true that Charlie had to pay some heavy 'backhanders' along the way to ensure that no one grassed him up.

Meanwhile, the musical chairs-type switching of other Great Train Robber inmates across the country continued. In one bizarre move, a black London taxi with a heavily armed escort was used to transport Tommy Wisbey from Oxford Prison to Armley in Leeds.

By this time, police had tapped phones, searched ships, tailed relatives, questioned criminals and alerted law enforcement agencies in 12 countries in their hunt for Charlie, but had come up with absolutely nothing. He'd so far been reported to be in hiding in the Midlands, London, Scotland, Ireland, Spain, Holland, Morocco and Mexico.

Charlie had deliberately 'muddied the waters' by trying to lay a false trail. He even let it be known he'd told Pat and the girls to forget him and that they would never see him again. This message was issued through writer Peta Fordham, whose barrister husband had defended four of the train robbers during their trials. Peta's book, *The Robber's Tale*, described the accused with a large dose of ambiguity. She even wrote that 'The events were so vividly in the minds of the actors that they remember, like Henry V's men at Agincourt, with advantages, what feats they did that day.' Renowned British novelist Piers Paul Read later reflected on the gang in a similar vein: 'Politically, one might describe the train robbers as Saxons still fighting the Normans.'

Scotland Yard even made a worldwide television appeal to 24 countries via America's new Early Bird satellite system 22,300 miles into space. Members of the Federal Bureau of Investigation (FBI) watched in their headquarters in Washington as Scotland Yard's Commander, Ernest Millen, talked about Charlie and the other missing men: Reynolds, Buster Edwards and Jimmy White. A deadpan Millen stated on camera: 'These men are Londoners and speak with cockney accents. We know that they are all familiar with and frequent the playgrounds and sun-spots of Europe and the Americas.'

The cameras then switched to the FBI and one agent asked Millen: 'Is there any indication that these men have ever been in the United States?' Back to Millen as photographs of the four missing robbers flashed on the screen: 'They will go anywhere to enjoy themselves and escape arrest.' And so it went on.

Back in London, the Home Office tried to salvage some credibility by announcing they'd foiled another escape plot involving Charlie's old friend Gordon Goody, who was being held at Manchester's Strangeways Prison. Few details were released about the alleged attempt and Goody himself later dismissed it as rubbish. He also insisted that both Charlie and Buster Edwards had been murdered since breaking out of jail. 'There's an awful lot of money involved and they'll stop at nothing,' said Goody, who was about to be moved to the recently completed top-security wing at Durham Jail, which even featured closed-circuit TV to keep an eye on the dangerous inmates. Goody knew how tough it was to be a train robber inside prison and hoped that none of his mates ever got caught. Telling the world they'd been murdered was his way of helping them stay on their toes.

Then there was a dramatic 'sighting' of Charlie in South America. British newspapers reported that a shaven-headed Briton had been released by police in Uruguay after he'd changed a bundle of British currency in a local bank. Was it Charlie?

Back at her mother's East End home, Pat was asked about the man being questioned in South America. She told reporters: 'Honestly, I don't know whether it's Charlie or not. I have not heard from him. I have no idea where he is and I don't suppose I ever shall have.' The rumours from Uruguay would not go away. A few days later, newspapers claimed Charlie had teamed up with fellow escapees Bruce Reynolds, Buster Edwards and Jimmy White in South America. In the end, Scotland Yard had to officially deny the story after admitting they'd received no information from the Montevideo police.

In mid-May 1965, a beautiful South African model called Else Smith told police that she'd been engaged to Charlie Wilson for months. She also alleged that she'd only broken off the relationship when she heard Pat and their daughters were flying to Johannesburg to join him. 'I was deeply hurt,' Smith told reporters. She claimed she'd been with Charlie since he'd arrived in South Africa at the end of the previous year. 'After an engagement party, he told me he was one of the train robbers. He said he was the only one who knew where the bulk of the money was stored. Three times he planned to fly to London but cancelled his flights because he said things were not right over there.'

Else claimed Charlie did eventually fly to London on 10 March, but returned two days later saying he had failed to pick up his share of the robbery cash. She added: 'But when I learned about his wife, I refused to speak to him.' When suspicious reporters showed Miss Smith photos of Charlie amongst other train robbers she immediately picked him out, but the story was never properly substantiated – although some of Charlie's old pals wouldn't have been surprised if Charlie had been spinning a few yarns to a pretty girl. It was certainly possible Charlie did pass through South Africa during the early months of his escape. After all, hadn't Frenchy advised him to visit every place he was considering as a long-term home?

The only investigator who remained quietly poised and extremely focused on his hunt for Charlie was Detective Chief Superintendent Tommy Butler, who believed he'd get his man in the end. His inquiries into Charlie's escape had already led him to a number of countries and he believed it was only a matter of time before Charlie slipped up.

Butler was given authorisation for at least four different phone taps on criminals known to be close to Charlie. He was convinced Charlie received 'wages' once a month from a 'moneyman' in London, sometimes by courier, sometimes by post. Butler remained highly unimpressed by the 'Charlie is dead' stories which were still doing the rounds. As he told the *Daily Sketch*: 'We have heard several reports from underworld contacts that he is dead. There is only one way to prove or disprove these stories. That is to find Wilson – dead or alive.'

In July 1965, eleven months after Charlie crept out of Winson Green, Ronnie Biggs pulled off an equally outrageous escape from Wandsworth Prison in south London. Until the train robbery, Biggs had owned a small painting and decorating business in Surrey, where he'd lived with his wife and two small children. Biggs was not one of the most important members of the Great Train Robbery team, but he'd been a popular figure.

Biggs's escape from Wandsworth was as dramatic as Charlie's had been smooth: as prisoners exercised in the prison yard, a furniture van drew up alongside the wall of the prison and an armed man leapt onto the roof of the van. He then dropped a tubular ladder into the yard below. Four prisoners ran towards the ladder, scrambled up and jumped down onto the van. Biggs and the three other inmates then poured through a hole in the roof into the back of the lorry and, half a mile later, split up and fled in three waiting cars.

Ronnie Biggs's escape was without doubt another nail in the Establishment's coffin. A headline and introduction in the *Daily Express* summed it up perfectly:

> FREED AT GUNPOINT
> The Train Robbers snatched another of their £2,500,000 gang from prison yesterday – at gunpoint, in daylight, in public, in the heart of London.'

Biggs's successful breakout, despite the supposed 24-hour lockdown on all the train robbers following Charlie's escape, simply added to the robbers' legendary status. How could they keep humiliating the authorities and expect to get away with it?

Ronnie's escape was also good news for Charlie because the police switched much of their attention away from him. The headlines that followed Biggs for many years turned out to be even bigger and bolder than for Charlie.

5

In November 1965, Charlie flew into Mexico City to meet Bruce Reynolds and Buster Edwards. Reynolds barely recognised Charlie when he went to meet him at the airport. In his autobiography, *Crossing The Line*, Reynolds later recalled: 'He had always been big, over six foot and powerfully built, but he turned up with a fantastic tan, ginger hair and a dyed ginger beard. He also wore small wire-rimmed glasses, which looked incongruous, and I thought, "My God – what have you done to yourself?"' Charlie and Reynolds – pals since schooldays – were delighted to see each other. 'Who would have thought that 30 years later we'd be sitting in Mexico City, he an escaped convict and me on the run?' added Reynolds.

Charlie stayed more than six weeks in Mexico City and was soon back to his old wisecracking self. His take on why he hadn't had any plastic surgery is worth repeating here: 'I heard Buster had plastic surgery. I was interested in it myself, until I found out it cost twenty grand. Fuck twenty grand – I'll get Joey to hit me in the face with a shovel and then go to St Thomas's and let them sort it out.'

Charlie told Reynolds and Edwards he'd decided to settle in Canada because Pat 'wasn't too keen on foreigners' and the city of Montreal seemed the best place for them. Charlie said Mexico would never be suitable because he hated not being able to speak the local language and wasn't too keen on the food, either. Pat and the girls were still back in England at this time, but Charlie told his old friends he was certain he could smuggle them out to start a new life in North America.

Charlie and his pals enjoyed some lively nights out in Mexico City and even went on a road trip down to the wealthy tourist resort of Acapulco in a brand new Cadillac. But Charlie's constant moaning about Mexico eventually began to irritate the two other train robbers. He complained about everything from the people to the weather and became morose over Christmas because he wasn't with his family. Charlie also loathed the numerous street beggars and lost his temper at the smallest thing; even a row with a waiter threatened to turn into a stand-up fight. He left soon afterwards with a set of newly issued Canadian immigration papers, all made out in a false identity. Buster Edwards was quite relieved to see Charlie go because he'd taken a fancy to Edwards' young, attractive Mexican maid, who'd started walking around Edwards' house in Charlie's shoes. It seemed that Charlie could desperately miss his family *and* lust after beautiful women at the same time.

In January 1966, Charlie arrived in Montreal via Brussels as a new immigrant using a fake passport in the name of Ronald Alloway. That same year, 63,290 other people emigrated to Canada from Britain. Three weeks after Charlie left Mexico, Bruce Reynolds took a flight north to see him. Charlie met his pal at the airport with a new girlfriend, an attractive nurse. It seemed to Reynolds that 'Cheeky Charlie' always had at least one mistress on the go. Reynolds explained in his autobiography: 'This girl was pleasant with a good sense of humour, although seeing them together, all lovey-dovey, I worried that they were too familiar.' When Reynolds got back to Charlie's rented flat in a leafy Montreal suburb, Reynolds took his friend aside and asked if he had told her anything about himself. Charlie replied that of course he hadn't, but later that same day, Charlie boasted to Bruce

Reynolds that his girlfriend was also having an affair with a Montreal police chief. Reynolds wasn't amused.

'Are you crazy?' he exploded at Charlie.

'Nah, it's OK, Bruce, really. He doesn't know who I am. Although it's funny, he said to her one night, "I know who your boyfriend is. He's Ronald Edwards, the English geezer, isn't he?"'

Reynolds' jaw dropped.

'I mean, who the fuck's Ronald Edwards?' said Charlie, laughing and not even noticing the expression on his old friend's face.

'I'll tell you who it is,' said Reynolds. 'It's fuckin' Buster!' Very few people – including Charlie – realised that Buster Edwards' real name was Ronald.

'Christ! What am I gonna do?' asked a shocked Charlie.

'Well, I don't think I fancy staying here with you, Charlie,' said Reynolds. That afternoon he flew back to Mexico City and told Charlie to 'move house, lose the girl and, for fuck's sake, be more careful'.

★ ★ ★

With Charlie now officially one of the world's most-wanted men, Pat became a virtual recluse at her mother's home in Brady Street, Whitechapel. The house only had two bedrooms, so with six people living under one roof it wasn't easy. Then, one morning, a telegram arrived addressed to her. Pat recalled: 'Like most people, I got a sinking feeling in my stomach every time I opened one of those little buff envelopes.' Pat went upstairs to the bedroom she shared with the three girls, sat down on the edge of the bed and started slowly tearing it open with her trembling fingers. The message was short and simple, but it made Pat's heart pound: 'I AM OK DO NOT WORRY STOP LOVE TO ALL AND LEANDER MA BELLE MICHELLE STOP RON'.

Pat burst into tears and fell back on the bed. The name Ron meant absolutely nothing to her, but those words 'Ma Belle Michelle' meant everything. As Pat later explained: 'The only people in the whole world who knew that was Charlie's pet name for our youngest daughter were Charlie and myself. The telegram had to be from my husband.'

Pat told no one about the message, not even her mother. Frenchy then contacted her and told her to change her name to 'Alloway' by deed poll. She explained: 'I was certain then that a reunion with Charlie was now only a matter of time.'

Weeks then went by without any fresh news. One day as Pat was window shopping along Oxford Street, in London's West End, a middle-aged woman asked if she knew the way to Bond Street. As Pat was directing her, the woman interrupted, saying: 'Never mind. If you'd like to follow me, I'll take you to see Ron.'

Pat was flabbergasted and began to shake violently. She recalled: 'It seemed as if my legs wouldn't hold the weight of my body and I thought I was going to collapse.' The mystery woman saw the state of Pat and immediately hailed a taxi for them both. The cab travelled to the corner of William Mews in Knightsbridge, then the two women walked 200 yards down William Street into Lowndes Square where a black Jaguar Mark 10 limousine was waiting.

The woman leaned in and spoke to the driver, who then reached across and swung open the front passenger door, flashed a broad smile and said: 'OK, Mrs Alloway. Ron's waiting for you.' The woman simply turned and walked away.

Inside the car, Pat sat in silence. She remarked later: 'For most of the time, we seemed to be going back over the same route as that taken by the taxi.' Then the vehicle stopped outside an apartment building. The driver escorted Pat into a building where they caught the lift to a top-floor flat. As Pat walked in the front door, Charlie strode across the room with his arms outstretched. Pat felt her knees buckling beneath her and had to be held as she started sobbing. 'Don't worry, love. Everything will be all right now,' said Charlie.

Pat noted later that Charlie seemed to have grown much older since the last time she'd seen him. Then he told her, 'Charles Wilson has died from now on, love. My new surname is . . .'

Pat interrupted: 'Well, my new surname is Alloway, so you'll have to get used to that.'

Charlie smiled. Of course, he already knew she'd changed her name by deed poll. He told Pat he'd been all over South America, the United States and Canada searching for a place they could settle down in. Charlie explained: 'Canada's the place for us. There's a town there near Montreal which has everything. If you think you can get used to the hard winters and deep snow, it's ideal. The kids can go skiing and sledging and the scenery's fantastic. Then, in the summer, it'll be water skiing, swimming and riding. We'll all love it, Pat.'

That first meeting only lasted 30 minutes, but Charlie promised Pat that they'd soon all be together once more as a complete family unit. As she was driven away, Pat said she turned to look up at the apartment block and wondered if it really was going to happen like her husband said.

One week later, Pat was out walking near her mother's home when a dark-blue Zodiac with the same driver from the previous meeting with Charlie collected her and took her to see Charlie again. But this time when Pat said, 'Hello, Ron,' Charlie didn't react or utter a word or immediately spring to his feet. Pat nervously asked him if something was wrong. Charlie – well dressed in a checked sports shirt and a pair of tailored blue mohair slacks – laughed out loud, and finally leapt up and kissed her. 'Not a thing, love,' he said. 'I just wanted to test you. You called me Ron – not Charlie. That's good.'

As the driver fixed the couple drinks, Charlie told Pat what he had planned for them. He wanted her to go home and find someone to look after the three girls for a couple of days. Pat was to return to the flat and stay with him while they discussed their future. She was also to bring along every detail concerning her change of name and get 24 snaps of herself from an instant photo booth.

Pat asked for some explanation but Charlie told her, 'Just get 'em, love. Don't ask no questions.'

Pat went home, got a friend to look after the girls and said she was off to Surrey for two days to try and find a house to buy. Then she travelled by Tube to London's Baker Street Station where she fed one half-crown after another into the slot of the instant photo booth. A few minutes later, she was thumbing through the pictures, finding it hard to stop laughing out loud as she looked sadder and more fed up in each successive photo. Pat recalls: 'By the time I got to the last set, I looked as if I'd just been to my own funeral.'

That evening she met up with Charlie again at the flat where he cooked her a meal and they opened a bottle of vintage wine. They even had their photograph taken together. Pat recalls: 'Looking back, I suppose it was a risky thing to do – I was so happy at the time I hardly gave it a thought.'

After two days together, Pat headed back to the East End with instructions to visit a café at Paddington Station at a pre-agreed time four days later. In that café, Pat was approached by a young woman who said little, but left a large envelope on the table where Pat was sitting. It contained a passport in the name Barbara Joan Alloway although Pat had changed her name to Patricia Ann Alloway. There was also a type-written note saying: 'Be at Slough Mainline Station 4.15 p.m. Wednesday.'

That Wednesday morning, Pat got up especially early and made breakfast for their three daughters and then told her mother she was taking them to the zoo for the day and might then go and stay with a friend in the country. Moments after her mother left the house, Pat crammed some make-up and changes of clothing into one small overnight bag and rushed out with the children. They then caught the Tube to Paddington, followed by a train to Slough where Pat and the children waited near the station bus stop. Ten minutes later, the driver who'd taken her to meet Charlie earlier pulled up in a black Jaguar.

Within minutes, they were driving along quiet roads lined with hedges and fields. Eventually, they turned up a long driveway which led up to a vast mansion nestled amongst beautifully mowed lawns and lavish flowerbeds. Pat and the girls were greeted at the front door by an elegantly dressed, well-spoken lady. 'Hello, Mrs Alloway,' she said. It was the same woman who'd delivered the passport at the café.

For the next few days, Charlie and Pat's daughters played happily in the grounds of the mansion. They'd been warned not to go beyond the end of the drive. Pat, meanwhile, was growing impatient with all the waiting. Three days later, Pat's host called her into the drawing room and introduced her to an extremely handsome-looking man in his early 30s. Speaking with a heavy French accent, he said: 'These are all the documents you will need, Mrs Alloway. Everything to get you through immigration: plane tickets, health documents. All you have to do is keep the children occupied.'

Pat knew their next stop was the airport, so questioned where Ron was. 'You will see Ron very shortly. Remember, he said not to worry,' came the reply. Pat was then shown three big suitcases and told to go to the main bedroom of the house and pick out anything she wanted for the journey. All the sizes were correct.

Two hours later, Pat – whose natural blonde hair had been dyed auburn – found herself alone at Heathrow Airport having been directed to a check-in desk by her driver. The first stop was Amsterdam from where they transferred onto a non-stop flight to Montreal. During the seven-hour flight, Pat was a bundle of nerves.

When oldest daughter Cheryl wrote her real name in a colouring book next to her, Pat leaned across in a panic and whispered for her to cross it out. Cheryl pleaded with her mother and wouldn't give it to her, until Pat eventually snatched it off her without anyone else noticing. By the time Pat and the girls arrived in Montreal, she felt even more stressed. Pat recalled: 'I kept thinking, suppose there's no one there to meet me? What if Charlie was there and Scotland Yard knew about it? Suppose the immigration officers found something wrong with our documents and started asking questions?' The only money Pat had on her was a £5 note.

Pat and her daughters got through immigration without a hitch, although in the Arrivals Hall there didn't seem to be a friendly face in sight. Just then, Tracey spotted a big American car parked just outside and yelled: 'Look over there!' Standing beside the car was a bearded man with bright, sparkling blue eyes. It was Charlie.

'Hello, loves,' he shouted across the hall.

Pat struggled to hold back tears as Charlie grabbed and kissed Cheryl and Tracey. When he got to Pat he said, 'Told you not to worry, didn't I! Told you everything would be all right.' Then, taking little Leander into his arms, he tried to kiss her, but she pulled away from him.

'Who dat?' she asked. 'Who dat man?'

Charlie laughed and handed Leander back to Pat. Then he picked up their cases and led his family out to his huge, gas-guzzling metallic-blue Pontiac Parisienne outside.

Pat was delighted by the beautiful house Charlie had rented for them in the township of Hudson Heights. She recalls: 'The view from it and the scenery was unbelievable. It was a secluded spot all on its own and surrounded on all sides by tall pine trees.'

As Pat walked into the lounge she found a bouquet of her favourite chrysanthemums and two potted plants. A pink ribbon adorned each one and a printed message on the card read: 'Welcome home – all of you. Love Ron. Now there is no need to worry!' Pat burst into tears.

Charlie was determined to remain financially secure in Canada. His money was back in London with an old friend whom he'd known since the '50s. They'd invested in some legitimate businesses such as betting shops, restaurants and, it was later rumoured, a part-share in a chain of provincial newspapers, but not long after Pat and the girls arrived in Canada, Charlie found out that this same business partner had been investing so erratically that Charlie's cash-share from the Great Train Robbery was down to just £30,000. He'd even had to pay a 10 per cent fee to his associate back in London to ensure all his money got to him. Charlie was unable to do much about it because he was on the lam and couldn't risk any more secret trips to London for the time being. As one of his oldest friends explained: 'Half the money they nicked on the Great Train Robbery went to straightening people up. They was mugged, including Charlie. Wisbey was the only one who didn't lose a fortune because his brother looked after the money. The rest of them ended up giving most of it away. They never saw it. They got taken to the cleaners by so-called friends.' Others reckoned Charlie invested part of the train robbery money into government bonds and that he received sufficient interest to 'keep him going' nicely.

So with money worries apparently looming, Charlie decided to go back to what he knew best. When Bruce Reynolds and his wife came to stay with them in Canada, Charlie told his old friend about his money problems and how he hoped to pull off a couple of 'jobs' in Canada to make ends meet. A contact had told Charlie about the movements of several large consignments of Canadian dollars which had been spent in New York and were then shipped back to Montreal. Charlie established that just two security men picked up half-a-dozen sacks of the money each month. Charlie and Bruce Reynolds staked out the shipment company where the money arrived from New York and then watched as the mailbags were unloaded into an estate car before being driven into central Montreal. They talked up a decent plan, but then Charlie decided it was too risky and the robbery was shelved. Some of his friends later claimed that he'd ditched the job because he didn't want to risk losing Pat and the girls again. Bruce Reynolds recalled: 'The Wilsons were a very happy family. Chas idolised his wife, Pat, and their three daughters. His family life was, and always had been, sacrosanct. Sure, he played around, but never to the detriment of his wife and family. In all respects, he was a great father and a good husband.'

6

Having decided against a life of crime in Canada, Charlie began working at a Montreal firm that sold sterling silver and glassware. Then he spotted a plot of land amongst snow-clad hills and a dense forest in the tiny community of Rigaud, 40 miles from Montreal. Charlie answered a billboard put up by the Mountain Ranches Development Company and was invited to view the land by Perry Bedbrook, the 50-year-old director of the firm. Charlie bought a half-acre plot for £1,640 plus £9,170 for his new house to be built over the following six months. The balance of £7,600 on the land and house was to be covered by a mortgage with the Central Mortgage Corporation – a federal agency – which checked Ron Alloway's credit rating and found him a safe risk after Charlie told Bedbrook he got $10,000-a-year interest from a property deal back in the UK.

Perry Bedbrook recalled: 'Ron was a gentle character, such a good friend. Hell, I guaranteed his mortgage, found the man to design his home, got it built for him at cost price.' Bedbrook also introduced Charlie to the local golf club. Bedbrook later commented that Charlie was a lousy golfer but a lovely guy. Others who met Charlie at that time note he always made a point of saying his life was in Canada now, so there was nothing to discuss about the past. Charlie went out of his way to prevent his short temper from fusing because he knew that any aggravation could mark the beginning of the end for him, Pat and the girls. And Charlie still always had bundles of money near him in case of emergencies. He even asked the builder of his new home to ensure that he added a special airtight room complete with a built-in waist-high safe in the basement.

★ ★ ★

Starting a new life in Canada might have seemed a dream come true, but there was one overwhelming problem for Charlie and Pat Wilson – their three young daughters. Charlie knew they could accidentally give them away in a split second, so within a short time of arriving in Canada, he got the girls sitting on separate cushions in the lounge of their rented home and began asking them over and over again: 'What's my name?' Eventually, they all answered 'Ronald Alloway', but it wasn't easy. Pat recalled: 'We played this game incessantly for days until the children were perfect nearly every time. Even sudden trick questions over lunch or at bedtime couldn't catch them out, although occasionally one of the girls would slip up. In that case, the other two would receive a "prize" of a bar of chocolate.'

Charlie then switched jobs from the silver and glassware business to being a car salesman, also in Montreal city. Pat later claimed Charlie was on such a low salary, he couldn't afford to buy expensive clothes or toys for the girls. But every now and again, Charlie would turn up with yet another bundle of cash from London and the family would go on a shopping spree. Charlie also paid to have a high stone wall built around the family's new house in Rigaud. It also had a garage for the family's two cars, a Volkswagen and Charlie's latest purchase, a brand new gleaming white Cadillac. The stone and timber house was perfectly perched high on a hill above picture-postcard Rigaud, with rolling valleys stretching into an endless and breathtaking view from the horizon to a forest filled with huddles of snow-frosted pine trees. The house was completed ahead of schedule. Charlie and Pat quickly became close friends with neighbour and local police chief Charles Pooley. Pooley and his wife even dropped in on the Wilsons for a glass of wine once. Afterwards, Charlie turned to Pat and said: 'I hope he never finds out who he's been drinking with!'

There were a few much closer shaves, though: like the time Charlie and Pat took oldest daughter Cheryl for an X-ray to make sure her hole-in-the-heart problem had not worsened since their arrival in Canada. At a Montreal hospital, Pat completely forgot her new identity until Charlie chipped in with 'Mrs Alloway, Barbara Joan Alloway'. Then he added, by way of explanation, 'I'm sorry, my wife is rather worried. She hates hospitals, you see.' Pat was so traumatised by forgetting her new name that she refused to ever visit Montreal again.

But for Charlie, who'd always loved the hustle and bustle of the city and the raucous, excited crush of a racetrack crowd, the idyllic countryside almost drove him crazy with boredom. Most mornings, Charlie would drive the children down the hill to the black-and-orange school bus that took them with their classmates to school in nearby Hudson. Charlie found it difficult mixing with law-abiding citizens in such a predominantly respectable middle-class community. Sometimes he'd slip away to Montreal's Blue Bonnet and Richelieu racetracks, 35 miles from the US border, but his loneliness was outmatched by his desire to stay free. As the months progressed, he spent more and more time just with Pat and the children; Cheryl, now twelve, Tracey, ten, and Leander, five. 'He did sometimes seem withdrawn and a bit strained,' recalls neighbour Russell Hodgson, part owner of the Mountain Ranches Country Club, close to where the Wilsons lived. 'He never said much, but I knew what the trouble was. He was bored.'

Charlie was thankful he'd discovered the joys of reading while in prison. He ploughed his way through at least one novel a week, one particular favourite being Len Deighton's *Billion Dollar Brain*. There were other, sleazier pieces of reading material kept hidden away from the children's eyes in the bedroom. Charlie had enjoyed pornographic magazines ever since his time in prison in the '50s. Nothing too sordid, but he found them strangely satisfying.

★ ★ ★

Back in Britain, the Great Train Robbery had now been added to the adventures of Robin Hood and Dick Turpin in British national mythology. At Madame Tussauds, one of the most popular new attractions was Charlie and Ronnie Biggs, sitting next to each other on a park bench. There seemed to be no end to the stories building up around the gang, particularly those who were still on the lam.

By the middle of 1966, the police issued fresh 'Wanted' posters for all the missing train robbers, appealing to people going on holiday and offering them rewards totalling £225,000 if they helped capture the criminals. Jimmy White was the first of them to be captured when police got a tip he was staying at a block of flats in Grand Parade, Littlestone-on-Sea, in Kent.

Then on Monday, 19 September 1966, Buster Edwards surrendered to police after carefully negotiating a lower sentence with Tommy Butler. His gamble paid off and he got 15 years. The police – particularly Butler – had proved they were as determined as ever to capture the rest of the gang. Charlie, Bruce Reynolds and Ronnie Biggs were now the only ones left on the run. But how much longer could they last?

Reynolds visited Charlie and his family again in Rigaud during Christmas 1966. In his memoirs, Reynolds recalls one day when they took a bunch of noisy children from the village in Charlie's big white Cadillac to a Christmas carol service. Reynolds says they laughed about what the children's parents would make of it if they knew who they were, making their way through the snow. He remembers Charlie laughing out loud and slapping the steering wheel. He loved a joke and adored the feeling that he was still getting one over on the real world.

Charlie gave the girls a pet cat called Fluffy for Christmas that year. He also carved the turkey with great energy and enthusiasm. 'And he even did the washing up; there was nothing he wouldn't do for his family and friends,' Reynolds recalls.

★ ★ ★

The publicity surrounding the robbers on the run seemed to calm down and Charlie's life itself followed suit, 1967 being surely the quietest year of his adult life. The key to Charlie's survival was to ensure that any money from the UK had to travel a very devious route because the police were still monitoring his London associates. Charlie's hideaway in Canada would only become known to police if his 'money suppliers' gave him away.

There were exceptions to Charlie's strict rules about making sure no evidence of the family's previous identity existed in Canada, however. Pat still had a locket around her neck with a photograph of Charlie without the beard he grew as a disguise. It was almost identical to the 'Wanted' picture issued by police after Charlie's escape from Winson Green. One night, a neighbour visited Charlie and Pat's house with his wife and young daughter. The little girl tried to open the locket as she sat on Pat's knee. As Charlie later wrote to a friend: 'We were all sweating that night!'

The Wilson house was guarded by an Alsatian and a Dobermann pinscher because dog-lover Charlie could never get out of the habit of watching his back. He also liked to know Pat and the girls had good protection whenever he was away from home.

Charlie and Pat tried not to court too many friendships in the small community of Rigaud because they felt that if their secret was ever revealed, it would lead to great bitterness and resentment. As Pat later explained, the locals would be justified in feeling that they had deceived them, but the neighbours and townsfolk of Rigaud were intrigued by the young British family. They were frequently invited into other people's homes for drinks during the sub-zero winter evenings and to barbeques and swimming sessions on baking summer weekends.

One evening, during the summer of 1967, as the Wilson daughters played happily at the lakeside with a neighbour's children, Charlie and Pat found themselves sitting around an open log fire at the water's edge, preparing supper. She glanced across at Charlie and noticed he was staring into the leaping flames, deep in thought. Then he noticed her, looked up, leaned across and whispered to her: 'These are such good friends, love. Whatever happens, I'm sure they'll stick by you.' She shivered in spite of the warmth of the night and the blazing logs; she'd always had a nagging fear that their life now was too good to last for ever.

Pat was often frustrated, even angry, about the predicament she found herself in. She confided to one friend that she and Charlie never properly discussed what would happen if he ever got recaptured. 'It was just a silence between us. It was never mentioned,' she complained. And Pat later said pointedly: 'I have always been of the opinion that a hard day's work doesn't harm anyone and you would always be a lot happier leading a normal life.' Like a lot of married couples, there were serious communication problems between Charlie and Pat. It was just that, with them, the stakes were a lot higher.

Even in Rigaud, Charlie occasionally let slip a hint of his real character. Perry Bedbrook recalls that Charlie made it clear he liked to count every penny and was not from a wealthy background. Charlie admitted to some neighbours and friends in Rigaud he was worried about the devaluation of the pound back in Britain and intended to start a business in Canada. Soon after this, Charlie agreed to invest $2,000 in a property business venture with his new friend Perry Bedbrook.

Charlie also met a Polish priest who wanted to build a new church in Rigaud. He persuaded Charlie to invest some money in a fund which would go towards the upkeep of the Roman Catholic parish and pay him back a modest rate of interest in the process. Charlie saw it as a very convenient way to launder money in the short term. Charlie was then elected a member of the exclusive Mountain Ranches Country Club. Was he actually starting to enjoy middle-class respectability? In North America, he was no longer the old lag who talked cockney rhyming slang and called himself 'Charlie the Greengrocer' from south London. In Rigaud, he was known as a wealthy businessman and the neighbours treated him as one of their own. For the first time in his life, Charlie Wilson was considered a fine, upstanding citizen.

★ ★ ★

In London, the tenacious Tommy Butler was still hard at work trying to capture Charlie Wilson. His attitude was perfectly summed up when one of Butler's younger detectives joked about Charlie's escape in the big, cluttered Flying Squad office at Scotland Yard, saying, 'We put 'em in – someone else gets 'em out.'

Butler, hurrying through to his small, spartan room nearby, rounded on the young policeman. 'This is no joke,' he said, with a grim expression on his face.

In late 1967, Butler launched Operation Perpendicular, the secret codename used by Scotland Yard for the recapture of Charlie Wilson. Only two other officers – Assistant Commissioner Peter Brodie and Commander Ernest Millen – knew about the latest plan to track the train robber. Strict instructions were given that any message coming into the Yard with the code signal Operation Perpendicular should be given only to those two officers. Butler even got his impending retirement suspended by Met Commissioner Sir Joseph Simpson on his 55th birthday in order to continue the hunt for Charlie Wilson.

Throughout all this, Butler continued to work on mountains of paperwork into the small hours and remained willing to meet underworld informants at any time of the day or night. He still prided himself on always being there at the final arrest.

Stories in newspapers about Charlie and the other two runaway train robbers, Reynolds and Biggs, were gradually being given much less prominence. By 20 November 1967, a report claiming Charlie had spent a few days in the West End of London made just one paragraph in the *Daily Mirror*. Everyone now presumed Charlie was sunning himself a long way from Britain and was out of harm's way. Why on earth would he risk everything to return to London?

Just after Christmas that year, Charlie travelled into Montreal on business and was sitting in a bar supping a drink when someone tapped him on the shoulder – Bruce Reynolds. Charlie later recalled: 'He was there, large as life – and not even disguised. I don't mind telling you it was a bit of a shock. But he was quite at ease. "I thought I'd come and see how you and Pat are doing," he said. "Are you OK for money?"'

The two men sat chatting about their families for at least half an hour with Charlie looking apprehensively over Reynolds' shoulder every few seconds. It was a flying visit and Reynolds eventually said his goodbyes and left. Charlie told Pat all about it later that same day, but voiced his concerns about the visit being 'much too risky'. Both Charlie and Pat had a strange feeling that the net was closing in on them, although they didn't know why.

All Pat cared about was that Charlie never again split up the family. She remained very much in love with Charlie and, in many ways, being in Canada had been good for their marriage because he had fewer opportunities to stray. She summed up her take on Charlie a few years later when she said: 'I always knew Charlie had the brains and the ability to be a master criminal, just as, in my heart of hearts, I suppose I always knew he'd get caught. I loved him dearly and he reciprocated that love. He was a kind father and a marvellous husband.' But even the loyal Pat conceded '. . . behind that shining exterior lay a darker side to Charlie, a man secretly craving excitement and danger, and with an overwhelming desire to organise men of similar temperament; a man who sought out others prepared to stop at virtually nothing to get on easy street for the rest of their lives'. And there lay the heart of the problem for Charlie: joining the local Rotary Club and swinging a few golf clubs around on a Saturday afternoon just didn't satisfy his urge for excitement in life. So, in the end, he broke his own golden rule and contacted a few old familiar faces back in London. Surely he could get away with enticing some of them over to see him in Rigaud?

7

It was a discussion between two people in the south of France that first alerted Tommy Butler to the possibility Charlie might be in Canada. Detectives had been unofficially shadowing two of Charlie's London associates when they overheard a conversation which clearly indicated the country where Wilson was hiding. Butler was already well aware that Pat and the children had disappeared from London and were most likely reunited with Charlie and living somewhere as a family unit. Just knowing Charlie was in Canada wasn't enough, though, because it was one hell of a big country. Butler therefore sought out all his most reliable south London informants and tried to find out if they'd heard anything on the grapevine. When one grass told Butler that Pat's cousin and Charlie's one-time business partner Georgie Osborne was planning a trip to Canada, he knew immediately that Osborne must be on his way to see Charlie.

When Osborne arrived in Montreal on a flight from Europe, his movements were plotted by the Royal Canadian Mounted Police who reported back to Butler and the Flying Squad that Osborne was staying with a character called Alloway, who resembled Charlie. Tommy Butler asked the Mounties to keep a close watch, but not to go near Charlie for the moment. Butler was hoping that if he monitored them for long enough, Charlie's old mate Bruce Reynolds might also pop up on the horizon and then he could nab both runaway train robbers at the same time. For more than three weeks, Butler sat back and waited. His Scotland Yard superiors then panicked that Charlie might slip the net, and put immense pressure on Butler to arrest him as quickly as possible. They were furious that Butler was risking Charlie's getaway on a hunch he might nab Reynolds at the same time. In mid-January 1968, Tommy Butler deliberately planted an article in British national newspapers in the hope it would put Charlie off his guard. The story claimed that Charlie had been spotted in Tangier, in Morocco, and had enjoyed a casual drink and a chat with an unnamed 'traveller'.

Over in Canada, Charlie and Pat were entertaining Georgie Osborne blissfully unaware that a Mounties team was watching their every move. Charlie even introduced Osborne to friend Perry Bedbrook.

Tommy Butler arrived in Montreal with his colleague Detective Sergeant Eddie Fuller the day after the Moroccan article was published in the UK. The next day, they watched from a distance as Pat stood outside in the snow waving the girls off as Charlie drove them down the hill to the school bus in his Cadillac. Later that same day, Pat spotted four men trying to fix a snowmobile which seemed to have broken down. As she later explained: 'A little shiver of fear ran through me because it was so rare to see anyone out in such cold weather.' She didn't bother mentioning it to Charlie, though, because they 'didn't really ever discuss that side of things,' as she later said.

Two days later, the family Alsatian, Cadillac Rocky, who had a kennel outside the front of the house, barked uncontrollably most of the day, only going silent after darkness fell. The following Tuesday, Pat spotted the same men whose snowmobile had earlier broken down. This time, they seemed to be driving a Dormobile van down the Wilsons' quiet lane. Again, Pat didn't tell Charlie about the strangers.

It was on Thursday morning, 25 January 1968 – day 1,261 of Charlie's freedom – that Tommy Butler made his move. Wearing snowshoes in temperatures of minus nineteen, he clambered through the two-foot-deep drifts in the forest near Charlie's house and watched Charlie walk out to his Cadillac. Even in thick, nylon quilted clothing, it was bitterly cold. Butler later said he could see Charlie's piercing blue eyes sparkling in the strong winter sunlight. Butler had local Mounties stationed in key positions around the house although the police operation itself had been a closely guarded secret (not even Charlie's neighbour, the local provincial police chief, knew about it). Butler was now certain the man in that house was Charlie Wilson, so it was time to spring his carefully planned trap.

A few minutes later, Charlie left the house to take Cheryl and Tracey to meet the school bus. As he drove down the hill, he spotted a blue van, which had half run off the road and was stuck in deep snow. Three men were trying to push it out. As Charlie later recalled, 'I thought, "Poor devils, I'll give 'em a hand on the way back."'

He dropped Cheryl and Tracey at the school bus, then went back up the hill and stopped his car by the men pushing the van and asked if they needed some help.

'Yes, please. We can't shift it at all,' came the reply.

As Charlie heaved and helped push the van, a voice behind him said: 'Good morning, Charlie. Want some help?'

At first, Charlie hadn't a clue who was talking to him. As Tommy Butler later said: 'I looked more like an Eskimo than a Yard man.'

Charlie recalled: 'I didn't recognise the voice, but the word "Charlie" made me freeze. Then, as I straightened up and half turned, I looked straight into the face of Tommy Butler from Scotland Yard.'

At first, Charlie staggered and gasped with surprise, then, typically, he straightened up. 'Morning, Tom,' he said. 'Fancy seeing you out in all this cold snow. You'll catch your death!'

Charlie was then seized from behind by Ted Fuller and made to stand facing his car with his hands on the roof while he was searched. A couple of minutes later, Charlie, Butler, Fuller and at least half a dozen undercover Canadian detectives walked up to the front door of his house. Pat recalls: 'Charlie had only been out about 15 minutes when the front doorbell rang. I went to answer it in a housecoat and nightie. As I opened the door, six big men were standing there in the snow.'

'Mrs Alloway?' one asked. 'May we come in? I think you know what it's all about.'

Pat recalled: 'I didn't cry. I just replied quietly, "Please, do come into the lounge."'

As Pat looked beyond the detectives, she saw Charlie talking to his greatest foe – Tommy Butler. Pat later admitted to an overwhelming feeling of relief. 'The strain, the tension, it all went. I still had many things to worry about, but I could begin to live a normal life again.' Butler then appeared at the front door and politely wished Pat a good morning, telling her not to worry.

Moments later, Charlie walked in, handcuffed to detective Ted Fuller. 'Sorry, darling,' he said. 'Still, don't worry. Everything will be OK. Tell the girls I'm goin' back to England for a while and they should look after their mum and be good.'

Youngest daughter Leander had come running downstairs when she heard the noise of the men wiping the snow off their boots as they came in. Pat told her her dad was going away for a while. Leander immediately asked why he was leaving them and Charlie explained that it was to buy her a black poodle and a white bird. Moments later, Charlie was taken away in a squad car to a holding cell at Montreal's main police station. Pat was allowed to remain at the house with a police guard.

Less than an hour after the arrest, a message arrived at Scotland

Yard on the desk of Assistant Commander Peter Brodie. When decoded, it said simply, 'Wilson has been recaptured.'

The following morning, Tommy Butler returned to the Wilson household with Charlie to make a thorough search of the property. Detectives removed jewellery and cash, plus the house deeds and car logbooks. Then Rocky, the Alsatian, provided some light relief. Pat explained: 'I felt I'd be unable to cope with the children, my worries *and* the dogs, so with Charlie's permission, I offered both dogs to the Royal Canadian Mounted Police, who'd come with Tommy Butler.'

One young officer took Rocky and promised Pat and Charlie he'd train him up as a police dog. A few moments later, the animal was driven off in a police cruiser sitting upright in the front seat with his paws on the dashboard, looking really proud of himself. Charlie grinned and shouted 'Turncoat!' after him.

Back in Montreal that afternoon, Tommy Butler hoped Canadian authorities would swiftly grant Scotland Yard a deportation order so that Charlie could be returned to the UK the following day. Pat and the girls were facing a similar request. They were moved to a hotel in the city under close scrutiny from immigration officials and were expected to leave Canada within three or four days.

Police told reporters they'd recovered a cache worth more than C$35,000 (£15,000) in Charlie's house in Rigaud. About C$20,000 (£8,000) of it was in Bahamian dollars and over $14,000 (£7,000) in US dollars, plus a much smaller amount in local currency.

Back at the house, the only sign of life was Fluffy, the family cat, who'd returned to the property after earlier fleeing into the snow-covered forest when strangers had first appeared. Multiple footprints clearly showed where the police team and Tommy Butler had organised their swoop, surrounding the house from all directions. Other tracks showed how the men had moved in an encircling movement so as to cover every window and door.

Through the windows of the house, it was possible to see the rich natural wood finishes on the ground floor. The house was quite spartan and lacking in real soft furnishings. Someone in the village said after Charlie's arrest that the Wilsons had lived with what looked like 'lower-class British-type furniture'. On a coffee table, amongst overflowing ashtrays filled with Pat's cigarette butts, lay an open letter addressed to Mr Ronald Alloway. Further inside, it was as if everything was frozen in time. The beds were unmade, plates and cups were still on the table, and there were clothes and shoes strewn across the bedroom floors. Expensive women's clothes filled the wardrobe in the main bedroom. On the dressing-room table lay the Book of Common Prayer and a book of hymns.

Each of the three girls had her own bedroom which was filled with toys and dolls. But those family touches were shaken by the presence of two guns which had, amazingly, been left lying on the couple's bed by police – a Winchester rifle and a Browning shotgun.

The kitchen housed every modern convenience; the dining room was formally set out; the sitting room contained a top-of-the-range stereo and television – on the mantelpiece were a jar of pennies and a model of a Rolls-Royce Silver Cloud; skis for everyone in the family leaned against the wall of the garage.

A few days later, a young British journalist discovered a cupboard shelf in the main bedroom filled with picture albums which provided a fascinating insight into Charlie's activities while on the run. Pictures clearly showed Charlie with runaway train robbery suspect Bruce Reynolds. One shot in Charlie's album pictured Reynolds and his wife at the Stardust Hotel in Las Vegas. At that time, there had been virtually no trace of Bruce Reynolds since the Great Train Robbery five years earlier.

* * *

At Charlie's extradition hearing, held in the harbour master's office at Sutherland Pier, deep in Montreal's dockland, investigating officer M. Jacques Pepin was told that Charlie had used a false passport to enter Canada illegally on 8 January 1966, by sea from England and Belgium. It took only a few moments for M. Leo Vachon, a director of immigration, to declare him an illegal immigrant. Tommy Butler decided to move swiftly and get Charlie and himself booked on the following day's flight to London.

Charlie, by now 36, looked unusually distraught. As he was led handcuffed to a police officer from the small office where the deportation order was made, he covered his face with a handkerchief, keeping his head bent low. A large sign hanging from a freighter at the dockside said 'A Merry Christmas and a Happy New Year' as the police car took Charlie to the city's police headquarters, where he was returned to a basement cell until his departure.

Inside the same Montreal building, Tommy Butler began mapping out elaborate security measures with his bosses back at Scotland Yard to ensure that Charlie never escaped again. Back in Rigaud, Perry Bedbrook said of Charlie: 'A nice guy like that could make money without stealing. All his friends are dumbfounded and a little mad because he conned us.'

That evening, Charlie and Pat had a tearful reunion in his basement cell. They talked about selling their house in Rigaud and Pat said she was determined to get home to London as soon as possible, even accepting the deportation order, which meant she'd have to pay her own way home. Tommy Butler showed great sympathy towards Pat and the children, saying at the time it was the kids who would suffer. He hoped the authorities would do all they could to make things easy for them. On the other hand, Butler insisted there wasn't room on the plane for the family the following day, when he and Charlie would be returning to Britain. No way did he want the media to snap Charlie and Pat coming off the same airliner when they arrived back in London.

Up until this moment, no one had actually asked how a foreign police officer, unaided by any search warrant or other judicial authorisation, had been able to enter a house in Canada and take possession of a wanted man and his personal effects with a view to taking them out of the country. It wasn't until early the following morning that lawyers acting for Pat went with a senior court bailiff to the airport to try and stop Butler and his sidekick Fuller from taking Charlie back to London. The bailiff even boarded the jet, but was unceremoniously asked to leave by airline staff shortly before take-off. Tommy Butler had known all along that once he nabbed Charlie, speed was of the essence. It was only after that plane took off that he knew he really had his man.

Charlie and his two Scotland Yard escorts travelled economy class, sitting near the rear of the Boeing 707. Charlie had shaved off his beard and looked tanned, fit and surprisingly cheerful. Butler even unlocked his handcuffs for the duration of the flight. Other passengers watched curiously as Charlie tucked into a supper of smoked salmon and fillet steak, washed down with white wine. 'The cabin staff warned passengers to keep away, but naturally they were very curious,' explained Roy White, the senior steward. One passenger, Mr Perry Landucci, who was flying on to India, said that Charlie looked relaxed and had chatted quite happily with the detectives. One curious passenger asked him whether he regretted the train robbery to which Charlie chirpily replied: 'Course it wasn't worth it. Look at me now. I know it wasn't worth it.'

At one stage, Charlie leaned into the aisle as a pretty hostess passed by and asked for her telephone number. She laughed because she was already engaged – to a police detective. It was typical bravado from Charlie, who, even in the middle of a crisis, still had an eye for a pretty girl.

When Charlie was asked how he'd escaped from Winson Green, he smiled and, with a sidelong glance at the inscrutable Tommy Butler, said: 'I don't know, do I? I was asleep at the time. That's right, one minute I was fast asleep in my bed and the next I was standing outside the wall.' He cheekily offered two journalists his wife's story of life on the run for £30,000, explaining: 'I don't want the money myself. Where I'm going, it won't be any good to me. I want it for the wife and children.' There were other questions thrown at Charlie which he evaded. On the subject of the whereabouts of his old friend Bruce Reynolds, he said he hadn't a clue.

Daily Express photographer Terry Fincher managed to get a brilliant picture of Charlie sitting alongside Tommy Butler which ran the following day with the front-page headline: 'BACK TO JAIL WITH A GRIN!'

Behind the wisecracks and smiles, Charlie was genuinely worried about Pat and their daughters. He admitted to one passenger on the plane that she was 'a girl in a million, a great old woman'. He went on: 'We've been apart for a long time before and she's always been waiting.' Charlie sombrely presumed Pat wouldn't be allowed to see him for some time, at least until the media frenzy had died down.

Charlie had earlier played his usual cheeky cockney routine, but here was another side to him. He later explained in interviews that he was annoyed with himself for getting caught and felt bad about Pat and the children. When Butler insisted on locking his handcuffs as the plane touched down in Prestwick, Scotland, for refuelling, Charlie ensured his handcuffed wrist was low between himself and Butler and asked the detective to drape a carrier bag across the chain before passengers disembarked. As the captain came on the speaker system and wished his departing passengers a safe journey to their final destination, Charlie said he smiled: for the first time in nearly four years he knew exactly where he was heading.

At the airport, a heavy guard was mounted as 65 passengers left the plane and more press, TV and radio men swarmed inside. Extra police officers were also on hand to travel with Charlie and the two Scotland Yard detectives. Forty minutes later, the plane took off for London. Charlie then switched back to his light-hearted side, even autographing a newspaper for one of the stewards. He joked with the chief steward, Dennis Hill, saying, 'Do you like your job? I'll swap places with you any time.' When a steward handed one of Butler's colleagues his change from a duty-free purchase, Charlie managed a quip about serial numbers, saying, 'Want me to check the serial number? I'm an expert on banknotes.'

It would have taken a platoon of commandos to break the security screen thrown around London's Heathrow Airport, organised in case Charlie's underworld pals tried to spring him yet again. Squads of plain-clothed police, airport security men and Special Branch officers were circulating in the airport bars and lounges in the Terminal 3 building, watching for familiar faces from the underworld.

As the Boeing 707 taxied to Gate 121, three green Rovers slid forward towards the plane. At the same time, two van loads of policemen and dogs ringed the aircraft. From rooftops, detectives watched the crowds. Police radio cars took up strategic posts around the airliner.

As the mobile steps were rolled to the aircraft door, six detectives ran up into the plane while other passengers filed off. Then came Charlie Wilson, moving along the gangway towards the front of the plane. He even had time to pat a three-year-old boy playfully on the head before winking at him. Then he ducked his head under an overcoat to stop prying cameras from getting a shot of his face as he was led, handcuffed, down the steps. At the bottom, Tommy Butler handed his prisoner over to a Flying Squad team led by Detective Inspector Ronald Hardy, who immediately directed Charlie into one of the waiting cars.

For the other passengers, mainly Canadian, it had been a memorable day. 'Better than the movies,' said one traveller. 'If they had train robbers on every flight, I'd fly BOAC every time!'

The photo in the following day's *Daily Mail* said it all: Charlie with a blanket over his head, flashbulbs blinking, cameramen behind and in front of him, police ringing the aeroplane, squad cars at the ready. What a homecoming!

Tommy Butler watched as the police convoy pulled across the tarmac and headed off for Parkhurst Prison on the Isle of Wight. He then turned and headed for the airport administration building where he needed to clear the items he'd brought back from Canada with officials. These included jewellery, which they intended to trace back to its original owners, to see if it was bought with Great Train Robbery cash or simply stolen. However, Tommy Butler also now had some more important fish to fry. He summed it up in five words: 'Ronnie Biggs and Bruce Reynolds.' He was planning to take off for the south of France the following day to check out a tip concerning Reynolds.

Four alternative routes for Charlie's police convoy from Heathrow Airport to Parkhurst had been planned. As one BOAC official pointed out: 'Wilson is VIC – Very Important Cargo.' The car with Charlie sped out of the airport onto the A4 road and headed towards Winchester, en route for Portsmouth and the final over-the-water lap to Parkhurst. Behind the Rover came a red Humber Snipe, crammed with armed detectives. Motorcycle police brought up the rear and a little further back were other police cars making sure the press pack didn't get too close.

The cavalcade seemed to be making good progress when just outside Portsmouth the lead car in the convoy stopped suddenly to avoid a pedestrian and four other vehicles following it went straight into the back of it. The car carrying Charlie had a broken fan belt and was unable to continue, so he was transferred to the Humber with his police escort, since it had only been slightly damaged. No one was hurt.

The ferry *Camber Queen* was still lumbering its way over from the Isle of Wight when the convoy eventually arrived at Portsmouth Harbour with 20 minutes to spare. Charlie and his escort had to sit it out while dozens of detectives kept a close eye on the fast-gathering crowd of onlookers. Sunday lunchtime drinkers in pubs next to the harbour abandoned their pints and strolled over to see why there were so many police cars seeing off the one o'clock boat to Fishbourne. One woman, more curious than the rest, stepped up and tapped on the Humber's window. There was no response from Charlie or the four detectives guarding him.

Unlike earlier, there was no attempt to cover Charlie's head. He looked fresh and cheerful, and when the *Camber Queen* finally arrived, he watched with interest as the first cars struggled off the ramp. Charlie had a 4s 6d one-way ticket bought for him while the detectives each had a 9s return, and a £3 15s day return for the Flying Squad Humber, registration number GLO 10C, which was to be the first vehicle on board. Five more police vehicles, including a police dog van and three police motorcycles, drove onto the wooden ramp to make the 45-minute trip to Fishbourne. Other ferry passengers peeped into the car and this time Charlie smiled and waved back. Then cameras came out and snaps of the famous train robber were taken for the family album. But Charlie was not allowed to get out of the car and stretch his legs. When he asked for a snack, a police officer fetched tea, a meat patty and biscuits from the below-decks buffet bar and brought it back to the car. Charlie had to use his left hand for his food and tea because his right remained handcuffed to a detective.

As the *Camber Queen* finally edged its way into the harbour, motorcycle police began revving up and the police van stood by. Then the Humber engine sparked up and the convoy moved off the ferry to begin the last five miles of its journey to Parkhurst.

In London, Charlie's capture provoked a mass of fresh newspaper headlines demanding that more should be done to recover the missing Great Train Robbery millions. Much of the money found in Charlie's Canadian home couldn't actually be confiscated because it didn't come directly from the Great Train Robbery mailbags.

Meanwhile, Charlie's dad, Bill Wilson, was telling journalists he was glad his rascal of a son was home. 'At least he can't get in any more trouble,' he said. But Bill Wilson's comments were tinged with sadness because Charlie hadn't seen his father for more than ten years. 'I hardly recognised him when I saw his pictures in the papers last week,' Bill told another newspaper. He had no plans to see his son in Parkhurst, though: 'Let him get in touch with us. He's had plenty of chances to do so. We would do all we could to help him, but he has never approached us.'

Perhaps the most disturbing newspaper image was a photo of Pat and her daughters in the back of a car in Montreal with the caption: 'What it meant to three bewildered little girls.'

Still in Canada, Pat found to her surprise that none of her local friends and neighbours had turned their backs on her. She'd gone out of her way not to ask for their help, but it came anyway. Neighbour John Ashfield and his wife provided the children with a safe haven after the police and Fleet Street invaded the isolated community. Others drove Cheryl and Tracey to school through thick snow. Even their Rigaud police chief friend invited Charlie's daughters to tea with their own children to allow Pat a few extra hours to clear the house and work out her plans for the future.

Over at Cheryl and Tracey's school, Hudson Heights High, the two children never once suffered any bullying or cruel remarks about their dad, the escaped convict. Local people even drew up a petition immediately after Charlie's arrest asking that the girls and Pat be allowed to stay in Canada. Clergymen, local officials and police officers were amongst the 500 signatories. As a result, Pat was told she could stay on in Canada until the following summer if she wanted. However, she'd already decided that she needed to get back to London as soon as possible.

Back in Britain, Fleet Street had calculated that, of the £2.6 million or thereabouts stolen in the Great Train Robbery, only £648,948 had ever been recovered. In today's terms, that means the blaggers had still got away with in excess of £30 million.

8

Just after 2 p.m. on 26 January 1968, in bright sunshine, the Flying Squad Humber carrying Charlie Wilson passed police patrolling the perimeter wall of Parkhurst Prison and headed through the gates. After almost three and a half years it was all over. Stretching blankly ahead was a 30-year stay back in bleak Britain. Parkhurst, the old island retreat, built in the first half of the nineteenth century, lay in a huge hollow and was renowned for the sinking feeling it gave its inmates.

Twenty warders, one of them with a lone Alsatian, lined up inside the prison reception centre as Charlie strolled in. Charlie ignored the screws and leaned towards the dog and said, 'Hello, Rin Tin Tin. I must get to know you, we're going to be great friends.'

Moments later, Charlie swapped his smart suit for a grey flannel prison uniform as a crowd of staff watched open-mouthed as if they were in the presence of a Hollywood star. The interest in Charlie had been so intense that prison authorities tried to water down the 'Welcome home' scenario by not allowing Charlie to meet any inmates on that first day. Instead, he was immediately put in a holding cell. Charlie was so exhausted from the dramas of the previous few days that he fell asleep virtually the moment his head hit the rock-hard HMP-issue pillow.

It wasn't until after a breakfast of steaming hot porridge in his icy cold cell on his first full day inside that Charlie was taken to see Governor Alastair Miller and the prison doctor. They were polite but businesslike, well aware that the warmest of greetings awaited Charlie once he was back amongst his own. Governor Miller had earlier promised waiting reporters: 'He is not going to have any different treatment from any other prisoner. He will be put to work. His tasks could be anything from cleaning floors, carpentry or any other prison industry.'

Less than 100 yards away, building work on the new high-security wing at Parkhurst – known as the 'Cage' – had just been completed and it now housed many of Charlie's train robber pals. There had been a ripple of excitement amongst the 17 high-risk inmates in the Cage since news of Charlie's arrival had filtered through the prison grapevine. Those inmates included Gordon Goody, Roy James, Jimmy Hussey, Roger Cordrey and Tommy Wisbey. There were also some other notorious criminals, including gunman Walter 'Angel' Probyn, police killer Harry Roberts, child murderers Straffen and Smith, and Soviet spy Peter Kruger. The last time Charlie had seen any of his robbery pals was at their trial back in 1964.

An almighty cheer went up when Charlie was escorted into the Cage by two burly prison officers during the mid-morning break. This was followed by the rattling of cups on the metal fencing around the gangways. Charlie looked up and smiled, a tad embarrassed but also grateful that so many of the chaps were on his side. His old mates greeted him with shouts of 'Hard luck, Charlie' and 'Let's 'ave another go, Chas' as he walked around shaking inmates' hands. Soon, they were all discussing his exploits. Later that first day, Charlie was allowed to choose a prison job making toys for sick children in the local hospitals.

All the warders in the Cage were hand-picked and if one fell sick or had special leave, his duties were shared between his colleagues on overtime. Some weeks, staff could earn an extra £20 in overtime. All this was supposed to make it more difficult to bribe them. This new high-security block was elaborately guarded with closed-circuit television covering all 28 cells, corridors, recreation rooms, workshops and outside walls. The cells were relatively light, spacious and comfortable. All the officers carried portable radio sets connected to the central control room and guard dogs patrolled the perimeter during the night. Charlie knew they'd be keeping a special eye on him.

So it was in this atmosphere that Charlie tried to settle down to prison life. Escape was virtually impossible and while he might have thought about it constantly, the reality was that he was probably inside for keeps now. The gym was the most important room as far as keep-fit fanatic Charlie was concerned. It had brown-tinted, heavy-glass windows set high up on the walls and Charlie was allowed to do exercise with one other inmate – they were only able to train in pairs and were never told who their partners were in advance. Beneath the block, there was even a garden where prisoners could grow their own vegetables. During the recreation period, Charlie was able to catch up with some of the newspaper coverage of his return to Britain.

Charlie and the other prisoners in the Cage were completely cut off from the 470 other mainstream Parkhurst inmates. In effect, the area was a prison within a prison. The main aim was to ensure that escape was a complete impossibility. One senior official at the prison described the life of inmates in there as 'sheer hell'. To make matters worse, Charlie didn't know if he'd automatically qualify for ten years' remission because it was up to the Home Office to decide how much of his original sentence he had to serve because of his escape.

As Charlie languished in a cold British prison cell on the Isle of Wight, the only heartening bit of news was a letter from Pat saying how good his old neighbours and friends back in Canada had been to her and the girls. Charlie later wrote to one friend: 'When I was told how good everybody was, I was so choked, I could not say anything. I am not the hardest man in the world, or the softest. But I had tears in my eyes. It was not easy for me not to burst out crying.'

Charlie undoubtedly found that first week in Parkhurst extremely difficult to handle, despite the warm welcome from the other inmates. He later admitted he felt an overwhelming sense of guilt about how much he had put his family through. Now, he was faced with a huge stretch behind bars and the pressure got to him for probably the first time in his life. Seven days after arriving in the jail, Charlie was treated for serious psychological problems which doctors put down to delayed shock following his return from Canada. All those years of bottling up his feelings in order to protect his family had come to a head and sent him into a deep depression.

Charlie's condition wasn't helped when Tommy Butler decided to interrogate him about the missing millions from the Great Train Robbery. Butler and other senior Scotland Yard officers believed they could crack 'the Silent One' with the right approach. They also wanted Charlie to help them find Bruce Reynolds and reveal the secrets of his original escape from Winson Green. Despite Charlie's psychological problems during those early days and weeks in Parkhurst, he was not for turning. His inbuilt hatred of grasses had left him as defiant of the police as ever.

There was also the highly sensitive subject of Charlie's daughters, whom police believed must know some of those answers. Obviously they couldn't interrogate the children, but some senior officers deliberately leaked information to one newspaper to try and provoke Charlie into cooperating with them. They put forward a 'suggestion' to the *Sunday Express* that Charlie had brainwashed his children. A Harley Street psychologist called Mr William Ousley was even quoted in the newspaper as saying: 'It is possible that the children were benignly brainwashed. The first stage would be to make a flat contradiction. Never, for example, tell them that their name is not Wilson but Alloway, although it would have to be much more subtle than that.'

In Parkhurst, Charlie was outraged that anyone would suggest he'd intimidate his daughters and even asked his lawyer to try and sue the *Express*. Charlie then heard the article had been 'suggested' to the paper by a couple of detectives. Their scheme backfired spectacularly when Charlie refused to see the police without a solicitor being present and reverted to his silent mode whenever in the prison interview room.

That initial shock of being back in prison never really faded, with Charlie facing up to his long sentence with a combination of bitterness and anger. He still considered the Great Train Robbery to have been an extravagant caper fuelled by a gambler's optimism that the gang would get away with all the loot. Charlie hoped that if public opinion was still behind them, then he'd never have to serve out his full sentence. Certainly, there was still widespread indignation that the robbers were being more severely punished than many murderers, rapists and spies. The well-known Methodist leader Lord Soper described the sentences as 'miserable, dreadful and unchristian', but Charlie knew that public opinion wasn't going to serve the sentence for him.

Not long after Pat's arrival back in Britain, she travelled down to the Isle of Wight only to discover that under strict new regulations at Parkhurst, she wasn't even allowed to embrace Charlie because of a two-inch-thick bullet-proof glass screen between them. Charlie felt he and the other robbers were being treated like animals, although this hardened his resolve not to let *them* – the Establishment – beat him. Inside prison, however, reputations meant little and many screws administered their own form of punishment to star inmate Charlie. To start with, he was often served cold food, sometimes missing certain ingredients. Then he and other train robbers were only allowed to exercise in a small, inner yard where you couldn't see any grass or even hear the trees rustling in the wind.

Eventually, Charlie refused to go out in the exercise yard at all as a protest against the restrictions. He undoubtedly suffered like the others, but was such a resilient character he rarely showed his emotions to the 'enemy'. Charlie remained as calculating in his approach to his confinement as he had been towards crime. He constantly slipped messages out to his associates and tried to set up other crimes from within the four walls of the prison.

Not long after Charlie's recapture, the *News of the World* took up Charlie's earlier offer to publish his wife's life story and ended up paying Pat £30,000 – exactly what he'd asked for on the flight from Montreal. On Sunday, 25 February 1968, the paper splashed the first episode of Pat's story, determined to get good value for money with a vast banner headline that read: 'MRS CHARLIE WILSON TELLS THE LOT – SCOOP OF THE YEAR'.

After 13 difficult years of marriage, Pat was pledging to reveal all – well, not everything, just enough to ensure she and the kids had some Fleet Street cash to keep them going for a while. In her introduction, Pat wrote: 'It will be a relief to write the story. For as long as I can remember, I've had a permanent headache from the strain of keeping it quiet.' Pat even admitted Charlie had been in frequent contact with Bruce Reynolds, the only man who still hadn't been caught for his role in the Great Train Robbery. Overall, Pat was careful never to reveal any of the train robber's inside secrets and Charlie later told an associate that he considered the *News of the World* deal to be 'money for old rope'.

Pat desperately needed the money because Tommy Butler had confiscated much of the cash and property found in their house in Canada. Also, banks who'd lost money during the Great Train Robbery were threatening court proceedings to try and claim any other money left over. Pat eventually won a legal battle to keep £2,000 of the money found by detectives in Canada, but this followed secret talks between Charlie and the authorities in Parkhurst. Charlie had insisted that none of the money found in Canada had come from the train robbery, but agreed to the settlement to help Pat.

Back inside Parkhurst, Charlie concentrated on the small luxuries which made life more tolerable. He saved up his paltry earnings from the prison workshop to buy belly of pork, which he'd then cook with vegetables from the garden on a stove on the prison landing. There was also a library boasting over 20,000 books and avid reader Charlie went through at least two novels a week.

But then, despite Charlie's supreme fitness, he began to have slight breathing difficulties, diagnosed by the prison doctor as the very early stages of emphysema, which doctors suspected was caused by the incessant smoke Charlie had come into contact with over the years, not only from Pat but from most of his fellow prisoners. Charlie was warned that the condition would eventually deteriorate and seriously affect his lifestyle. He requested not to sleep in cells next to smokers because of how it affected his lungs at night, but at the time 80 per cent of Britain's prison population smoked so it was difficult to accommodate Charlie's request. His skin also became tainted grey from the lack of sunlight in prison. He told one long-standing friend that prison was like being 'pickled in fuckin' vinegar'.

Charlie and the rest of the train robbery gang became even closer friends inside, because their infamy set them apart from other inmates. Charlie was immensely proud that not one of them had grassed any information to the police and that had helped bond them together as an even closer unit, much to the irritation of the staff. Home Secretary Jim Callaghan still hadn't made up his mind if Charlie was going to be further punished for his breakout from Winson Green.

As those first few months inside passed, Charlie's laid back, often jovial temperament returned. He tried to give the impression he'd accepted the prison regime while actually he continued plotting all sorts of criminal enterprises. And reading a newspaper every day reminded Charlie that perhaps he had slightly misinterpreted the public attitude towards the Great Train Robbers. Most normal, law-abiding people had been entertained by the gang's antics and considered their sentences too severe, but few actually felt sorry for thieves who'd got away with more than two million quid.

Back then the pain and anguish suffered by Pat and their daughters – caught up in the aftermath of the Great Train Robbery – was rarely touched upon. Many seemed to assume that men so allegedly brutal in their treatment of driver Jack Mills would be equally unprincipled when it came to their own families. Nothing could be further from the truth. Charlie and the others had risked imprisonment by carrying out the crime in the first place, but their families had no choice in the matter. The way in which they all suffered in the ten-year period after the crime was committed infuriated Charlie and the other gang members.

Pat continued to feel terribly isolated because the robbery's whirlwind of notoriety had left her with just a handful of friends and family prepared to help her and the children survive. Pat remained a quiet, shy, dependent, domesticated lady, who'd left every major decision in the past to her husband. As the years passed, many other train robbers' wives found maintaining relationships even harder. Gordon Goody's fiancée, also called Pat, eventually married another man with the tacit approval of Goody, who reasoned that it was better for her in the long term, even though she still visited him in prison long after her wedding.

Others told their partners to forget them or even consider them dead so they could go away and get on with their lives. When one of the other wives started talking in riddles which Pat could not understand it soon became clear that the poor woman was so stressed by her husband's incarceration she was having a nervous breakdown. At least Pat Wilson was able to live with her daughters in a relatively secure environment at her mother's house.

Pat stuck by Charlie because she did not know any other way of life and she never once considered a relationship with another man. That devotion now meant spending much of her time either alone or with her own family. Her life centred around visits to Charlie in Parkhurst. Yet the weeks of anticipation, combined with the long travel time and just 30 minutes with Charlie either through glass or under supervision by a team of hefty-looking screws, took its emotional toll. Pat also became increasingly worried about how thin Charlie was getting, even though he always had a smile and a joke for her.

Like most inmates' wives, Pat loathed the journey to Parkhurst, which involved a train from Waterloo to Portsmouth, a ferry over to the Isle of Wight followed by a journey on the local bus or a taxi. Sometimes she'd get to Waterloo with her three daughters feeling so distraught that she wondered if she could go through with yet another visit. She also lived in dread of getting to the prison to find something awful had happened to Charlie.

Back in London, Cheryl, Tracey and Leander were being openly derided at school because their old man was that runaway train robber. All three Wilson daughters would grow up to be vital and attractive women determined not to marry criminals who'd end up in prison half their lives. It didn't seem fair that they should suffer for their father's crimes. Pat was bringing up their daughters single-handedly with an allowance provided by a friend of Charlie, who was holding onto the *News of the World* cash in case the authorities tried to take it away. Like all the train robbers' wives, Pat was too terrified to open a bank account in case any money was confiscated.

Pat virtually never went out socially, unless chaperoned by other robbers' wives or girlfriends, which was a rare event in itself. Pat saw her role as mother and housewife, not star-struck criminal's moll. But then Pat's life had always revolved around Charlie; she knew no other way.

Over in France, the only train robber never to face a criminal trial – Bruce Reynolds – was making his own plans to return to Britain. His wife had already moved to a mews flat off Gloucester Road in south

Kensington, west London. Reynolds joined her several weeks later, entering the country via Shannon in Ireland. He was eventually picked up by Tommy Butler staying in a rented house in Torquay in Devon.

Reynolds was sentenced to 25 years at his trial in January 1969. The fact it was five years less than Charlie and the original trial defendants had received in 1964 once again raised questions about the sentencing anomalies. Meanwhile, Britain's forces of law and order still made it clear what they thought of the train robbers: Chief Constable of County Durham Alec Muir reckoned it would be more humane to shoot the gang members. He told a Durham University Liberal Club meeting he'd be more likely to kill a train robber than shoot a German during the last war. Naturally, Muir's comments sparked a storm of protest. The Great Train Robbery was never out of the public eye for long.

On 24 October 1969 Charlie and two of the other gang members, Jimmy Hussey and Roy James, got caught up in a riot that erupted in the Cage after other inmates began protesting about conditions. For forty terrifying minutes that evening, seven members of staff at Parkhurst were held captive by furious inmates. One prisoner came within a whisker of slitting a prison officer's throat. Charlie, Hussey and James barricaded themselves in their cells as part of their protest against conditions. Eyewitnesses later claimed inmates were screaming abuse as the staff began dismantling doors. Then fists flew and beds, mattresses and chairs were thrown. Charlie and the other protesting inmates were seized, one by one, and locked in other unused cells. Two officers ended up with suspected hand fractures and another had a badly cut face. None of the prisoners was seriously hurt.

Charlie was placed in solitary confinement after the prison flare-up, but he was more worried that he might not get any parole on his 30-year sentence following his escape. He even asked his solicitor to write to the Home Secretary asking for consideration for parole. 'Without that, I'm fucked,' Charlie told one old friend. 'I know I can never go on my toes again, but if I can't see an end to being in here then I might as well give up on life.'

Charlie was eventually interviewed by two visiting Justices who travelled to Parkhurst to talk about his sentence. They decided that Charlie should lose only six months of remission on his sentence because of his earlier escape. Six months for three and half years on the run might seem a reasonable deal, but in reality it actually meant Charlie getting a release day four years later than if he'd never escaped from jail. Prisoners' sentences are always automatically suspended when they're on the run, only starting up again the day they are rearrested. At least Charlie was assured he'd qualify for parole within ten years.

Eventually, Charlie was allowed back to his usual cell in the Cage. Despite suffering slight discomfort from his emphysema, Charlie continued to exercise furiously, almost narcissistically boosting his already muscular physique with a punishing regime that he intended to keep up for the rest of his life. Every time Charlie did a press-up, he saw it as a mark of defiance against the system. In his mind, they'd never beat him. Ever.

Inside Parkhurst, the new younger generation of professional robbers intrigued Charlie. People like Mickey Green, who'd been part of the 'Wembley Mob', a bunch of blaggers who were London's most successful bank robbers until one of their team turned grass. Green was another schemer like Charlie, always looking ahead to the main chance. Green was happy to bide his time in Parkhurst, safe in the knowledge that once he got out there was money to steal and girls to bed. Mickey was the original gold-medallion man with a penchant for flash cars and sparkling jewellery, but he gave Charlie hope that there was a life to look forward to after he finally got released.

Two other characters Charlie came across in Parkhurst were young robbers 'Mad Mickey' Blackmore, from Camberwell in south London, and Roy 'The Lump' Adkins, from Notting Hill, west London. They and many others inside the Cage looked up to Charlie as a hero because of his dramatic escape and involvement in the Great Train Robbery. Charlie had already invested some of his little remaining train robbery cash in new crimes and even promised financial backing to Blackmore and Adkins if they came up with any big targets to rob on their release.

Blackmore had been well known in south London criminal circles since his early 20s, when he appeared in court in London accused of stealing a £15,000 emerald ring in a raid on the famous Grosvenor Hotel in the West End. Blackmore from Camberwell New Road only got caught for the jewellery theft because he forgot to switch on his car lights two days after the robbery and was stopped by police. They found a bullet under his back seat. A subsequent police raid on his home uncovered a .22 pistol and a Russian 9mm and 'Mad Mickey' ended up in Parkhurst for five years.

Great Train Robber Bruce Reynolds was sent to Parkhurst shortly after the riot, but he was kept apart from the other robbers at first as part of strict prison policy. Eventually, the governor agreed to allow Reynolds to meet Charlie well away from the prying eyes of the Cage in the so-called 'nonce' wing where child molesters and other special-category inmates were kept. Reynolds later recalled that Charlie looked fit and carried a plentiful supply of chocolate, including Mars bars and Cadbury's Fruit and Nut. These were luxuries that Reynolds had not been allowed since his arrest.

Charlie, a dedicated non-smoker, was surprised to see that Reynolds had succumbed to the dreaded weed. The two men discussed their families and Charlie reiterated how much he'd relied on Pat and missed her now he was banged up again. Charlie's face turned to stone, though, as he told Reynolds he was convinced someone had grassed him up to Tommy Butler and that was how he'd been tracked down in Canada.

In February 1970, one of Charlie's prisonmates, a recently released armed robber called Bobby King, was part of a nine-man team that raided a Barclays Bank in Ilford, Essex. The job had been carefully rehearsed for more than six weeks. King had earlier been briefed on the art of armed robbery by Charlie when the two men were inside Parkhurst. King and the other robbers even copied certain aspects of Charlie's infamous 1962 Heathrow robbery by dressing in smart suits and bowler hats. The robbery netted more than £50,000 in cash and underworld sources later claimed that Charlie earned a £10,000 cut of the loot because he'd helped plan and bankroll the job from prison.

By the late '60s and early '70s, bank robbers had become the new criminal aristocracy, admired by up-and-coming young villains, fancied by the prettiest girls in the most expensive West End clubs and bars. It was all a far cry from dinosaurs like Charlie, locked up on long stretches. These new, cocky young villains played The Doors and T-Rex on their flashy eight-track car stereos and marched across the nation's pavements brandishing sawn-off shotguns. Charlie's attitude was that just because he was locked up didn't mean he couldn't have a piece of the action.

As the months turned to years inside Parkhurst, Charlie's power and influence within the prison walls grew immensely. He focused on the weak, impressionable members of staff prepared to turn a blind eye to certain things. In Charlie's case that meant a plentiful supply of everything from porn magazines to chocolate. He even managed to get baby oil brought into him because he didn't like using soap to wash his face – he believed it would age him quicker. Whenever Charlie wanted to talk about any sensitive subjects with a visitor, he'd promise the warders a 'drink' if they'd stand back so they couldn't hear what he was talking about.

In the summer of 1970, Charlie and the rest of the train robbery boys in Parkhurst gave a loud cheer when news filtered through the prison that Ronnie Biggs had once again evaded capture, this time in Melbourne, Australia, where he'd moved with his wife and children, then disappeared as the authorities were closing in. Biggs may have been considered a junior member of the train gang, but knowing his antics were infuriating higher powers was a real morale booster for the others.

There were other, more serious, aspects of the robbery that continued to haunt the blaggers even after they were all banged up. Just after Biggs slipped out of Australia, train driver Jack Mills died. The media claimed his death had been caused, in part, by the beating he got at the hands of the train robbers that night in Cheddington in 1963. The question of who injured Mills and whether he suffered later illnesses as a result of that incident remained a highly contentious issue even after his death. In the years following the robbery, Mills was also plagued by suggestions he'd dramatised his injuries and consequent physical disabilities when giving evidence at the main trial in 1964. Charlie and the rest of the train robbers were adamant that his injuries during the robbery had been very slight and believed that he was put under pressure by police to exaggerate what happened to ensure they all got heavy sentences.

Tommy Butler's death, also in 1970, at the age of just 57, sparked a completely different reaction from friends and foes alike. Even 'enemies' like Charlie sent their respects. Criminals felt no anger towards Butler because of his absolute fairness. When Bruce Reynolds had been jailed, his solicitor even thanked Butler in open court for the kindness and courtesy he'd shown Reynolds' wife and son. Ironically, Tommy Butler died on the very same day that Ronnie Biggs's on-the-run memoirs were being published in *The Sun*. The newspaper's serialisation was authenticated by a copy of Biggs's thumbprint, published alongside a front-page article.

It was at this point that Charlie and some of the others started to change their opinions of Ronnie Biggs. 'They thought he should have kept his trap shut. Talking about the actual robbery was a risky undertaking because there were still people out there who'd never been nicked for it,' explained one of Charlie's oldest pals.

9

Whilst still in Parkhurst in 1972, Charlie met a Colombian called Carlos who'd been convicted of cocaine trafficking in London. At first, Charlie was unfriendly towards the South American because he was what Charlie termed a 'druggie'. Back in those days, so-called 'real criminals' robbed banks and trains, they definitely didn't deal in drugs. Charlie believed at the time that narcotics were never to be touched, either personally or professionally, but charming Carlos, a tall, handsome, dark-haired man, who talked in an educated, upper-class English accent, had a friendly manner which eventually put Charlie at ease. Carlos was intrigued by the Great Train Robbery, so Charlie told him all about it and how he'd ended up with one of the longest prison sentences in British criminal history.

Carlos then explained to Charlie some of the basic, economic reasons why cocaine dealing made good criminal sense. 'What's the point in risking your life to rob a bank or hold up a train when you can make ten times that money and never even have to touch the product?' Carlos told Charlie. Carlos explained cocaine was such a dominant industry back in Colombia that a handful of small-time thieves and hustlers in the country's second and third cities, Medellín and Cali, were already handling hundreds of millions of pounds' worth of coke flowing out of South America every year. Carlos predicted that within ten years cocaine would be one of the biggest-selling products in the world. The Brits had to get a piece of the narcotics trade or else foreigners like Carlos were going to make all the big money. The younger British robbers inside Parkhurst with Charlie – 'Mad Mickey' Blackmore, Mickey Green and Roy 'The Lump' Adkins – had already decided they would take the drugs route on their release from prison. Charlie, however, remained far from convinced.

In 1974, Ronnie Biggs got himself arrested in Brazil and it looked as if the last of the on-the-run train robbers would soon be inside a British jail. But Scotland Yard's Detective Chief Superintendent Jack

Slipper had to fly back to London empty-handed because the Home Office had not prepared the right paperwork and Biggs announced his Brazilian girlfriend was pregnant with his child, which meant he could not legally be extradited under Brazilian law.

Charlie and the other robbers were delighted that Biggs had avoided being brought back to Britain, but Biggs's big mouth got him into trouble again when one well-known criminal, whose identity was revealed in a book written by Biggs, swore to tear him into little pieces if he ever saw him again. A lot of the growing animosity towards Biggs came because he was a relatively unimportant member of the gang and yet had become the most infamous thanks to his escape and subsequent life in Brazil. Charlie certainly didn't appreciate being fed a non-stop diet of Biggs stories every time he picked up a newspaper. Ronnie Biggs had undoubtedly become an obsession with the Great British public.

That same year, 1974, Buster Edwards and Jimmy White were both released from prison after serving nine years of their original sentences. Charlie and other train robbers thought it was out of order since both men had been amongst the last robbers to be caught.

Meanwhile, Charlie continued to look around for more ways to make money. There is clear evidence to suggest that in the mid-1970s Charlie part-financed a large shipment of cannabis into the UK from his prison cell. Around the same time, there were also rumours Charlie had made a sizeable 'investment' in the Bank of America robbery in Mayfair in April 1976, when eight smartly dressed men in suits got away with £8 million.

By 1976, all the train robbers, except Charlie and Bruce Reynolds, had been released. Charlie was then transferred to Long Lartin, a top-security prison near Evesham in Gloucestershire, and told that his release was scheduled for some time over the following two years. Long Lartin was a much smaller and more restrictive prison than Parkhurst, but Charlie knew he had to keep his head down and his nose clean if he wanted to earn parole.

In Rio de Janeiro, Ronnie Biggs was managing very nicely by cashing in on his notoriety with books, recording contracts, even an advertisement for British Leyland cars. In Charlie's world, you said little and tried to plan for the future, you didn't go around blabbing about your past exploits. So when the released gang members were offered £10,000 each to help respected author Piers Paul Read write a book about the train robbery, Charlie was far from pleased. Eventually, the others promised him a share of the proceeds and Charlie reluctantly agreed to let them form themselves into a limited company. Charlie was a sleeping partner because jail regulations did not allow inmates to conduct business from their cells.

As one of Charlie's oldest friends later explained: 'Charlie wasn't the quiet man for nothing. He was very old fashioned in that way and didn't feel it was right to boast about the robbery in public, but Biggs was grabbing all the limelight – and most of the cash – on the back of what others had done. It just didn't seem fair.' Charlie agreed to help with the Piers Paul Read book on condition the author did not carry too much detail about him. It was a typical back-scratching deal by Charlie.

Roy James, Jimmy White, Jim Hussey, Tommy Wisbey, Gordon Goody, Roger Cordrey and Buster Edwards all believed the book would be the first of many projects in which they'd make money by offering 'technical advice' to anybody wishing to write or film any aspect of the robbery. An agent was appointed who would also negotiate deals for newspaper stories, features, photos and, possibly, another book, which the robbers wanted to write themselves. When an MP was quoted describing the Piers Paul Read book deal as 'monstrous', Charlie accused his old mates of making things even worse for him and Bruce Reynolds. 'Charlie reckoned every time there was a story in the papers about the robbery, it meant his chances of parole took another knock,' said one old friend.

Virtually every article that was ever published about the Great Train Robbery still claimed driver Jack Mills was battered with an iron bar during the raid and never properly recovered from his injuries. Mills's widow was wheeled out by newspapers and television reporters whenever there was a suggestion the robbers were about to cash in on their crime. As she told the *News of the World*: 'You can imagine my feelings when I hear the robbers are being paid big money for their story, as though they did something splendid and brave. They ruined the life of a good, hard-working man.' Whenever Mills's name came up, Charlie seethed because he'd personally taken the time to try and make sure Mills was all right after he'd been hit. 'Charlie felt that Mills should never have been touched. He saw himself as a professional soldier doing a job, but he always said that Mills didn't deserve to be hit,' explained one old friend.

Inside Long Lartin, Charlie developed newly found skills as a talented artist. His speciality was startlingly lifelike portraits of celebrities such as Tom Jones and Barbra Streisand. He also proved a dab hand at copying some of the Old Masters. He was so good at duplicating northern artist Lowry's matchstick figures that one fellow inmate told him to try and flog them as fakes. Charlie didn't want to give the authorities an excuse not to release him at the earliest possible date, however.

Inside Long Lartin, Charlie met an Indian drug smuggler called Surya 'Chris' Krishnarma, who'd made a point of getting to know some of the heavier British criminals inside the prison. Charlie had already had a 'good tickle' out of his earlier cannabis deal and was interested in possibly investing in more drug deals in the future. Krishnarma claimed he had the connections to line up top-quality drug shipments. He was also an expert tester of the produce. Charlie reckoned Krishnarma could be a very useful character to employ in the future, even though he was still not wholly convinced that drugs were the future for organised crime.

Charlie was eventually transferred from Long Lartin to Coldingley Prison in Bisley, Surrey, to further prepare him for his release. Coldingley was relatively new and was the first prison in the UK to give prisoners specific training for life after they were released. Charlie joined a course to pursue a new career in jewellery making, as well as studying French. He soon boasted that he could read and understand entire French novels. Charlie insisted to the prison governor that after his release, he would work as a market packer and then eventually start a jewellery business. He believed there was no shortage of investors willing to back him. Around this time, Charlie also heard that he'd become a grandfather, which made him feel even more desperate to be released back into the real world.

★ ★ ★

Training as a jewellery designer inside prison fed Charlie's fertile mind and precious metals, especially gold, became Charlie's latest obsession. He still wanted to see if there was a way to make money without having to go down the drugs route and perhaps gold was where his future lay.

It is reported that 90 per cent of all the gold produced, estimated to amount to some 2,000 million ounces, can still be accounted for: 45 per cent of it lying in central banks, where it is kept as a guarantee of economic stability for the governments in question (the Old Lady of Threadneedle Street, for instance, never let her reserves drop below 500,000 kilos); 25 per cent remaining in private hands (those of either powerful international conglomerates or hugely wealthy individuals);

and 20 per cent used in jewellery, religious artefacts and dentistry. Even the missing 10 per cent has not vanished without trace – much of it is entombed on the floor of the ocean waiting to be rediscovered. With all these odds stacked against him, Charlie Wilson, the ultimate gambler, became addicted to the gold market as he prepared for his release.

Charlie taught himself everything there was to know about gold. He heard from one criminal associate that the precious metal had recently become a favourite commodity with which to swindle the British government out of VAT.

Charlie heard on the grapevine that there was a variety of scams that could easily be operated in order to deprive the VAT man of his share. One was to smuggle gold into the country, then sell it to a reputable dealer, the 15 per cent VAT filling the pockets of the smugglers. Another scam was to draw up documents showing that the gold had been exported immediately after its arrival in Britain, which meant it was not liable for VAT. The honest trader, meanwhile, would still have to pay the 15 per cent VAT to the 'company' selling him the metal, usually a firm based in short-let office accommodation which would fold within a matter of months without making any VAT returns.

Gold was particularly suitable to such scams because its high value meant large returns with a minimum of delay. It also had an official price, fixed twice daily by the London gold market, so the smugglers didn't have to worry about commercial competitors undercutting their prices. It was also compact and easy to transport.

In the late 1970s, VAT frauds in general had one further major attraction – the maximum penalty for indulging in the racket was just two years' imprisonment. Small wonder, then, that VAT fraud involving gold was becoming very popular amongst well-organised, professional criminals like Charlie.

There were problems with handling gold, though. Charlie's careful research showed that the true origin of ingots of gold had to be disguised and that meant removing identification numbers and assay marks. Many ingots carried their own individually designed hallmarks to signify their purity and, in some cases, a serial number. Absolutely pure gold did not exist. Some contamination was always present, however expertly the metal had been refined, but bars with the number 9999 meant they were 99.99 per cent pure, the highest level to which the metal could be refined; 999 bars, known in the trade as ten-tola bars (a tola being an ancient Indian unit of weight) were only marginally less perfect.

In order to pull off any scam involving gold, as well as removing the identifying marks, Charlie would have to disguise the purity of the bars. Failure to do so would lead legitimate traders to quickly become suspicious that the quantities they were being asked to buy were either smuggled or stolen. That meant Charlie needed specialised smelting equipment, the sort used by only a handful of people in Britain, most of them in the Hatton Garden area of central London, internationally renowned as a centre for the jewellery trade. Such shops were on their guard against suspicious customers ordering smelters, so Charlie would have to tread carefully. 'The irony is that it's the Frommers [Jews] in their Hatton Garden shops who were the first ones to pull off the VAT scam,' explained the friend who first gave Charlie the idea. 'I told him it was a brilliant scam and that a lot of us were doin' it at the time.'

In August 1977, Charlie was transferred to Pentonville Prison in preparation for his release on parole. He'd lined up a job carrying fruit and vegetables around at a stall owned by Jimmy Rose, whom he'd known since the 1950s when they were banged up together. He knew it wasn't going to be easy for the first few months because he'd be under strict parole conditions, but Charlie had big plans for the future.

Charlie had lent Rose £40,000 back in 1964. He was now living in a comfortable detached house in Pett's Wood, Kent, which he'd used to set up a successful road-haulage business that eventually made him a millionaire. Rose's fortune came partly thanks to a profitable sideline in smuggling, and Charlie had already got Rose to agree to repay the debt by allowing him to use some of those lorries to run smuggled goods into the UK from Europe. Charlie couldn't wait to get back into the 'real world' once again.

PART 3

BACK IN THE REAL WORLD: 1978–83

Charlie wasn't content to be a soldier of crime,
not merely one of the workers. He wanted only
one role – Commander in Chief of Crime.

Pat Wilson

1

Charlie stepped out between the gates, heard them sliding shut behind him and no doubt thought to himself, 'Well, mate, you're on your tod now. No more nice, gentle screws to bring you breakfast, dinner and tea, and tuck you up in bed at night.' His old windcheater felt cold after the thick prison uniform. He paused for a few seconds outside the building and looked back at the gates. Then he shivered, not from the cold but as his old man used to say, 'because someone just walked over your grave, son'. That was the only encouragement Charlie needed to get the hell out of that place before they changed their minds and dragged him back inside again.

Charlie later admitted he was 'bloody terrified' to finally be free. All he had, as far as the cozzers were concerned, was the suit he was standing in and a holdall containing a razor, a clean shirt and some clean underwear – all care of Her Majesty's Prison Service – plus £100 cash from his workshop duties because he'd sent all the rest to Pat and the girls.

Charlie had hit middle-age and had three daughters who'd grown up without him, but the strange thing was, as he later admitted, he didn't really feel that old. One old-timer he'd shared a cell with at Pentonville told him he reckoned life in the slammer kept you young and healthy. He had a point. 'The outside world moves at a hell of a pace,' said the wise old lag. 'Meanwhile, we're all stuck in here frozen in time. No reason to get old if you ain't got the problems they have out there.'

The other cons always said it was the air you first noticed when you were out. Air doesn't always have to smell of disinfectant, they said. Charlie also thought about the sounds he'd left behind. Prisons were bloody noisy places, night and day: doors crashing open and closed, the mesh in the stairwell clattering when anyone moved along the galleries, people bawling all the time, kicking up a racket because everyone – the screws and the inmates – was bored out of their skulls.

Back on the streets of London, it was still too early for the main rush hour, but commuters and lorries were already starting to jam up the city streets. And then there were the black cabs. They looked almost the same except some of them weren't black any more. Luckily, they still made that same familiar diesel clunking noise: engines, tyres, exhaust . . . peace and quiet, London style.

At Waterloo, Charlie got a number 49 bus to the Central After Care Association; if he hadn't, he would have been banged up again within 24 hours for violating his parole licence. He sat in the drab waiting room opposite a couple of old lags puffing away on roll-ups. It was just like being back in the joint. He'd been the only inmate on his floor at Parkhurst who didn't live on cancer sticks. Charlie hated smoking so much. Eventually, Charlie saw his parole officer and informed him that he had work as a porter carrying fruit and vegetables for Jimmy Rose. He didn't bother saying that Rose was one of his oldest criminal associates.

Afterwards, Charlie headed to a nearby caff and forced himself to put away some bacon and eggs. He hadn't eaten anything since his last lousy plate of porridge at five that morning, but he still found it hard to get a normal breakfast down on account of it being so rich. It would be a few days before he could handle food on the outside.

None of the pedestrians seemed to even notice Charlie, but he couldn't stop looking at all of them. Different clothes, different colours, different faces, different buildings, different cars. A different world. Just then, Charlie's mind switched to more pressing matters. He was a man with a mission. A mission to make money.

A few nights later, Charlie enjoyed a special homecoming party hosted by his old friend Joey Pyle at Nosher Powell's pub, the Prince of Wales, in Tooting, south London. A lot of the old faces were there, but Pat took centre stage. In later interviews, Charlie said he couldn't keep his eyes off her. He genuinely wondered how he'd managed to hold onto such a gem of a woman. He knew there were many times he hadn't deserved her. He'd always worn his wedding band even when out chasing other girls. It was a reminder of who really mattered in his life.

Nosher said later that Charlie behaved 'as if he hadn't even been away' that day: 'I came out from behind the bar and gave him a hug. He'd been to the dogs earlier and was flush. He kept sayin' "You all right, Nosh? Any problems? Need some dosh?" [I replied] "Nah, Charlie. Just good to see yer back, mate."'

English life had changed drastically for the better since Charlie's incarceration in 1968: the rigid distinctions in dress and manner between one class and another had given way to an informality that Charlie would take some time adjusting to. He'd dusted down his old suits and ties only to find that most people now stuck to jeans and a T-shirt.

While some of the other train robbers who'd got out earlier still seemed unsettled, Charlie slipped back into domestic life with ease. He still looked on all his daughters as children and was soft and indulgent with them, even though two of them had moved out of the house. There were the usual clashes about boyfriends and clothes and lifestyle, but the Wilson family managed to pick up the pieces very well, all things considered.

There was soon a definite sense of anticlimax following the initial euphoria of Charlie's release. Pat had changed to a certain degree – she was far more streetwise and savvy than she had been before Charlie's capture in Canada. Pat was also not quite so prepared to give her husband complete, unquestioning support. She wanted to know more about what he was up to because she didn't want him to be put away ever again. Not that Charlie took much notice. He was soon popping out until all hours and it became clear that while Pat might have changed a little, there was nothing she could do to alter Charlie's criminal habits.

2

By the time Charlie was released from prison, the level of corruption at Scotland Yard's Flying Squad had reached such endemic proportions that rumours began circulating in police and underworld circles that officers in London had been indirectly involved in a robbery which took place in 1978 at the *Daily Mirror* newspaper offices in Holborn Circus, in which a guard was killed and £200,000 was stolen. Officers were also connected to an earlier payroll snatch at the *Daily Express* offices in Fleet Street in which £175,000 was stolen. Then there was a robbery at Williams & Glynns Bank in the City in which £225,000 was taken.

The Flying Squad had been in existence so long that the Squad's nickname in rhyming slang, the 'Sweeney' (from Flying Squad–Sweeney Todd, the notorious Fleet Street barber who turned his customers into meat pies), was generally regarded as a cliché. But after the likes of Tommy Butler had disappeared, the image of the Flying Squad as courageous men dedicated to upholding the law took a bit of a battering. Over the following ten years, a climate arose in which the Squad's detectives were often viewed with as much suspicion as the criminals they dealt with. The activities of a number of corrupt officers played straight into the hands of professional criminals, tainting the reputation of many of the Yard's most honest officers.

Police suspicions about the honesty of the London detective force had first properly emerged in 1969, when *The Times*, then a newspaper of the ruling powers, published a story accusing a detective inspector and two detective sergeants of corruption. In November 1971, the *Sunday People* ran a series of articles about the men behind London's burgeoning pornography trade, including a leading pornographer called Jimmy Humphreys. The paper accused them of corrupt dealings with officers. The same newspaper then revealed that Commander Kenneth Drury, then head of the Flying Squad, had been on holiday in Cyprus and Humphreys – a man with nine convictions to his name, including a spell in Dartmoor Prison – had been his host.

Drury was served with disciplinary papers and suspended. He immediately resigned rather than face a full disciplinary hearing, but before doing so he wrote an article for the *News of the World* claiming that Humphreys had been one of his informants. The furious pornographer, aware of the effect that such a claim could have on his criminal reputation, responded a week later through the columns of the same paper saying that the opposite was the case – he had never received any money from Drury, but instead had wined and dined the police chief on a total of 58 occasions and had always picked up the bill.

Flying Squad chief Drury insisted it was 'absolutely essential' for him and his officers to mix socially with people connected with the criminal fraternity. Drury said: 'You cannot expect them to give information about crimes if you ostracise them except when you want information from them.'

The problem with the Drury philosophy was that it left detectives wide open to accusations of corruption. Some criminals, like Charlie Wilson, would only ever appear to help the police in order to divert attention from their own activities and ensure a degree of protection from prosecution. Blatant corruption, which Charlie abhorred, was occurring more frequently, with detectives either turning a blind eye to what was going on in return for a cut of the action or, if the information led to the recovery of stolen property, pocketing some of the reward money which detectives would claim on the informant's behalf.

There were still strategically placed officers who could, for a fee, ensure bail was granted or hold back evidence and details about past convictions from a court. It was also possible to have details of a case being made against the accused passed on or a warning given about police operations in which he or she could be compromised. Corrupt officers held onto a proportion of whatever valuables they recovered during an inquiry, too.

The Flying Squad was now to be completely overhauled. Instead of dealing with serious crimes in general, they'd tackle armed robberies only. The Squad's officers would form a central robbery squad based within a coordinating unit inside Scotland Yard, plus four smaller groups strategically placed around London. The newly appointed Met Deputy Assistant Commissioner (DAC), David Powis, also ordered a crackdown on those corrupt policemen creaming reward money meant for informants. In future, all payments amounting to more than £500 would be handed over by the DAC himself.

For the Charlie Wilsons of this world, the Flying Squad's corruption problems were further evidence that the old enemy occupied the same moral ground as the very people they were supposed to be bringing to justice. Charlie was far from convinced that the Flying Squad would suddenly become honourable and honest overnight.

The Met as a whole had already been warned that if it didn't put its house in order, others would move in and do the job for it. Waiting in the wings was MI5, the security service, on the lookout for new areas to add to its empire. MI5 had already informed the Home Office that it considered itself ably equipped to tackle major organised crime, but was unwilling to share its secrets with police officers, whom it didn't trust.

In March 1980, Charlie was ordered to pay tax on the £30,000 Pat had received from the *News of the World* for those articles published 12 years earlier about her life on the run. They'd both always presumed that because Pat and the children had still officially been residents in Canada at the time, they wouldn't have to pay tax. Charlie was particularly incensed that the decision came from Lord Denning, Master of the Rolls, who'd turned down Charlie's appeal against his original sentence before his escape from Winson Green. Denning, sitting with Lord Justice Walker and Lord Justice Dunn, said people 'regretted the practice of some newspapers in paying money to criminals or their wives so as to get a sensational story to publish'. The overriding message to Charlie was: 'It's legal and the payments are taxable.' Charlie saw it as yet more evidence that the Establishment was still after him.

Now he needed to earn some big money, and fast. Maybe it was worth putting that gold VAT scam he'd heard about in prison to the test?

3

Shortly after leaving prison, Charlie moved with Pat to a small first-floor flat in a quiet street in suburban Twickenham, west of London. He was obsessed with keeping a low profile and determined not to bring attention to himself, and he certainly wasn't going to splash out on a big mansion, even if he could afford it. Charlie assured his parole officer the move to Twickenham was further proof that he was going straight, but the truth was that Charlie had a lot of schemes up his sleeve and didn't want loud-mouthed regulars in his old haunts knowing what he was up to.

One of the few familiar faces he'd kept in regular contact with was fellow Great Train Robber Roy James – still known to many as 'The Weasel'. James had learned to be a silversmith while in prison and had then become a successful Hatton Garden jeweller after his release in 1975. Now in his mid-40s, James lived in a comfortable detached house in Highfield Road, Purley, Surrey, south of London, and was also a director of a manufacturing company called Illuminate Ltd.

Over the following few months, Charlie and Roy James personally imported more than 76,000 Maple Leaf gold coins and krugerrands into the UK. The coins were VAT-exempted and then melted down to swindle Customs and Excise of their 15 per cent tax, exactly the way Charlie had worked out when he was inside. A series of big robberies in London and the south-east had actually helped finance the purchase of the gold coins in quantities of up to 1,000 at a time. The key to the operation was that the gang's frontman used a false name, then disappeared off the face of the earth before Customs and Excise called for the VAT charged on the sale of the gold which had been created by melting down the coins. In the end, Charlie's gang bought approximately £16 million worth of Maple Leaf coins and krugerrands legitimately. As one detective said at the time: 'It was a brilliantly simple operation.' Others were not so impressed. One of Charlie's oldest friends, who'd first mentioned the VAT scam to him, explained: 'Charlie never did things by halves. Instead of just letting it tick away nice and gently, he went out and bought millions of pounds worth of coins every month. It was a sure way of being noticed by all the wrong people.'

Charlie had no idea that Customs officers had been probing the gold coins VAT swindling racket since he'd bought his first shipment. In one dramatic incident in Hatton Garden, Scotland Yard detectives assisting Customs men stopped a London taxi cab which was carrying a passenger and gold bars. Another taxi was stopped under similar circumstances the following night and more gold bullion seized. When Charlie and James turned up in the middle of the Customs investigation, detectives couldn't believe their luck: the Great Train Robbers were up to their old tricks again.

On 4 April 1983, Charlie was arrested after a couple of the less-important players in the operation confirmed his role to police. Charlie immediately swore revenge on whoever had grassed him up and, as usual, refused to say a word to police investigators. He and six other men, including Roy James, were eventually charged with conspiracy to defraud the Customs and Excise Department over VAT claims on gold bullion and all were remanded in custody at Clerkenwell Magistrates' Court until 8 April. On the 7th, Pat visited Charlie in Brixton Prison to tell him that his dad had died, never having reconciled things with his son. Charlie was extremely upset by his father's death, especially as he was banged up on what he considered trumped-up charges. An application to attend his father's funeral in south London was refused, which further added to Charlie's hatred towards the Establishment.

During one early appearance at Clerkenwell Magistrates' Court, Charlie made quite an impression on a young detective sergeant called Richard Kirby who was dealing with a gang of armed robbers also appearing at the same court. He recalled: 'I do not subscribe to the popularly held belief that police officers hold a sneaking regard for some of the jobs pulled off by armed robbers in general and the Great Train Robbers in particular. During my dealings with the perpetrators of armed robbery and the misery that they inflicted upon their victims, I came to the inescapable conclusion that armed robbers, very much like their terrorist counterparts, are nothing more than shit, who ought to be locked up and the key mislaid for ever. But on the few occasions that I saw Charlie Wilson, I must admit that I was impressed by his personality . . .

'At every court appearance, Charlie and Roy James were immaculately dressed. Their tastefully cut suits were sharply pressed, their linen was fresh, their ties sober and their conservative black shoes possessed a gleam which would not have disgraced a guardsman. An onlooker, unaware of their identities and antecedents, would have felt rather embarrassed for them, regarding them as being two undeniably tough-looking businessmen who had somehow inexplicably strayed into somewhat seedy surroundings.

'And each week a prison van delivered them to the Magistrates' Court where they would emerge from their cells like film stars, about to go on set for a day's filming. As they strolled down the cell passageway to court, they exhibited the manners of princes, chatting calmly and graciously with the gaoler.

'"Morning, George. How's your back?" asked Charlie.

'"Much better, thanks, Mr Wilson. That new doctor I told you about's a good 'un."

'"And how's the missus? That was a nasty operation she had."

'"Coming along nicely, thanks for asking, Mr Wilson."'

Ahead of Charlie and Roy James were DS Kirby's gang of robbers. 'An unwholesome bunch they were,' recalls Kirby. 'They screamed filth at the Stipendiary Magistrate, spat at the elderly matron and wiped their excrement over their cell-door handles. They were never going to be granted bail in a thousand years and were viewed by everybody with utter contempt.' Kirby went on: 'Charlie and Roy were their exact antithesis. They went into court, courteously put forward the most cogent reasons for being granted bail and the Magistrate who was, of course, fully aware of their past transgressions would patiently listen to the whole of their application before replying, "Gentlemen, I have listened with great interest to your compelling arguments, but I am afraid that you've failed to convince me that you should be granted bail. You'll both be remanded in custody for seven days."

'Then Charlie would reply, "Thank you for your attention, Your Worship" and with a slight bow, he and Roy James strolled back towards the cell passageway. On the way back to the cells, the conversation between Charlie and the gaoler would resume, with no trace of the bitter disappointment Charlie must have felt after not getting bail.

"'Well, George, see you next week, then."

"'Yes, that's if you don't get bail from a judge in chambers, Mr Wilson. I thought you put up some good points today. Thought you were going to make bail, this time."

"'Ah, well, the beak's prejudiced, isn't he, George? That other lot, they give robbers a bad name, don't they? All the best, then.'"

Kirby admitted that his encounters with Charlie and Roy evolved into a 'weekly treat' for him. Charlie eventually decided he'd had enough of Kirby's gang of robbers, whose appalling behaviour was certainly not helping his chances of bail. Kirby takes up the story again: 'The lunatic conspirators were in mid-rant in court and Charlie, aware that they were poisoning the well for anybody else who desired bail, was quietly simmering.

'A few minutes later one of the robbers approached Charlie as he waited his turn to go into the dock, "Yo, Charlie, how's it goin'?" Charlie raised a weary eyebrow, but the robber pressed on regardless. "You done a bit of time for rob-ber-y, innit Charlie? What you say, Charlie? You gonna get a result, man?"'

Kirby explained: 'Charlie, who by now had accepted that he and Roy James would be granted bail when goldfish grew tits, looked pretty irritated. Then he turned to my prisoner and quietly and forcefully replied, "Fuck off, you cunt!" The cell passageway at Clerkenwell Magistrates' Court echoed to the sound of howls of laughter!'

★ ★ ★

In the middle of Charlie's gold coin 'problems', two historic robberies were carried out in Britain which threatened for the first time to overshadow the exploits of the Great Train Robbery. Charlie later told friends he would have dearly loved to be involved in both of them.

The first was the Security Express heist on Easter Monday, 2 April 1983, when armed robbers struck the supposedly impregnable Security Express depot in Shoreditch, east London. Charlie later claimed he'd had a chance to help the financing of this one, but had pulled away in the early stages because he was under so much heat from the police at the time. Once again, as in the Great Train Robbery, there were suggestions that an Army-major type had been the brains behind the raid. Almost £6 million was stolen, but only a small amount of the money was ever found, despite Security Express offering a £500,000 reward.

Just after the raid was carried out, Charlie faced his Old Bailey trial on the gold coins scam. He denied conspiring to defraud Customs and Excise, but two months into proceedings a retrial was ordered by the judge after new evidence emerged which put the prosecution in some doubt. Charlie had by this time spent the majority of the previous 12 months in prison on remand and had even begun thinking seriously about escaping again.

Inside two prisons, Hull and Brixton, Charlie came across his armed robber pal from Parkhurst, 'Mad Mickey' Blackmore. The two men became friendly, even though Blackmore was a bit of a loose cannon. Blackmore told Charlie that he'd already lined up some new business for his release. 'Drugs, Charlie. That's where all the money is,' he said. Charlie already knew that – his problems with the gold scam had convinced him he should have gone down that road a lot earlier.

Then Charlie offered a fellow inmate called Tommy Mason £5,000 to smuggle a consignment of cocaine from Spain to the UK. The 35-year-old east Londoner later claimed Charlie put the word out in the prison that he was looking for men to bring drugs back from Spain, which suggests that Charlie's earlier prejudices against dealing in drugs were rapidly changing. Mason later explained: 'Charlie said they had to be hard men who could be relied on to look after themselves and not to grass if they were caught. I told him I was interested, so he gave me the name of a man to contact in south London when I got out.'

Mason claimed that he later met the contact and another man in a pub. They gave him a couple of travelling bags and £500 expenses. He was then ordered to fly to Majorca, go to a bar called the Amazonas in the capital Palma and wait to be approached. Mason followed the instructions and eventually two men, one English, one Spanish, introduced themselves. Mason later explained that they told him they would pack the contraband into his bag, if he still wanted to do the job. He was then to fly back to London and await contact from someone who would come and take it from him in exchange for £5,000.

He explained that he asked them how much he would be carrying but they said he had no need to know. 'In the end, I lost my nerve,' he said. 'I needed the money, but without knowing what I might be risking, I decided it wasn't worth the gamble. They weren't too pleased with me, but I doubt if it really bothered them because I know they fixed up a constant stream of people to-ing and fro-ing between Spain and Britain.'

The new hearing of the VAT scam began at the Old Bailey in October 1983, and the second of those historic robberies occurred in the middle of that trial. On 26 November 1983 at 6.25 a.m., a gang of south-east London robbers, well known to Charlie Wilson, raided a Brinks Mat security warehouse near Heathrow Airport, neutralised alarms and headed for the unit's vault where they found a carpet of drab grey containers, no bigger than shoeboxes, bound with metal straps and labelled with handwritten identification codes. There were 60 boxes in all, containing 2,670 kilos of gold worth £26,369,778. There were also hundreds of thousands of pounds in used banknotes locked in three safes. One pouch contained traveller's cheques worth $250,000. In the other was a stash of polished and rough diamonds worth at least £100,000. They'd expected riches, but nothing like this. The Brinks Mat robbery, ruthless in its conception and brilliant in its execution, had just landed them with the biggest haul in British criminal history.

In January 1984, Roy James was cleared at the Old Bailey of involvement in the gold coin VAT fraud. Charlie, who'd spent months glaring at the public gallery and press corps all assembled to watch his downfall, remained convinced he was heading for yet another custodial sentence, especially since he'd already been described in court as the mastermind of the alleged conspiracy to swindle, although Judge Richard Lowry, QC, had at least directed that the criminal background of the defendants should not be published until after the verdicts.

However, this time the jury failed to reach a verdict and Charlie was released on bail. The public prosecutor took the decision to abandon proceedings because of the not-insignificant matter of public expense, although the charges against Charlie were to be left on file.

Charlie also secretly agreed with Customs officials that he'd settle a vast outstanding VAT tax bill. The prosecution said Customs were satisfied with the offer and would no longer prosecute Charlie for the outstanding offence. Judge Richard Lowry, QC, told the court: 'It seems proper, sensible and correct to allow the indictment to lie on file.' No one would confirm the details of the deal between Charlie and the VAT men, and one of their spokesman insisted: 'The amount is a matter between the tax payer and ourselves, but we have the power to stay proceedings if we wish.'

Charlie tried to maintain a dignified response outside court. 'I am very relieved,' he told waiting reporters, 'but there will be no champagne celebration – more likely lemonade.'

Newspaper headlines like 'SECRET DEAL FREES TRAIN ROBBER ON £2.4M CHARGE' did nothing to cheer up Charlie since they clearly implied Charlie had been up to no good. Another headline, 'TRAIN ROBBER WILSON BEATS £17 MILLION GOLD

CHARGE', made it clear Charlie's pocket was about to take a real hammering, but at least he wasn't on his way back to prison.

4

Charlie Wilson might have just escaped by the skin of his teeth, but he was facing a VAT bill of at least £400,000, which destroyed any dream of a quiet retirement for him and Pat. Police and Customs officers had deliberately pushed for Charlie to be hit where it hurt most – in his pocket. He would have to hand over the full amount to Customs and Excise or the gold coin case could go to a third trial.

Charlie's solicitor George MacKenzie insisted the payment was made without any admission of liability or guilt. Charlie had always considered VAT nothing more than tax, which he'd avoided paying all of his life. As one old friend later explained: 'You have to understand Charlie had never paid income tax in his life. So when a chance came along to make a few bob by melting down those gold coins he went for it, unable to fully appreciate that the Customs people would come after him.'

As with anything involving the Great Train Robbers, a public outcry was whipped up by Fleet Street, who were outraged that Charlie had effectively managed to buy himself out of trouble. The chairman of the Labour Party, Eric Heffer, told one paper: 'It's a bloody disgrace. It is a classic example of the kind of society we live in.'

Charlie's old friend Joey Pyle later recalled: 'I remember bumping into Charlie one day just after the gold coin trial . . . he had a big fine to pay and he said it was a fuckin' lot of money. He seemed a bit shocked by it.'

Pat was even forced to give evidence regarding her own finances at a bankruptcy hearing in London because Customs and Excise were determined to prove Charlie could afford to pay the settlement he'd made after the trial. Pat had since relaxed her 'rule' about bank accounts and the court heard she had £180,000 saved, which was immediately frozen. Charlie sat outside in the corridor throughout the 30-minute hearing whilst Pat, shaking and with tears in her eyes, was interrogated by the registrar.

Charlie was far from happy. He told one old friend: 'I think I'd rather have done some more bird than pay the bastards all that money. Now I'm back to square one. Potless with a family to support.' Charlie then started looking around for some other 'businesses'.

Shortly after Charlie's acquittal, Great Train Robber Bruce Reynolds found himself back in jail on a drugs charge. A jury at Snaresbrook Crown Court eventually found him guilty of supplying amphetamine sulphate and he was sentenced to three years.

Charlie's two trials utterly convinced him that the authorities were still after him and he didn't know who to trust any more. He firmly believed that the long arm of the law would keep chasing him for the rest of his life. He even started thinking about a move abroad.

However, this paranoia was about to be fuelled even further. On 4 October 1984, Charlie and his former Parkhurst jailmate Colin King were arrested for plotting a robbery and being in possession of two sawn-off shotguns. A Flying Squad surveillance team alleged they'd seen Charlie passing a bag containing the shotguns to King in a south London café. According to police, the bag was later seen in a green van parked near King's home in Bedford Road in Sidcup, Kent. Detectives also said they found a scrap of paper with three index numbers on it in Charlie's car. The third number, which had a line through it, was the registration of a Group Four cash-in-transit van. Confronted with this evidence, both men were alleged by police to have made statements. Charlie was refused bail and found himself back in the slammer yet again.

At their trial three months later, the court was told it wasn't possible to lock the van. Why, therefore, would the bag have been left in the vehicle in the first place? Charlie's defence team then reconstructed the police's alleged surveillance of the van and discovered they could not have seen what was going on inside it unless they'd been standing right next to the vehicle. Mr Alan Rawley, the QC for Charlie's co-defendant King, told the Old Bailey there'd clearly been 'a fit-up, and a deliberate one'.

Then Charlie's counsel, Stephen Solley, said 'the real horror in the case' was the piece of paper, bearing vehicle registration numbers, allegedly discovered in Charlie's car. 'That piece of paper was never found. It is a piece of paper written by an officer knowing, as he did and must have done, that the index number was not only of a Group Four van but another wholly innocent vehicle.' The two other numbers read out in court related to innocent vehicles in Cheltenham. If the line running through the third number AFH 782Y was removed it became DFH 782Y, which was also registered in Cheltenham. There were also no fingerprints linking Charlie to the guns or the van.

Prosecutor for the Crown, Mr Rodney Smith, denied the case had been pursued spitefully. On 5 June 1985, Charlie and King were cleared of plotting a robbery and having sawn-off shotguns after the prosecution agreed there were 'disquieting features' about the case. A detective sergeant and detective constable involved in Charlie's arrest were later suspended and charged with serious offences. After the case, one prosecuting counsel even admitted it had been 'a deliberate fit-up'.

Charlie hid his face with a newspaper to avoid the flashing cameras as he left court following his Old Bailey acquittal. He'd been in custody for more than three months.

Later, Charlie summed it up perfectly: 'It was a fuckin' joke. They thought they could fit me up, but thank gawd they didn't get away with it.' Later claims on a television documentary also questioned the honesty of some of the other Flying Squad officers involved in the case.

Back at their modest home in Twickenham, Charlie and Pat were bombarded with so many press callers they referred all enquiries to their solicitor George MacKenzie. Reporters who visited the property were surprised to find that the Wilsons occupied just the top half of a 1950s semi-detached house and that Charlie had described himself to neighbours as a car dealer.

For the first time in almost two years, Charlie didn't have to report to the local police station. He planned to take Pat on a special holiday to Spain where he'd bought an apartment in Neuva Andalucia, near Marbella, on the Costa del Sol. Charlie told Pat he wanted them to make a full-time move to the sunshine.

Bruce Reynolds explained: 'Charlie didn't want any aggro. After his release in 1979, he'd had plenty of it. He knew they'd never leave him alone – so off he went to Spain.' Joey Pyle was even less surprised when Charlie packed his bags. 'He'd had enough. The way the police treated him was a disgrace. He had to get away from London. I never saw him again after he moved, but I knew it was the right move for him. A man can only take so much. But then Charlie was a right good money getter. I never knew him to be skint. He'd always pick himself up off the floor and start again. Charlie was that type of man.'

The weather on the Costa del Sol usually comprised sun, more sun, and yet more sun. The days were long and nights hot and windy for most of the months of the year. Charlie adored the 40-mile stretch of golden beaches and bars which had become synonymous with fugitives from the British justice system. He wasn't overly keen on rubbing shoulders with Britain's most-wanted men because he liked to keep a low profile, but since he wasn't actually wanted for any crimes, there was no reason for anyone to harass him.

In some ways the Costa del Crime was already a cliché, but the activities of many British criminals were threatening to blow a hole in the idea of a nirvana for villains, where the chaps could still enjoy all the pleasures of home – satellite footy, Carling Black Label, bacon butties and *The Sun*. Back in the summer of 1978, the extradition agreement between Spain and Great Britain had collapsed and that had opened the floodgates. The agreement had broken down because Spain felt Britain was making it too difficult for the Spanish to retrieve their fugitives from the UK.

That turned Spain into a safe haven for criminals: close enough for the family to come out and visit yet far enough away to avoid the attentions of the police. Scotland Yard reckoned that by the mid-'80s there were at least 100 men on the Costa del Sol whom they would like to interview. Across the Mediterranean was Morocco, from where vast quantities of cannabis could be smuggled into Britain for a huge profit. Across the Atlantic were plentiful supplies of cocaine, the evil marching powder of South America.

By the time Charlie headed for the Marbella area, the Costa del Sol had already turned into Europe's California – sunny, spoiled, decadent and dangerous. True, some nasty lowlifers had popped up alongside the old faces, but that was only to be expected in a place where fish and chips were as popular as paella.

PART 4

COSTA DEL CRIME: 1984–90

In each of us, two natures are at war – the good and the evil. All our lives the fight goes on between them, and one of them must conquer. But in our own hands lies the power to choose – what we want most to be, we are.

The Strange Case of Dr Jekyll and Mr Hyde,
Robert Louis Stevenson

1

Charlie Wilson was already a shrewd, artful crook when a seismic shift in criminal opportunity presented itself in the mid-'80s: Europe discovered cocaine. Coke was the fashionable 'drug of choice' for people from all backgrounds. The cocaine business had already turned dozens of Colombians into multimillionaires and Charlie believed it was now his turn to grab a piece of the action. With the US cracking down heavily on the drugs flooding across their borders, Spain was the new gateway for the majority of the world's cocaine. Charlie had bold plans to be one of the big boys in Europe, controlling the cocaine flowing into Britain via Spain and South America.

At an age when most men are contemplating a life of uninterrupted retirement, a small group of greying British villains in Spain were trying to get a piece of the European-wide, multi-million-pound drug industry growing in their backyard. The profits were phenomenal. Cannabis, for example, could be bought for £250 a kilo in North Africa and sold in the UK for upwards of £4,000. An investment of £20,000 in a shipment of cocaine would bring a return of £160,000. Usually, four investors worked together to buy a hundred kilos at a time.

Cocaine use in the United States had peaked in 1985. The gradual decline which followed instigated the Colombian cartels' complete swing to Europe as the next main territory to conquer. The money generated by street sales of cocaine – all cash-and-carry, no cheques, credit cards or charge accounts – had made the coke trade the commercial colossus of the world.

It could be sold for £60 a gram – that's just a 28th of an ounce; 15–20 modest lines worth, sufficient to induce a heightened sense of well-being for an evening at an intimate party. The 125 tonnes of the drug being sold that year would be cut up to 4 times by successive dealers to eventually generate retail revenue of something in the region of £30 billion a year. The cocaine business was the sixth largest private enterprise in the US Top 500. Companies like Boeing, Proctor

& Gamble and Chrysler Motors came after the drug on the 'rich list' of industries. By the mid-1980s, there was so much profit and so many shipments going into the UK that criminals like Charlie calculated they could afford to lose one third of their produce and still make tens of millions of pounds in profit each year.

At first, Charlie became someone happy to 'buy into' loads. That meant he made his living from partly financing other people's deals and having virtually no direct contact with the actual drugs. He also sometimes took a 20 per cent stake in large consignments of cannabis from Morocco. In order to get the really big money, however, he was going to have to get his fingers dirty. He didn't care whether it was puff or coke and let it be known on the Costa del Crime that he was willing to pay cash upfront.

Not long after this, Charlie got a call about 15 tonnes of Lebanese cannabis resin hidden in a cave on the Costa Brava by a bunch of young wannabes. He organised a search party to drive up the coast and locate the drugs, steal them and then sell them through to the UK. This was what life on the Costa del Crime was all about.

Charlie also contacted associates including his old mate Jimmy Rose, whose team of smugglers were so successful they were known inside criminal circles as 'The Rose Organisation', renowned for transporting virtually anything across continents without any problems. Charlie also met with the Haynes family, notorious drug smugglers. Michael Haynes, from Egham in Surrey, and his sons, Andrew and Stephen, were part of an international family-run drugs ring. Michael was later arrested on the French border with a woman called Susan Smith after being tailed from the Costa del Sol. Police found 36 kilos of cannabis hidden in secret compartments beneath his car.

These smuggling teams were extremely adept at persuading innocent one-off couriers – known as 'mules' – to smuggle drugs into Britain by plane, knowing full well that there were other smugglers on board with much more valuable consignments of drugs. The mules would sometimes be sacrificed to Customs inspectors so the big-time smugglers had more chance of getting through. Another smugglers' trick was to get a lorry to pick up a perfectly innocent-sounding cargo, then tip off the local police who'd arrest the driver, who had no idea the concrete blocks he was carrying contained cannabis. 'That way the cozzers think they're winning the battle against drugs while all the big consignments are still getting through,' explained one veteran smuggler. A classic Costa del Sol drugs delivery set-up involved a smuggling team renting a villa near the coast, close to where the narcotics would be delivered by boat. They turned the villa into a temporary 'drugs warehouse' and prepared at least half a dozen cars to carry the drugs back to the UK.

Initially, Charlie was a 'banker' to one of the large hash trafficking firms operating between North Africa and Spain. In Marbella slang, small groups despatching 20 kilos of cannabis a week to Britain were known as 'hash gangs', while those that moved 30 or more kilos were known as 'firms'. Most firms were doing runs once a fortnight and there was a huge amount of money at stake, but, as one smuggler explained: 'If you fell foul of the people running it, they'd kill you no matter who you were.'

Charlie kept such a low profile on the Costa del Sol that the Spanish police had no idea the former Great Train Robber was even living on their manor. Soon, Charlie was making regular, discreet visits to Tangiers in Morocco, where it is not thought he spent his time looking round the kasbah or the Museum of Antiquities. Tangiers was the main trading post for top-quality marijuana grown in the remote heights of the nearby Rif Mountains and then smuggled into Spain.

Charlie's efforts to remain in the shadows in Spain weren't helped by the ever-increasing number of lurid newspaper headlines reminding the British public that southern Spain was virtually awash with his criminal associates. The *News of the World* published an article headlined: 'THE UNTOUCHABLES – 100 MEN WHO FLED COPS LIVE IT UP ON COSTA DEL CRIME.' Charlie wasn't among the men named, but he was personally acquainted with at least half of them.

One of Charlie's most powerful new friends on the Costa del Crime was bank robber-turned-drug baron Tony White. South Londoner White, in his mid-40s and nicknamed the 'King of Catford', had been cleared of involvement in the Brinks Mat robbery, although an Old Bailey jury dubbed him a 'dishonest man with an appalling criminal record' who had come into substantial wealth after the raid. He was also in the frame for a number of other notorious blaggings in London. Following Brinks Mat, White was sued by insurers Lloyds in the London High Court, who named him as one of the Brinks Mat gang, and he was ordered to pay them millions of pounds in compensation although no one knows to this day if he ever came up with any of the cash. White moved to Spain after Brinks Mat. His house on the Costa del Crime, appropriately called The Little White House, was a massive spread and he sent his children to Aloha College, an expensive fee-paying British school. White was later arrested by Costa del Sol police on money-laundering charges and detectives who raided White's mansion found a secret Scotland Yard surveillance report clearly implying he had a number of senior British police officers in his pocket.

Tony White relied heavily on Brian Doran, a 42-year-old Scottish-born villain who'd once run a travel agency in Glasgow. He was known as 'The Professor' because of his university education and degree in Latin American studies, plus his ability to speak four languages. Doran, later jailed for 25 years over cocaine deals worth in excess of £30 million, had left Scotland in 1982 and set up a bar in Marbella, where he began to nurture contacts amongst the Colombian cartels. When, in the mid-1980s, a huge consignment of drugs was found in a Costa del Sol house connected to his name, he fled to Colombia before he could be arrested. It was his Colombian connections that now made him such an important player.

Also out in Spain at the time was Freddie Foreman, who cut a smart figure in his silk suits, cigars and dark glasses. Some even reckoned that the renowned British gangster flick *The Long Good Friday*, with Bob Hoskins playing the lead, was based on his life story. Foreman – known as 'The Mean Machine' – ran an exclusive hostelry called the Eagles Country Club for the chaps in Marbella and was vice-president of the town's boxing club. 'Off duty' he was known for his charm and good manners. Foreman had been tried at the Old Bailey in 1969 with Kray twins Reggie and Ronnie, and jailed for ten years for being an accessory to the murder of Jack 'The Hat' McVitie. On his release, with remission, in 1975, detectives quickly re-arrested him on suspicion of the murder of Ginger Marks, but the following October he and three others were cleared of the crime. Foreman moved abroad, first to Tenerife, followed by the United States, where he remained until January 1982, when he arrived on the Costa del Crime.

Another old mate whom Charlie linked up with in Spain was one-time Parkhurst resident Mickey Green, former Wembley bank robber-turned-drug baron. By the mid-'80s, he was already worth many millions, owned 11 yachts, a Rolls-Royce and half-a-dozen other luxury motors. Green still described himself as a car dealer, but lived lavishly in a huge villa near Marbella. Green also part-owned a nightclub overlooking the marina at Puerto Banus, near Marbella, and spent much of his time cruising the port in his expensive cars looking for blonde dolly birds. Green – later described by Eire's Criminal Assets Bureau as one of the world's biggest cocaine traffickers – had become so adept at escaping justice since his time, ten years earlier, as a notorious London armed robber, that authorities had nicknamed him 'The Pimpernel'. Green also had alleged links to the Mafia and

Colombian drug cartels. As one of his Costa del Crime friends later explained: 'Mickey was from the old school. He'd done well for himself and kept on his toes for much of the time. And luck was certainly on his side.'

Green, now in his mid-40s, had over the years been shadowed by British, Dutch and French law enforcement agencies. There was even a rumour he kept £1 million in French francs hidden in a box in the flowerbed of his Marbella villa. British Customs agents had been pursuing Green for years and were sure they'd get him in the end. One agent commented: 'It's just a matter of time. He thinks he's cleverer than us, but one day he'll make a mistake.'

One of Green's closest mates in the sunshine was another south Londoner who also knew Charlie called Frank Maple – tall, grey-haired and extremely stylish in a 1980s sort of way. Maple had fled to Spain after being named as the brains behind the Bank of America robbery of 1976, in which Charlie was rumoured to have invested. Maple had earlier spent three years in an Austrian jail for a £100,000 hotel robbery.

In June 1984, Spanish magazine *El Tempo* obtained a copy of Spanish legal paperwork filled in by Scotland Yard detectives investigating the previous year's Security Express heist at Shoreditch. Full details of the document were blasted across several pages of the glossy publication, blowing the cover of a Flying Squad team out on the Costa del Sol. The Spanish publication also printed a list of £500,000-plus investments on the Costa del Crime connected to numerous wanted British criminals. The financial breakdown had been compiled by the local police chief after weeks of surveillance with the London detectives.

A few days after publication of the article, at least a dozen well-known British criminals took a day trip on a boat from Puerto Banus. It was an extraordinary gathering of criminal heavyweights and the main topic of conversation was the magazine article, which had ruffled a few of their feathers. Charlie was grateful not be mentioned in the *El Tempo* article; further proof he'd been right to keep such a low profile in Spain.

Back in England, barely a month went by without mention of new seizures and lengthy jail sentences for drug offences. Amongst the faces getting caught up in the drugs game were Charlie's train robbery pals Tommy Wisbey and Jimmy Hussey, who were both dealing cocaine at the time. Tommy Wisbey later explained: 'We were against drugs all our lives, but as the years went on, towards the end of the '70s, it became more and more the "in" thing. Being involved in the Great

Train Robbery, our name was good. They knew we never grassed anyone, we had done our time without putting anyone in the frame.' Another old-time robber called Jack Browne put it this way: 'In the '60s, if you were a drug-taker, you could never be a proper thief. It just wasn't acceptable. But that had all changed by the time Charlie got out of prison. The old crims were getting heavily involved in the drugs game. The big money was no longer in going across the pavement or holding up a security van – drugs were a far steadier, low-risk option.'

Charlie's ambition to move up the drugs ladder for bigger financial rewards meant he needed to know more about the product, so he decided on a risky experiment which involved buying a small shipment of cocaine entirely by himself. He then had it weighed into grams before selling it onto the next link in the cocaine food chain. His kilo 'investment' was kept in a secret compartment in the spare bedroom of his Neuva Andalucia apartment. His return for that shipment was far higher than his earlier partnerships and Charlie stored the cash profit in an air-conditioning duct in the flat, which cut off the air supply to the rest of the building. It was necessary to avoid damaging the money or any remaining product and Charlie began to appreciate the complex system which brought cocaine to the dinner table.

★ ★ ★

When the drug barons emerged during the second half of the last century, cocaine had already been quickening the spirits and brains of South Americans for some 4,000 years. The coca plants themselves grew virtually everywhere in the moist tropical climate of the Andes – Peru, Ecuador, Chile, Bolivia and Colombia – but the really high quality produce tended to come from areas not too high above sea level. The growing had never been a problem; the biggest challenge for cocaine production was always transportation. To this day, pack animals and aeroplanes remain the best ways to move the drugs from their original source. In leaf form, the drug is bulky. Interim laboratories, therefore, some of them portable, were set up close to the growing fields to reduce the leaves to a cocaine paste, which could be shipped far more easily.

The paste then went through another process to produce an interim form of cocaine called 'base', making it 100 per cent pure cocaine alkaloid and very potent. From a marketing point of view, this form of cocaine still lacked versatility because it was too sticky to snort or inject. Creating street cocaine required one more operation, which involved dissolving the base in ether then combining it with acetone and hydrochloric acid. It was then allowed to sit out and dry into a white, crystalline substance. The result was Colombia's number one export – cocaine hydrochloride.

The drug glowed with an ethereal opalescence after being pressed into a rocklike form safe for travelling. The consumer would then chop it up with a razor blade or credit card on the face of a mirror and arrange it into inch-long lines of the infamous marching powder – a light, fragile, flaky substance like newly fallen snow.

Charlie had never forgotten how, ten years earlier, his Parkhurst jailmate Carlos had explained the economic end of the business. In order to produce a kilo of 100 per cent pure cocaine, which they were selling out of Colombia for $6,000, the combined cost of coca leaves, chemicals and cheap labour added up to less than $1,000. Once transported to northern Spain, it would go on the wholesale market for $50–60,000 a kilo.

Moving from wholesaling to retailing would see those astounding profits go even higher. After it was cut a number of times by interim dealers to boost the weight and maintain the profit margin, the end product often contained no more than 15–20 per cent actual cocaine. But that wasn't Charlie's problem. At the end of the day, when Charlie did his sums, he realised that by selling the coke for £60 a gram, with 1,000 grams to the kilo, and all the deals running smoothly, the kilo he purchased for £4,000 in Colombia would generate street sales in the UK of £200–300,000.

Finding the right supplier was the key. Without that source, none of it meant anything. 'Don't worry, my friend,' one Medellín cartel man on the Costa del Crime told Charlie. 'We can get you all the cocaine you want, if you have the money.'

The Medellín cartel had been formed in early 1982 after the Colombian guerrilla movement M-19 (Movimiento 19 de Abril) kidnapped a cocaine tycoon's sister. In response, a group called MAS (Muerte a Secuestradores), consisting of three cocaine barons called Jorge Ochoa, Carlos Lehder, and Pablo Escobar, was set up to counter the guerrillas. Their alliance soon became known as the Medellín cartel. 'It's a bit like General Motors; everything's connected,' explained one old hand from South America.

In 1985, Colombian President Betancur tried to rid his country of cocaine exporters after immense pressure from the United States government. It was then that the Medellín cartel turned to Europe, where a ripe, young market of wealthy upwardly mobile yuppies seemed the prime marketplace. Eurotrash and cocaine was as natural a combination as strawberries and cream.

In the mid-'80s, it was predominantly Spanish drug lords who were acting as middlemen for the South Americans and Charlie believed he could offer the Medellín cartel more security than them. He wanted to exploit the UK market, which at that time was supplied with cocaine by a number of gangs. The Colombians preferred not to supply the British market directly because they knew that, as foreigners, they would stand out and be asking for trouble. They needed a British 'partner' they could trust – a facilitator who knew how to get the stuff into the country safely and in much larger quantities than previously. Charlie seemed the perfect candidate: he had a colourful criminal background and held the respect of other villains, even the police. Charlie told the Medellín cartel reps in Spain he knew who to bribe and who to avoid in Britain. These were the sorts of connections the Colombians wanted.

Charlie knew that once he had the UK end of his operation properly set up, the money would start pouring in. He was convinced that for the second time since the Great Train Robbery, he was about to come into enormous riches. As one associate later explained: 'Charlie was patient. He had a plan and he was sticking to it like glue. If he played his cards right, he'd get fuckin' rich beyond his wildest dreams.' Charlie didn't even really care what he had to go through to achieve such wealth. None of it mattered any more. Here he was, a kid from south London, about to become a powerful world player in one of the most profitable industries in history. As Charlie himself would say, 'Can't be bad, can it?'

2

Many of Charlie's oldest south London associates on the Costa del Sol warned him against joining forces with the Medellín cartel. One smuggler, whom he'd known since they were tearaways together in south London, almost 30 years previously, told Charlie: 'Don't mess with 'em, Chas. I know what them fuckers are like. I wouldn't piss in their mouths if their throats were on fire. Keep away from them, for fuck's sake.' But Charlie and others from the underworld aristocracy ignored the warnings and began energetically throwing themselves into the drugs business, even though a few of them seemed happier wallowing in the sun with a sangria in one hand and a sawn-off in the other.

Another important figure Charlie became close to at this time was drugs baron Brian Wright, who'd first known Charlie when he worked as a teenage croupier at Charlie and Joey Pyle's Charterhouse Club in the early '60s. Wright, a racing fanatic with extensive drug connections, had kept in touch with Charlie down the years.

He was born and bred in Kilburn, London's premier Irish community in north London, and started work as a bookies' runner. In just 20 years, he'd transformed himself into a phenomenally successful gambler, well known at virtually every racetrack in the UK. One of Charlie's oldest criminal associates on the Costa del Crime commented that Charlie 'wanted to up the stakes' and he saw Brian Wright as the perfect way to get in at the top of the drugs game.

Wright even offered Charlie the use of his private boxes at a number of different race courses across southern England whenever he popped back to the UK for 'business meetings'. Wright also had a house near Charlie in Spain. In 1985, Wright was given a warning at one race course for placing large bets on behalf of a man who, as a licensed jockey, was not allowed to bet. In the days before TV cameras covered every race, it was easier for jockeys to 'strangle favourites' or pull off what they called 'anchor jobs'. And plenty were willing to take Brian Wright's bread for it.

In one later court case, Wright's criminal network was said to be responsible for importing up to two tonnes of cocaine a year. Numerous yachts were bought and subcontracted back to smugglers and it was said that Wright was virtually 'swimming in money'. Wright told Charlie how gang members used light aircraft to parachute cocaine drops of up to 600kg a time to waiting boats. Smaller speedboats would then take the produce to shore. Ocean-going yachts and other larger vessels in the Caribbean, Venezuela and South Africa also had to be summoned for long-haul journeys.

One of Wright's technicians later used a Global Positioning System to organise yacht-to-yacht drug transfers known as 'coopering'. These could take place off any coastline. The coopering process meant the gang could dodge Customs checks as transatlantic vessels – which were usually checked at ports – could dock 'clean'. In turn, Charlie was able to give Brian Wright lots of good advice about life in Spain and who the emerging players were. Wright introduced Charlie to a man called Ronald Soares, a middle-aged Brazilian who had a direct line of communication to Colombia's Medellín cartel. Another highly dangerous character Charlie met at this time was Roman Smolen, who was later arrested on board a boat that contained more than half a tonne of cocaine.

But, unknown to Charlie, there were problems brewing on the Costa del Sol. His associate Tony 'King of Catford' White was already notorious as the central figure of a south London crime culture that was almost Dickensian in its structure and rules, where meetings took place in private clubs and drinking dens, and where territorial claims were still recognised. Since arriving in Spain, however, White had let that cover drop and was flashing his cash around.

Customs and Excise investigators in the UK initially had Tony White and his associates in their sights because they were investigating the whereabouts of the proceeds of the £26 million Brinks Mat gold bullion robbery. The Customs operation had started as a fairly routine monitoring job of at least a dozen names. Previous attempts to trap this type of criminal had come to nothing, but it was becoming clear there were some huge drug deals going down.

Initial inquiries took UK Customs agents more than 5,000 miles across the Atlantic to Colombia, where White's friend Brian 'The Professor' Doran had set himself up as South American middleman for British criminals based in Spain. Doran, who liked only the best wine and designer clothes, was now a big fish and had even popped up on the US law enforcement agency radar. Doran had cultivated superb connections in Medellín, where cocaine was produced with the efficiency of an international corporation. Once accepted by the cartel, Doran was probably the most important link in the entire chain. Charlie didn't trust the cold-blooded South Americans, but he also knew he needed direct contact with them, so he asked Doran to set up a meet with the most legendary Medellín man of all, Pablo 'El Doctor' Escobar. Charlie wanted the Colombians to supply him directly and knew he needed Escobar's personal authority to distribute the drugs. He couldn't just ship a load over to Europe and expect everyone to welcome him with open arms.

In 1984, two US enforcement agencies watching drug barons in Colombia matched a man who flew into Medellín from Europe with Charlie's description. Charlie later told a friend that Escobar said he needed 'ambassadors' in the UK and Holland to represent his interests.

As one old-time villain out in Spain later explained: 'You needed these soldiers because they helped you distance yourself from any aggro with the police, Customs and suppliers. They were frontmen in a way.'

The street kids in the city of Medellín, Columbia, were prepared to do just about any job for the drug lords, including working as hired assassins specialising in motorcycle killings, during which the motorbike pulled alongside the intended victim's car and the kid on the back emptied his machine pistol into the interior of the vehicle before taking off into the chaos of the city traffic. Even for someone like Charlie, the danger levels in Medellín must have seemed disturbing. The number of violent deaths each year in the city during the mid-'80s exceeded 5,000 – 20 times the murder rate in London, which had a population 7 times the size.

Medellín had always played second fiddle to the Colombian capital Bogota, which made the inhabitants even more chippy and trigger-happy. The city may have had three universities and a stunning botanical garden, but most of its inhabitants lacked sophistication and money. When they left home, most boys in the family were told, 'If you succeed send money; if you fail, don't come home.'

Medellín was teeming with hustlers, smugglers, con men and wheeler-dealers, ranging from one-legged beggars, who flagged down tourists in taxis, to pickpockets and sharpsters pushing stolen TV sets along the street. Then there was Medellín cartel kingpin Pablo 'El Doctor' Escobar, allegedly so wealthy by the mid-1980s that he was rich enough to personally pay off Colombia's national debt of $13 billion – if the government would leave him alone.

Escobar was in some ways a man after Charlie's own heart. His childhood was one of dire poverty and he had first made his way in the world by digging up gravestones, grinding off the inscriptions and selling them cut-rate to people in the local market. What Charlie Wilson perhaps didn't fully appreciate was that by meeting Pablo Escobar, not to mention his two commanders-in-chief Jorge Ochoa and Carlos Lehder, he was dealing with the devil incarnate. Escobar once commissioned an employee to carry a briefcase onto a crowded airliner without telling him it was dynamite rigged to explode in mid-air. The resulting disaster killed more than 100 people travelling on a Colombian internal flight. Then there was the time Escobar's men were caught trying to buy 120 Stinger anti-aircraft missiles in Florida.

There is little detail available about Charlie's first visit to Colombia – it wasn't until after he arrived back in Spain that law enforcement agents took a closer interest in Charlie – but he undoubtedly thought he was on a mission to make millions of pounds and Escobar later told an associate that he believed Charlie could become one of the godfathers of European cocaine trafficking.

Charlie's next step after his return from Medellín was to meet the all-important Dutch connection, so he contacted Netherlands-based former blagger Roy 'The Lump' Adkins, whom he'd met in Parkhurst. West Londoner Adkins introduced Charlie to his boss Klaas Bruinsma in Amsterdam, where a violent and complex network of international drugs traffickers were based, thanks to Rotterdam being the world's largest harbour. The Netherlands had become a key transit country for drugs coming from Pakistan, South America, North Africa and just about everywhere in the world.

Most drugs did not stay there long because a far greater profit could be made selling them in Britain, Sweden and elsewhere in Europe. Klaas Bruinsma – known in Dutch criminal circles as 'The Preacher' – was believed to be one of the top six most-powerful drug barons in the world. He'd also personally killed a number of drug dealers and was suspected of ordering hits on at least half a dozen more.

In the late 1970s, Bruinsma joined forces with Charlie's old associate Adkins, a gangster with a wide circle of contacts in the British underworld. Adkins had always kept one step ahead of the police in the UK even though he'd been deeply involved in narcotics trafficking since coming out of prison in the early 1970s. 'Roy was known as "The Lump" because that's what he was. He wasn't a subtle sort of fella. He just charged in, all guns blazing,' explained one of Charlie's oldest associates. Adkins had operated first from Spain then moved to Holland. Bruinsma and Adkins even set up phoney businesses in source countries such as Morocco and Pakistan, and used them as cover to ship narcotics into Holland. The two men were so careful they never packed entire lorries with drugs, preferring instead to divide the produce amongst a number of smaller vehicles. Adkins was a fiery, abrasive character whose paranoia was fuelled by his own intake of cocaine. He'd also had some problems with a Colombian cocaine smuggling gang who'd accused him of ripping them off. He was irritated that Charlie thought he could just waltz in and get into bed with Escobar and the rest of the Medellín cartel, but for the moment he was content to play along with him. Another south London criminal involved with the Dutch connection was 'Mad Mickey' Blackmore, whom Charlie also knew from Parkhurst, as well as more recently on remand in Brixton and Hull prisons.

One senior Scotland Yard detective stumbled upon evidence of what

Charlie was up to in Holland when he was investigating the hit-man killing of a London businessman some years later. The detective explained that he went to Holland to find out more about Adkins, but instead uncovered information regarding frequent visits by Charlie Wilson to Amsterdam for drug meets with Adkins, Klaas Bruinsma and Mad Mickey.

Being seen in the company of people like Tony White and Mickey Green had put Charlie firmly in the sights of UK Customs investigators and members of the British National Drugs Intelligence Unit. America's Drugs Enforcement Agency (DEA) – which had been watching Brian Doran in Colombia for almost a year – also began asking questions about that man who matched Charlie's description who'd just visited Medellín. The DEA were capable of putting the entire group of criminals under a constant ring of surveillance, which involved staking out their secret meeting places, eavesdropping on their conversations in the street, photographing diary entries and money transfers to Colombia and elsewhere, as well as tracing bank accounts under false names to places as far afield as Geneva and the Cayman Islands. Investigators would eventually travel to many locations, from a five-star hotel in London's Knightsbridge to a Caribbean island. Even, in the case of Tony White, to a pie-and-eel shop in Kent. The operation to watch people like Charlie, White, Green and Doran was ongoing. It was the most highly ambitious project that Customs and Excise had ever undertaken and the technical expertise of the DEA was going to be an essential ingredient.

Charlie and other criminals on the Costa del Sol knew the UK police were out in Spain watching their movements, but they had no idea about the other agencies. The Spanish government was not enthusiastic about having any foreign law enforcement agencies on their territory, but they were even more irritated by the presence of so many British criminals. The weak link in this chain was the Spanish police.

If ever Charlie needed to know about the Yard's movements on his doorstep, he just picked up the phone and spoke to a man who in turn spoke to one of three Spanish officers 'in exchange for a beer'. Charlie had heard how badly the British police and their Spanish counterparts got on. The local cops were considered slow, dogmatic and ill-equipped to deal with the wealthy drug barons based on their doorstep.

The new police station in Marbella summed up the situation; it remained unfinished and was about five years behind schedule. The old copshop at the back of town was 'like something out of a spaghetti western' according to one British police officer who visited the building in the mid-1980s. Ex-Flying Squad detective Peter Wilton explained: 'The boss used to come into the station at about ten o'clock in the morning. It was a struggle for him to get up the stairs. He used to sit at his desk, light a cigarette and examine the solitary piece of paper in his in-tray for a while. Then he'd walk back down the stairs, go into the café next door and get a large brandy and a coffee, and stand there playing the fruit machines. After that, he would go home for his siesta. Sometimes, he would reappear at teatime and do another two minutes' work.'

Spanish police equipment was from an earlier era, as were the wages officers were paid, and many detectives in Marbella genuinely believed that these criminals the British authorities so desperately wanted to arrest were bringing money into the region, which meant jobs for the locals, so why not leave them alone? British police officers also got the impression that the Spanish were resentful towards them. It was in this atmosphere then that Charlie's old enemies in the Flying Squad tried to keep tabs on numerous familiar faces living on the Costa del Crime. No wonder Charlie and others believed they could remain one step ahead of the boys in blue. Liaison officer for all British police and Customs activities in Spain was Cliff Craig, based in Madrid. He found himself constantly juggling the needs of the British investigators with a certain level of diplomacy so that the Spanish government didn't stick them all on a plane back home. One team of Flying Squad officers even turned up in Spain during this time pretending to be tabloid journalists. The Costa del Sol, with its ever-increasing contingent of dodgy ex-pats, was a favourite watering hole for reporters from the UK.

Many officers believe to this day that there should be a British-manned police station on the Costa del Sol. Simple tasks, such as checking a British-registered vehicle, were an administrative nightmare for the Spanish and could take up to four weeks instead of the few minutes it would take for UK law enforcement officers.

The first team of London detectives to gather evidence about the activities of Charlie and his associates returned to London in 1986 with thick wads of documents, although they could do little without actually catching these high-powered criminals in the act of committing a crime. British police were also restricted by rules which meant if they persuaded a suspect to visit a police station in Spain, he or she would have to be interviewed by a Spanish officer while the British detectives waited in another room. But it was the way that the movements of most British officers in Spain were leaked to Charlie and other faces on the Costa del Sol that really made the UK police's blood boil.

In early 1986, Charlie's main Spanish police informant mentioned a new Scotland Yard investigation codenamed Operation Nightshade in which detectives were targeting British criminals involved in importing drugs and then laundering their proceeds. Charlie was told that the Yard had even set up special bank accounts in the names of false companies, which undercover detectives were planning to use to try and lure criminals into a trap. The Spanish police had a strict policy at that time of 'buy-or-bust', which meant that if they came upon someone in possession of drugs, the only way they could overlook the offence was to try and use that person to worm their way into a drugs organisation. That often led to undercover cops buying big shipments of drugs in order to continue an undercover operation.

In early 1986, Charlie met up with Indian drug smuggler 'Chris' Krishnarma, whom he'd known in Long Lartin prison almost ten years earlier. Krishnarma had made a point of getting to know a lot of the British criminals on the Costa del Sol. Charlie had always been impressed by Kirshnarma's knowledge of drugs and he was soon a regular breakfast-time caller at Charlie's home.

Another visitor was Charlie's old friend, master-smuggler Jimmy Rose and his wife Patty, who flew over from their home in Kent. Rose later admitted he was quite envious of Charlie's new life out in Spain: 'It was a good lifestyle and he didn't seem to have none of those problems with the law like you got back home. Charlie in his suntan seemed to have the perfect set up to me.' Charlie and Rose usually had a bit of business to discuss, so they'd have dinner with their respective wives and then slip off together to Puerto Banus where many of the bars were filled with familiar faces.

3

Back in the 1960s when Charlie first came to criminal prominence, the underworld was a solidly based sub-society with its own economic structures, class system and laws. By the mid-'80s, the rules had changed and the younger villains didn't think twice about threatening anyone, not just other criminals. By this time, the economy, judicial system and peace on the streets were all at risk from individuals whose power was increasing in inverse proportion to the police's ability to put them behind bars.

Now virtually every criminal had his own firepower and a minor industry had sprung up to accompany the demands of increasingly gun-conscious gangsters in both Spain and the UK. The number of contract killings on the streets suggested that professional criminals were prepared to commit the ultimate crime to achieve ascendancy in the underworld. Violent villains were clamouring to feast on the fattest prize in criminal history – narcotics.

Drugs, counterfeit money and guns – Spain had it all in abundance. More than a dozen heavy characters living within a stone's throw of Charlie's home in Neuva Andalucia had the potential to cause significant destabilisation to the drugs market in Europe and the UK. The police in both countries knew who they all were, but proving what they were up to was another matter.

In the summer of 1986, Charlie was introduced to a Medellín cartel accountant at the Atalaya Park Hotel, just off the main N340 coast road, west of Puerto Banus. Charlie met with the Colombian and his assistant in the vast lobby area. What none of them realised was that a US DEA officer was sitting across from the reception watching them and monitoring every word (although he had no idea who Charlie was at the time). The 'accountant' had all the usual Colombian features: pale white skin, lots of dark wavy hair and a small moustache. He was immaculately dressed, wore gold chains around his neck and a chunky Rolex on his right wrist.

After the initial hotel meeting, Charlie was asked back to a Medellín cartel-owned house in the hills behind Puerto Banus, close to the local bullring. It was a large two-storey hacienda, stucco fronted with a red-tiled roof, which they'd taken over from a Spanish cocaine dealer who owed them money. In the back garden was an Olympic-sized swimming pool and in the gated driveway an assortment of Ferraris, Lamborghinis and Rolls-Royces.

Around the pool were at least half a dozen women in various stages of undress. They were all dripping in gold, emeralds and diamonds, and a group of men were sitting nearby at a card table playing poker. Soon after arriving at the house, Charlie found himself alone in an upstairs office being pumped by two of the Colombians about his background. Charlie later told one friend that at first he wanted to tell the Colombians to 'fuck off', but realised that would probably be a stupid thing to do in their own backyard, literally. The man he now knew to be the accountant suggested that Charlie should start re-investing some of his earnings in a series of legitimate businesses recently set up by the Colombians in Spain. Charlie tactfully declined their kind offer, but knew only too well that the next time they came back to him it might be with an offer he couldn't refuse.

Also at the house that day was the most powerful Medellín man in mainland Europe, 35-year-old Cesar 'The Mexican' Arango. Arango organised numerous shipments from Colombia and lived in a beautiful former monastery 20 miles south of Barcelona with his wife Marleni Chaquea and their two young daughters. He owned numerous other residential and commercial properties in Spain and regularly made vast money transfers to offshore bank accounts.

About 60,000 Colombians entered Spain each year perfectly legally because it was the only European country where they did not require a visa. Madrid had become a haven for Colombian drug bosses, who were involved in regular, bloody gun battles in the Spanish capital.

The Colombians had a carefully planned strategy for everything; after each occasional arrest, the networks simply regrouped and business went on as usual. Everything was arranged by telephone in carefully worded code. The cocaine supply route was usually Colombia to the Caribbean, where it was dropped by air to be delivered to a Spanish fishing boat which then made the journey to Galicia, in northern Spain, where the 'mother ship' waited offshore for fast launches or smaller fishing boats to pick up the merchandise. They then sailed to hideouts amongst the hundreds of narrow inlets along the Galician coastline. Within days, the cocaine was being disguised in cans of hake and shellfish before heading off in articulated lorries all over Europe.

On ancient maps, Galicia was named Finisterre. At one time mariners believed that west of Rias, the rocky inlets swept by incessant drenching winds, was literally the end of the Earth. Navigating these waters remained a hazardous business, but, as Charlie discovered when he visited Galicia, it could also be a spectacularly profitable one too.

Many police chiefs and mayors in the Galicia region were in the Colombians' pockets. Laureano Oubina, a Spanish vineyard owner, later imprisoned for his role in a smuggling operation, admitted frequently hiring boats to collect cocaine from Costa Rica, Panama and Venezuela. One Colombian alleged to be 'the boss of bosses', called

Jose Ramon Prado Bugallo, was also later arrested in Galicia when five tonnes of cocaine were seized on a mother ship off the coast.

After arriving on the Spanish mainland, the drugs were usually stashed in underground hiding places, pits dug in little lanes or under piles of firewood in someone's back garden. Then the Colombians would send someone from Madrid to collect their produce by car. That person would take his cut, sell the drugs on and remit the profits in US dollars to his bosses back in Colombia. The rest was shared amongst the sailors and the distributors who passed it on to the traders all over Europe.

Charlie already had contacts in Galicia through his criminal associates on the Costa del Sol, who regularly sent up scruffy-looking soldiers in campervans to take drugs straight through France and across the Channel. The trade had been building steadily since the early 1980s, pushed by the Colombians' need for alternatives to the heavily controlled North American market and by ever-increasing demand for cocaine and cannabis in Europe. Enticed by the profits to be made, Charlie decided to make a visit to Spain's northernmost coastline and see if he could hammer out a deal for local facilities to cut out yet more middlemen.

Many of the *pueblos* (villages) on the western coast of Galicia suffered in the sixteenth and seventeenth centuries from attacks by English and Turkish pirates, so the presence of a few criminals like Charlie Wilson drew little or no attention. Take the picturesque village of O Grove – according to ancient maps, it was once an island, but little by little it has become united with the tip of *La Lanzadaon*, the mainland. In 1562, the Bubonic plague entered the port and wiped out the surrounding communities. This, and a succession of bad harvests, starved the remaining population and the landscape became barren of people once more.

It was only at the turn of the nineteenth century that the population returned to these isolated shores thanks to the fishing industry. Soon, cottages in villages such as Horreos sprang up, fronted by aerated storage buildings on stilts preventing rats getting into precious grain, vegetables and fruit preserved for the severe winters. These would later become ideal hiding places for narcotics.

Charlie was about to enter the lion's den. He wanted to run shipments of drugs without having to use many of the traditional middlemen and that meant taking far more risks. Just before Charlie travelled up to Galicia in 1986, Customs officials had boarded a rusty old trawler some 60 miles off the coast near Vigo and seized a tonne of cocaine. It was a rare victory for the authorities, and showed that not even Galicia was completely beyond the law.

Charlie's first stop was, bizarrely, an ice-cream parlour in the village of Cambados, a few miles along the coast from the town of Vilagarcia. He was waiting to be picked up by his Medellín contact. Colombians regularly turned up dead in these parts, but the riches amassed by some of the locals implied that cocaine had also brought people a great deal of wealth and happiness.

Charlie was eventually taken to the village of Vilanova de Arousa in a Ford pick-up truck, past its tiny harbour into a neighbourhood of mansions of staggering luxury, sprouting fat radio antennae behind spiked granite walls with electronically controlled gates. There were also luxury restaurants and nightclubs, most of which had undoubtedly been built with drug money. DEA sources say Charlie met Carlos Goyannes, a high-society playboy and the link man between Galician smugglers and Spain's coca jet set, who usually organised shipments of cocaine all over Europe.

Also while he was in northern Spain, Charlie needed to shake hands with ETA – the Spanish terrorist organisation whose brutal campaign for an independent Basque region had made the IRA look like a bunch of schoolboys. ETA's people were cold, dedicated killers, who'd slaughtered upwards of 500 people in almost 15 years of terrorism against the Spanish government.

In the early 1980s, some of Charlie's old criminal associates on the Costa del Sol had formed an uneasy alliance with ETA, who needed big injections of cash to buy explosives and arms. ETA had immersed themselves in the drugs trade in much the same way as the IRA did in Northern Ireland in the late 1970s. One drug smuggler recalled: 'ETA had to muscle in on the drugs business in order to survive and everyone knew they shot first and asked questions later. They'd turn up at meetings and say, "You're workin' with us." There was no "please" or "thank you."'

Another ex-smuggler on the Costa del Sol explained: 'At first, the Brits thought ETA would just be a bunch of college kids. But they're colder and tougher than any crims and the Brits had to really watch their backs.' Added the source: 'ETA's motivation was purely to buy enough weapons to kill as many Spanish officials as possible. Charlie Wilson and others made the mistake of thinking they could operate alongside ETA.' In late 1985, a beautiful brunette ETA member called Maria – known as 'The Tigress' in the Basque country – pulled a gun on two British gangsters during a heated meeting about drug shipments in a Marbella hotel room. Maria was later alleged to have been involved in 24 ETA murders – including 17 members of the Guardia Civil.

Charlie Wilson knew that without ETA waving his drugs through northern Spain he couldn't set up his supply route via Holland to the UK. Charlie even recruited a North African woman with connections to two of ETA's most senior members responsible for raising funds for their continual campaign against the Spanish government. The woman – in her early 30s – eventually became one of his lovers. Charlie had severe reservations about dealing with terrorists, but as he told one of his pals in Spain: 'This is business and I have to deal with these bastards, otherwise I can't get my produce through Europe.' One ETA member later told another British criminal on the Costa del Sol they thought Charlie was 'a mad and dangerous man'.

Charlie returned to the Costa del Sol from Galicia believing he'd set up a supply route that would earn him a fortune. And as word spread of Charlie's status as an up-and-coming drugs baron, other characters crawled out from under the woodwork. These included a notorious Israeli mafia man called Oleg, one of the biggest Ecstasy dealers in the world. Oleg had at least six homes on mainland Spain, but spent much of his time in luxury hotel suites with his wife and children out of harm's way in France. Ecstasy was just taking off in northern Europe at the time. Unlike heroin and cocaine, E could be sold to teenagers as a user-friendly drug. Being an amphetamine, it propelled the release of serotonin, a chemical that gives an immediate rush to the brain. Side effects included panic attacks and kidney, liver and heart problems.

Self-acclaimed E king Oleg was proud of the fact he rarely got his fingers dirty through one-to-one meetings with the distributors of his drugs. He'd even set up a ten-million-pound drug deal from inside his Spanish prison cell during a brief spell inside during the mid-1980s. Oleg made his first fortune when he took over several clandestine Ecstasy pill production laboratories in the Netherlands (thereby gaining control over the entire Ecstasy operation in the country). The pills were then driven overland to Spain, Belgium, France and Germany. A variety of courier services – from New York strippers and Spanish teenagers to pensioners – were used to sneak the drugs out of Europe to the US, Canada, Israel and Australia. Sometimes tablets were packed into picture frames and sent via ordinary international messenger services. The gang also trafficked cocaine and cannabis, and financed a group of Israeli armed robbers who targeted jewellery shops in all the main Spanish cities.

America's DEA had Oleg under observation so when he met Charlie in Malaga, its agents became even more convinced that Charlie's status should be upgraded to important surveillance target. The DEA had offices in 67 of the world's countries and was said by many to have more power than the KGB ever had. One of the organisation's main European offices was inside the United States Embassy in Madrid.

Just the phrase DEA sent a shiver down the spines of many European criminals. Cannabis dealer Howard Marks described them like this in his book *Mr Nice*: 'Why is the DEA so sadistic and inhuman? How can they happily and deliberately cause innocents [his family] to suffer? In the name of what? I must always remember the DEA are evil. They began as President Nixon's Mafia. They know what they're doing. I hate them. I'll fight them until I fucking die.' There was even talk on the Costa del Crime that the DEA intended opening a 'branch office' inside a newly created US bank office in Marbella. It was also rumoured that DEA agents thought themselves above the law and had taken part in torture/interrogation sessions alongside Spanish drug police. (American law enforcement agents were not allowed to participate in an actual foreign arrest or question those arrested in another country, they were just there to aid and assist the local force, but some criminals were convinced the DEA was capable of kidnapping villains if they felt the UK and Spanish police forces were not up to the job of incarcerating them.)

The DEA's involvement helped to further mobilise the law enforcement agencies representing the United States, Great Britain and Spain in an unprecedented international effort to crack down on the drugs that were flooding into Spain en route to the rest of Europe. One of the DEA's most energetic agents was Craig Lovato, who was based in Spain at the time. His office authorised Charlie's home phone to be tapped because it was felt he could prove a vital link to the Medellín cartel.

Over in Florida, Lovato's wife Wendy, who also worked for the DEA, was assisting Scotland Yard in their Brinks Mat robbery inquiries. It was these inquiries that had first alerted detectives to Charlie's activities in Spain. His criminal background meant little to the US officials, but the Yard were mightily impressed by Charlie's involvement. One Customs officer later divulged: 'The Yard guys were virtually in awe of Charlie Wilson and here he was popping up in the middle of a major Colombian coke investigation.'

The multinational squad of law enforcement agencies agreed to step up surveillance of a number of criminals, including Charlie, Tony White, Mickey Green, Brian Wright and Brian Doran. The DEA operation was so secret (and unofficial at that time) that it did not even have a codename. It wasn't long before law enforcement agents in Holland, Canada, Pakistan, the Philippines, Hong Kong, Thailand, Portugal and Australia were also involved.

The DEA believed that if they could gather enough evidence against Charlie then they might be able to 'turn' him – in other words persuade him to become an informant by offering a heavy prison sentence as an alternative. What the DEA completely failed to appreciate was that Charlie Wilson's entire criminal ethos was based on never grassing up another villain. So, a clutch of DEA agents, US spooks and UK Customs representatives were now on the trail of Charlie Wilson. Yet, for the moment, he seemed blissfully unaware of these new shadows.

In early 1987, DEA and UK Customs officers in Spain monitored a meeting between Charlie and Tony White's Colombian connection, Brian 'The Professor' Doran, in a bar in Fuengirola on the Costa del Sol. They overheard White's name being mentioned frequently. One senior Customs officer involved in the operation later explained: 'Charlie seemed to be trying to set up a huge coke deal, paying Doran as a consultant to smooth things with the Medellín cartel. But he was talking in cockney rhyming slang a lot of the time, so it was impossible to be certain of anything he was saying. It was as if he was being incredibly careful not to say anything incriminating.'

4

Flushed with new funds from a number of recent drug deals, Charlie decided to splash out on a villa for himself and Pat. Charlie's friend Freddie Foreman had heard about a property on a very sought-after *urbanization* just behind Marbella and mentioned it to Charlie when they bumped into each other in a bar. Charlie and Pat immediately went to look at the detached house on the *Urbanization Montana*, directly beneath the mountains that overshadow the Costa del Sol. To the east was Marbella old town, while to the west lay the British criminal fraternity's favourite haunt of Puerto Banus. The estate itself was filled with rutted roads lined with expensive properties hidden behind high walls and security gates, and protected by surveillance cameras and burglar alarms. It was definitely not the kind of area where you'd ask your neighbour what he did for a living.

The house itself was a rather small, nondescript-looking bungalow, but it was on a superb quarter-acre plot of land just far enough back from the road to provide complete privacy. On the other side, it backed onto a small woodland area which separated the property from a new development of flats being constructed in an adjoining street. Charlie paid a bargain 12 million pesetas (£48,000) cash for the property. He knew he'd have to spend at least double that to create their dream home, so there was no chance of an early retirement quite yet. He soon announced grand plans to turn it into a palace. He told Foreman the property had plenty of scope for improvement. Intriguingly, the house was number 13 in the street, but the previous owners had refused to use the number because it was unlucky. Charlie immediately named the property 'Chequers' because, as he later explained, 'The fuckin' British government have got all my money.'

Pat later explained: 'Charlie came here to find peace. We weren't a couple who entertained or joined the so-called Costa del Crime party set, but if we saw any of the English people, it was usually just to say "Hello" while we were passing in the street. Very rarely did we go to their homes. We lived like a retired couple. Our love for the children, dogs and each other was enough.'

It was certainly true that Pat rarely went out. She preferred to watch her favourite soap operas, beamed in from the UK through their huge white satellite dish positioned next to the swimming pool. Charlie, however, was regularly spotted out and about in Puerto Banus, drinking in the Navy Bar, a block back from the harbour and frequented by a lot of the chaps.

Charlie hired a beautiful Argentinian architect called Marti Franco to help design the rebuilding of Chequers and transform it from a small, single-storey home into a mansion. A skilled artist, Charlie even provided his own sketches of how he wanted the house to look, right down to a sitting-room area filled with furniture and an expensive Chinese-style rug. Marti Franco later recalled: 'It took more than a year to rebuild the house and we completely changed the shape of it. Charles paid cash for everything direct to the builder, including my fee at the end.'

Pat was away in London during a lot of the reconstruction work, so Charlie and Marti formed a close friendship. He even admitted his criminal past to her. She later recalled: 'At the beginning, I did not know who Charlie was. Then, as we became friends, he said to me, "Marti, I must tell you something before you hear it from someone else and get upset." So he told me he robbed a train and was put in jail for many years. Little by little, I got to know the whole story and when I saw Charlie working on his house every day, working, working, working, I started to feel pity for Charlie. Pity, pity, pity! Poor man. Years and years of his life in prison. I felt so sorry for the man. I even asked where is the money and he said it had all gone. I'm sure he was telling the truth. He said he gave a lot of the money to friends and they took it. But he made a lot of jokes about it. I'd always thought criminals were supposed to be terrible people, but he wasn't like that.'

Marti continued: 'Charles was always very polite, but he was clearly a workaholic. He was always thinking about what to do next. He told me he'd paid his dues in jail and had left England because every time anything happened he was blamed for it. He didn't mention any business he was involved in. He loved that house and made it clear he'd never sell it. In many ways, it was his life.'

Marti met Charlie's three daughters when they stayed at Chequers in the late summer of 1987. 'Charlie, Pat and their daughters all came over to my house for dinner. He was a good father and they clearly loved him.' But Marti was struck by how rarely Pat went out. 'She was always at home and didn't even go out to buy a newspaper. I thought that was a bit strange.'

Marti Franco insists she never met any of Charlie and Pat's friends visiting from England. 'They never talked about anything in the past. Pat was a very straight lady while Charles was much more mischievous, an amusing man with a good sense of humour. Naughty, but very nice. He made a lot of jokes. He was a professional criminal trying to run two lives at the same time. It must have been difficult.'

Charlie employed half a dozen builders full-time for many months and spent considerable sums of money renovating and rebuilding Chequers to transform it from a pokey, little bungalow into a garish hacienda, complete with gold-plated taps and Portugese pink marble in all the bathrooms. Hand-painted bone china ornaments and expensive imported Chinese rugs were everywhere. Another entire floor was put on the one-storey property featuring a turret with windows inlaid with coloured glass and two balconies.

At one end of the sitting room area was a wall covered entirely by a mirror, stretching from the floor to the ceiling, with a little shelf running across it. Underneath the shelf was a small button, which released a secret door down to a specially built basement. It was a small room about eight foot by six foot and not dissimilar to many prison cells Charlie had called home over the years. Charlie had a five-foot-high safe set into the wall of the basement and built a tiny window just large enough to give him a view of anyone approaching the house. Charlie's pride and joy, however, was a two-foot-thick, six-foot-high stone wall which he personally helped to build around the property.

Marti Franco drew up special plans for the basement room at Chequers. She recalled: 'Sure, I designed the cellar in the house. He never said why he needed it. Just for his things, like everybody else. It had a secret door which seemed kinda strange, but people have a right to do what they want in their own house and I never questioned it because I sort of knew it was his business and not mine.'

Despite the move to Spain, Charlie remained a creature of south London. No matter how successful he became or how his image developed on the Costa del Crime, his habits and attitudes came from back home. On the streets of south London, it was one thing to grow rich as a powerful villain with a reputation to match, but when Charlie sought respectability, his more polite neighbours in Marbella tried to avoid the issue. To them, Charlie was obviously a criminal who was still actively pursuing what he knew best. They soon noticed the late-night comings and goings at Chequers. Some had even heard about the secret basement he'd had built in the house where he no doubt stored all his ill-gotten gains. As one old associate said: 'You can't take the villain out of a south London character like Charlie, otherwise you're left with nothing.'

Those who visited Chequers said there were other 'strange' features in the house. One of Charlie's guests recalled: 'Charlie had the main bathroom floor raised above the level of the bedroom as if he kept something underneath it. The fireplace was also much deeper than the actual fire area, but that might just have been down to the design.'

Meanwhile, Charlie's good friend Mickey Green just couldn't seem to stay out of the headlines. In 1987, he was named by Spanish police as the criminal mastermind behind an extensive drugs network known as The Octopus. In a series of raids on Green and his associates in Spain, cannabis worth £2 million, 11 yachts and powerboats, a Rolls-Royce, a Porsche and five other cars were seized, and six Britons arrested. Green was also wanted for questioning about another VAT gold fraud, similar to the one Charlie had almost been imprisoned for in 1983. Green had been tipped off about the police raid and managed to flee the Costa del Sol before he could be arrested. Charlie was soon in touch with Green's people, offering to take all his boats and cars off his hands.

Charlie had always made it clear he'd rather die than face incarceration in a Spanish prison. He'd heard from Green how horrendous conditions were in places like Barcelona's notorious Modelo Prison where you were locked up virtually 24 hours a day with a bottle of water and little else. There was no daylight and no noise; not even a stone bench or a hole in the ground to use as a toilet.

When Mickey Green turned up in Paris a few months after his earlier disappearance from Spain, Interpol were alerted and French police swooped on his expensively decorated Left Bank apartment where they found gold bullion and cocaine, but no Mickey Green. He was later sentenced to 17 years in jail in his absence for possessing drugs and smuggling. Green's next stop was California, where he rented Rod Stewart's mansion under an alias. A few months later, FBI agents knocked down the front door of that house as he was lounging by the pool and arrested him. Green was put on a flight bound for France and that jail sentence, but managed to get off when the plane made a stopover at Ireland's Shannon Airport. Using an Irish passport, he slipped past Customs and headed for Dublin, where he had many contacts. Green then took full advantage of the weak extradition laws between Eire and France at the time and settled in Dublin. He was certainly living up to his nickname, 'The Pimpernel'.

* * *

Dawn streaked the Mediterranean with crimson as Charlie's white Toyota nosed its way through the back streets of Puerto Banus. It had been another heavy night and he was on his way home to Pat and the dogs. By this time, Charlie rarely attended business meetings on the Costa del Sol without being armed. His favourite stunt, just to make sure those present knew he was packing, was to greet his associates with a hug and let the metal weapon press into them. More often than not, it had the desired effect. At the time, Charlie kept at least three handguns in his basement, plus a sawn-off shotgun, which he'd been looking after for another criminal who'd got a five-year stretch back in London.

Charlie had admitted to one pal that he wished Spain was still ruled by the dictator Franco; the police had more authority then and the bad pennies never had a chance to develop into deadly criminals. Charlie, like thousands of British expatriates, was feeling the impact of a free, more liberal Spain. Of course, he hadn't retired to southern Spain to bask in the 320 days of sunshine the region can boast nor enjoy a peaceful life, but the problems he was starting to encounter with other criminals did make him wonder if it was all really worthwhile.

Charlie was caught up in the growing pains of an infant democracy. Sure, the living was easy amid the white-washed villas overlooking a rippling blue sea, and the wine and food remained cheap. The twentieth century, however, was moving on at such a startling pace that the entire area was threatening to turn itself into a seedy, crime-riddled version of Los Angeles, with appalling traffic problems and a bunch of psycho-bunny criminals on virtually every street corner.

Naturally, Charlie didn't see himself in that category. As far as he was concerned, he was a businessman doing what he did best. He didn't want to step on other people's toes; he just wanted to invest his money in shipments of whatever, then reap his reward for taking such big risks. The property sharks, drug dealers and bank busters showing up on his doorstep in paradise were an irritation. The old boys from back home were fine, but some of the newer faces really got on his nerves. He could even sympathise with local government officials who hated the label 'Costa del Crime'. Charlie wanted to maintain a low profile and any adverse publicity was certainly no good for his business.

He was particularly outraged by the way petty crime was creeping into local society: muggings were now commonplace in Marbella; burglary was so rife that anyone in a detached property was advised to keep dogs *and* a decent burglar alarm with connections to the nearest police station (Charlie naturally chose just to have dogs!). Add to this potent mix the fact that some of the scumbags Charlie was having to deal with would rob their own granny as soon as look at her and it's no wonder he began to feel a little paranoid about life in Spain. 'It's getting bad out here. The police need to sort out all this street crime,' Charlie told one old pal, without a hint of irony in his voice.

At least Charlie kept a lower profile than most other underworld figures residing on the Costa del Crime. The Spanish and English press had branded criminals Freddie Foreman, Ronnie Knight, John Mason, Ronnie Everett and Clifford Saxe as 'The Famous Five' because of their alleged links to the Security Express heist back in 1983. Charlie had tasted fame after the Great Train Robbery and knew it was short-lived and annoyed the police so much that they made even more effort to catch you.

One of Charlie's favourite off-the-beaten-track restaurants was Venta

Los Pacos, just down the hill from Chequers on the N340 main coast road. The restaurant was always packed with Spaniards enjoying loud conversation and numerous bottles of wine. Charlie's Spanish wasn't good, but he could just about communicate in restaurants. Pat was different: she didn't like this or most of the restaurants Charlie took her to. She didn't like foreign food and preferred it when Charlie cooked some meat on the barbeque and rustled up one of his finest mixed salads.

One popular watering hole with the chaps was Silks restaurant in Puerto Banus, which was run by ex-British, European and Commonwealth light-heavyweight boxing champion Eddie Avoth. When one young London face dared to barge his way into Silks without a booking, Freddie Foreman and a few others had sorted out the situation within minutes. The young hoodlum ended up in hospital, but Charlie avoided any direct involvement in the incident, preferring to keep a low profile as usual.

★ ★ ★

There were other, bigger problems looming for Charlie, though. Along with many other older criminals, he'd discovered that getting high made the night go with a certain bang. He'd broken the golden rule and started sampling the produce himself. However, unlike younger people discovering drugs for the first time, Charlie and many of the other middle-aged British gangsters in Spain were so flush with cash and had such easy access to drugs that they didn't just sample the produce, they consumed it by the bucketload.

Charlie was soon chairing meetings to discuss drug deals and then pulling out bags of cocaine and inviting everyone in the room to take a snort. 'Charlie wouldn't touch the stuff when he first came on the scene and that made some of the chaps a bit nervous,' explained one of his old friends. 'Then one day, this mouthy villain says to Charlie, "How do I know you ain't rippin' us off? You won't even try it yerself." So Charlie chops out a line and off he goes. Trouble was, he got a bit hooked on the stuff.'

Meetings to discuss new shipments of drugs were often reduced to hyped-up bartering matches where nothing much got achieved except greedy cokehead gangsters hoovering up massive lines of marching powder. Consuming large quantities of cocaine naturally didn't help Charlie's respiratory problems, the result of his emphysema.

By the mid-'80s, the use of cocaine had become so flagrant in the nightclubs of Marbella and Puerto Banus that it was taken for granted most people were using it. Charlie – once completely anti-drugs – was regularly starry-eyed and dry-mouthed, just like everyone else. He even laughed at his own expense when one wisecracking crook asked him, 'Do you want some Charlie, Charlie?'

Some characters were so blatant they'd snort the drug in the middle of a restaurant or club, then get abusive if the management complained. The sight of three or four hefty faces disappearing into the lavatory was commonplace. About the only time cocaine wasn't on the menu was when the chaps took their wives to Freddie Foreman's Eagles Country Club, near Puerto Banus, for a roast beef Sunday lunch. Another place Charlie liked to go during the day was Banana Beach, a *chiringuito* (beach bar) in Marbella where many Brits went to watch English football on satellite TV.

Charlie frequently stayed up all night drinking and snorting cocaine before rolling back home in the early hours, telling Pat he'd been involved in a heavy business meeting. She must have known he was lying, but chose not to confront him. Charlie never once discussed drugs with Pat, but told her he still intended to retire sooner rather than later.

For the moment, Charlie was right in the firing line; buying shipments of cocaine from the Medellín cartel and then arranging to have them smuggled out of northern Spain along the European pipeline via Holland to the UK. This highly lucrative operation meant Charlie was spending an increasing amount of time on planes or waiting at airports. He even admitted to a pal that things got so hectic that at one stage, he found himself waking up in a plane, after a brief sleep, and forgetting where he was heading. Charlie always travelled on a false passport and went through them at a rate of one every six months at a cost of £3,000 each.

Charlie must have known it was unwise to start taking cocaine himself. Few of the Colombian cartel members he dealt with ever touched coke. One of Charlie's most important South American contacts called it 'poison' and refused to enter into anything more mind altering than a glass of beer. The Colombians particularly disapproved of using the drug during business meetings.

Some of Charlie's associates in Spain say that his cocaine habit made him more short tempered and definitely affected his judgement. One night, Charlie accused his smuggling team of disloyalty when they were together in a clip joint in Puerto Banus. 'It's all going fuckin' bad on us,' he ranted. 'There's no fuckin' loyalty. You lot think I'm just a stupid old man.'

Meanwhile, Charlie continued playing the role of gracious host to regular visitors from London. His old mate Jimmy Rose returned on at least three occasions as well as some other familiar faces from south London, including his old Great Train Robber pal Buster Edwards. The arrival of such characters often heralded a bevvy of beautiful women to act as 'entertainment'.

That's when Charlie used a secret and notorious club specially set up by British criminals on the Costa del Sol to supply reliable prostitutes. Nicknamed the Wooden Horse Club, some of the girls who worked there also acted as drug couriers or helped to launder cash. Even undercover British police detectives working in the area had been known to pay for sex provided by the club. One villan, who was a regular at the Wooden Horse, explained: 'It was a bit like the Masons – only we were not coppers or shopkeepers and we had a lot more to spend.' Popular girls were often circulated amongst members and orgies were held in specially rented houses up in the hills behind Marbella.

The main escort services on the Costa del Crime advertised in the biggest selling English-language newspaper, *Sur In English*, and often after consuming their first line of the day, visiting criminals would be on the phone calling for the company of women. They usually preferred English girls, who'd charge between £40 and £80 an hour, starting with a blow job and moving through a list of sex acts that would test most people's physical endurance. When hookers arrived to meet Charlie and his pals, their eyes would feast on the cocaine piled high on tables. Then they'd usually call up their agency bosses and tell them they were going off duty, and would stay for as long as their client wanted. Charlie sometimes flew into Malaga Airport and dialled in an instant order for two girls to come over and service him at a nearby hotel.

The women would be wined and dined as well, usually in Puerto Banus, where dozens of expensive restaurants lined the waterfront and overlooked multi-million-pound yachts and luxury cars. Some of the British criminals at that time even had marriage-breaking affairs with hookers, who then went on to become their wives.

Charlie was already involved with a North African woman, whom he'd met initially through an escort service but who'd also turned out to have good contacts in Colombia. The two formed a close friendship for more than a year and Charlie even allowed the woman to stay in an apartment he owned in Puerto Banus. It was allegedly a very fiery relationship, though, punctuated with huge rows in public places during which she often threatened to tell the police about his activities.

Charlie was so far managing to balance drugs, sex and a vast input of cash with creditable panache. The Colombians seemed happy enough in their dealings with him. He had a reputation as a smart, reliable yet tough operator, but they suspected he might not be spending or saving his money wisely and the Colombians believed that the weakest link in the cocaine trade was always money.

Around this time, Charlie was introduced to a local nightclub entertainer called Mel Williams, a singer who'd lived on the Costa del Sol for more than ten years. Williams immediately asked Charlie if he could give him a quote for a book he was writing about his show-business adventures in Spain. Charlie's reply summed up the way he felt about his most famous criminal episode when he muttered, 'I wish the fuckin' train hadn't stopped.' When fellow train robber Gordon Goody was asked a similar question by Williams, his reply echoed Charlie's sentiments. Goody told Williams: 'The mailbag hanging up in this bar probably brings in more money.'

According to Williams, Charlie was extremely careful about who he talked to, only socialising with people he already knew. Williams says he didn't say much unless someone went up and talked to him specifically.

One of Charlie's criminal associates in Spain provided a remarkable interview, recorded on tape, which confirms much of what Charlie was up to in Spain. The source explained: 'The reason Charlie came here in the first place was because bank robbing was over. Drugs were the thing. He got himself a fancy pad, but he had to sustain it. Charlie started with an introduction to a third party, someone who was already in the game with contacts in Morocco and South America. Initially, it was small scale with another dealer under an umbrella. Charlie had to prove he was reliable and so he was put to the test. Holland was the European transit centre, so he had to go there to smooth things over.

'At the beginning, he financed the deals only partly himself. A classic example would be when he put up £50,000 and made £200,000 back. He'd give the £50,000 to a guy who gets his hands dirty by dealing direct. These fellas are called the "technicians". I know Charlie eventually got a share in a transport company near Estepona. He also paid to have puff stored in small coastal resorts between Marbella and Fuengirola, in villas rented for three months near the sea. As a front, there was even a typical family renting it for their hols, complete with kids playing in the pool.

'Many officers in the Guardia Civil were on the payroll. I remember one time we even took photos of the police helping carry bales of hash from a boat on the beach into the back of a four-wheel drive. They didn't mind posing. The villas had to always be close to the beach. Places like Cabopino and Elviria just east of Marbella were perfect. You needed a garage, a house with gates and a driveway. You could store between one and five tonnes of hash in a double garage. When it leaves the farmer in Morocco, it lies on the beach over there for a while. Then a separate team called *rancheros*, specialist Spanish motorboat drivers, in very fast powerboats, pick it up and bring it here. But it was great out here back then; everyone turned a blind eye on the Costa del Sol. The Spanish police didn't even view pot as anything serious. Five years was all they'd give you.

'In Amsterdam, transactions were made and money was handed over immediately. Charlie used to send one of his guys – a bagman – to pick up the cash to pay the lads in Amsterdam, so that all the shipments could get through without any hassles. The only thing to worry about after that was laundering the cash, but it was very easy to launder money back then. There were banks in Gibraltar where no questions were ever asked. I know one time Charlie turned up with half a million at a bank and no one cared. The Spanish had a fascination with the black economy because they have always been very suspicious of banks. Most locals used to keep their money under the mattress. And you could buy any property you wanted with cash back then and no one batted an eyelid.

'Another good way of laundering money was through selling second-hand German cars. Mercedes, Audis and BMWs were traditionally much cheaper in Germany than in Spain, so Charlie coughed up some cash for his boys to go over to buy three or four cars, all perfectly legal, and then drive them back here and flog them for a healthy profit. Charlie and some of the other London firms out here also bought houses and flats just on plan, then sold them on before they were actually built.'

Charlie's associate explained what each member of the team specialised in: 'Transport was separate and Jimmy Rose was the main man for that. Then you'd have the packer who'd fit the stuff in the vehicle. Charlie used one particular firm who had a canning machine in a garage and they'd put kilos of cocaine in tins labelled "canned tomatoes".

'Charlie was eventually turning a deal round every six weeks, so he was making a lot of wedge. There's no real link between pot and dickie [cocaine], but with Charlie he sort of progressed into coke. That's when people started coming to him saying they had deals for him. In them days, the profit on coke was £50,000 a kilo. A crate of coke would hold 20 kilos. That's £1 million clear profit. He trebled his money easy, but often it was much easier to deal in smaller quantities. Mind you, a crate of coke is a far sight easier to hide than the equivalent in puff, which is a two-ton truckload.

'We all knew Charlie was obsessed with dealing direct with the Colombians. We all thought he was fuckin' mad because they're right evil bastards, but Charlie didn't scare easy and he was after the big money. Charlie was back and forth to Amsterdam as well. He knew how important it was to keep those characters happy. Roy Adkins was overseeing everything that went through Holland on behalf of that evil bastard The Preacher [Bruinsma]. The blokes in Holland saw themselves as the account managers in a sense. Charlie was determined to squeeze at least a 50 per cent profit for himself out of every deal by buying coke direct, but he often didn't seem to appreciate that the middleman was worth his fee because he had to pay government bribes, police, transport. Often, Charlie really pushed his luck. He even had an apartment locally which was always kept empty with a false passport in case he had to do a quick runner. He never used bodyguards because he reckoned all they did was attract more trouble.'

The smuggling team member said it made good sense to be based in the Marbella area. He explained that it was like the upmarket crime centre, while Fuengirola and Torremolinos further down the coast were full of lowlife criminals. He continued: 'It's like the difference between the Old Kent Road and Knightsbridge. All the big deals happen in Marbella. Colombians, Russians, Irish; they're all here. These guys are like managing directors of companies. They walk around in suits, drive classy cars.'

He went on to explain they would often meet to do deals at places like the terminal at Malaga Airport, or one of the hotels nearby which rented out conference rooms by the hour. He said that Charlie even met a few of the chaps in the Directors Institute on Pall Mall, reinforcing their image of themselves as legitimate business-people, no different from the chairmen of multinational organisations.

Charlie's friend claimed the IRA were also active in Spain during the late 1980s. 'They were quite open. They stayed in hotels. Often they'd come here on holiday with their wife and kids and then pop down for a meeting with Charlie. But ETA were the big boys on the

Costa del Sol. They expected and got a piece of everything that went through their territory in northern Spain. They're much worse than the IRA. I know all this because I was in prison with a couple of ETA blokes and they said they had direct links to the Colombian cartels. Those ETA guys used to joke about all the bodies of the two-timing drug dealers they'd dumped in the mountains just behind Charlie's house.'

5

In the summer of 1987, law enforcement agencies intercepted telephone calls from Charlie's home to Florida and London, which led them to believe he was financing a huge cocaine shipment from South America. Still, Charlie was nothing if not cautious. He was extremely polite and only occasionally pulled any of his trademark wisecracks. He also spoke softly and calmly during most phone conversations, sometimes even slipping into cockney rhyming slang to confuse anyone who might be listening. Ultimately, Charlie's phone calls revealed he was arranging meetings in various parts of the world and, as one Customs officer commented, 'You can't nick someone for getting on an aeroplane.'

That same agent, who heard this and many of the surveillance tapes, later recalled that Charlie sounded like a pushy businessman working on his investments, or a company chairman keeping an eye on his empire. Whenever people called Charlie for decisions, he usually responded very calmly and swiftly. As the authorities continued to listen in, it became increasingly clear he was running a substantial drugs-smuggling empire.

The surveillance tapes also revealed Charlie's opinions of some of his criminal associates, and occasionally cast some suspicion that beatings, or worse, were being authorised in carefully constructed codes so as to confuse potential eavesdroppers.

When Medellín cartel chief-of-staff Carlos Lehder was arrested in Colombia and extradited to the States in the middle of 1987, it meant Charlie would have to deal more frequently with Lehder's crazy billionaire boss, Pablo 'El Doctor' Escobar. Charlie contacted middleman Brian 'The Professor' Doran in Colombia and asked if he could organise another meeting with Escobar. Doran warned Charlie that Escobar had become much more erratic since his last visit to Medellín, but Charlie wasn't put off.

Charlie's meeting with Escobar in Medellín in the summer of 1987 further convinced the DEA to step up its joint surveillance operation on Charlie and his British criminal associates on the Costa del Sol. At that time, the DEA in Colombia were using a number of Beechcraft light airplanes, which closely resembled standard two-prop commercial planes, equipped to carry six passengers. They were in fact spy planes, crammed with state-of-the-art electronic eavesdropping and direction-finding equipment. On board, operators worked at computers set up for listening once the planes had reached an altitude of between 20,000 and 25,000 feet.

The DEA confirmed Charlie's meeting with Escobar in Medellín through their agents on the ground rather than their eavesdropping equipment in Colombia. A later phone conversation between Doran and Charlie, however, included the following:

> Charlie: 'If you get this deal firmed up, I can find a home for it all.'
> Doran: 'Look, Chas, I can get you any amount you want. That's not the problem.'
> Charlie: 'What d'you mean?'
> Doran: 'The people out here don't like the idea of you changing the system.'
> Charlie, speaking quietly: 'Fuck the system.'

Law enforcement agents who were listening were astonished by Charlie's bravado. 'I remember thinking, he must be mad,' commented one UK Customs officer when he heard excerpts from the surveillance tapes. 'I really thought to myself, this bloke's got a death wish. You don't just walk into Colombia, bypass everyone, buy a mountain of coke and walk out again with it in your pocket. It's just not the way things are done out there.'

Law enforcement officials then switched their focus to Charlie's recent financial transactions. They turned up bank accounts everywhere from Gibraltar to the Cayman Islands, but where did all the cash come from? 'At first, we wondered if he was maybe fronting all this up for another, even richer villain,' explained a UK Customs source, 'but as we started to track his finances we realised he was heavily re-investing his own profits.'

Soon after arriving back in Spain, Charlie got a call via a translator from Pablo Escobar who came on the phone with his favourite phrase and standard greeting '*Que mas, caballero?*' (What's happening, man?)

Charlie later told a friend that Escobar had warned him that DEA agents might be on his tail, but Charlie didn't believe he was a big enough fish to warrant around-the-clock surveillance. Charlie had no idea that he'd already had one close shave with a woman drugs courier he'd used a few months earlier. She'd offered information about Charlie to British Customs after losing her position following an incident in a bar when he came on to her. Law enforcement agencies had considered her information to be so tainted that it was not even referred to in Charlie's file.

However, at this time Charlie undoubtedly thought someone was keeping tabs on him because he began using a special scanner to check for listening devices in phones or rooms he was using. His regular cocaine binges also helped fuel huge bouts of paranoia. The fatal cocktail of adrenalin and narcotics seemed about to implode.

6

Charlie's globetrotting exploits should have had a serious impact on his home life – he and Pat virtually never went out together by this stage – but as one neighbour later explained: 'Pat was not the sociable type and the longer they stayed in Spain, the less she seemed to go out.' It could be said that Pat had almost cocooned herself inside Chequers to block out what her husband was really up to. Pat had also long since given up asking Charlie awkward questions about his criminal activities.

One of the few occasions Charlie and Pat did go out as a couple was to Security Express robber Ronnie Knight's wedding reception, held on a baking-hot Saturday in June 1987 at a Marbella beachside restaurant called El Oceano. Sue was his second wife, his first being *Carry On* star Barbara Windsor. At midnight, a firework display with the words 'Ron' and 'Sue', surrounded by sparkling pink Catherine wheel hearts, dazzled in the moonlit sky. Everyone who was anyone on the Costa del Sol was there, including Freddie Foreman and his family, and Security Express suspects Ronnie Everett, John Mason and Clifford Saxe. Jimmy Hussey, another Great Train Robber, was also there. Many of the guests drew the line at posing for wedding day snaps, though; at least four of them were on the Spanish police's latest list of more than thirty Spanish-based Brits wanted in the UK.

Across the street in unmarked cars, members of Scotland Yard's Flying Squad indiscreetly watched and photographed all of the guests going in and out of the restaurant. Fleet Street was also out in full force, with long-range telephoto lenses spying from motor launches. An overhead helicopter whirled away as it circled the reception area. Charlie and Pat didn't stay long, although Charlie did stop and have a chat with old friend Brian Wright. Wright advised Charlie to watch his back when dealing with 'Mad Mickey' Blackmore and Roy 'The Lump' Adkins, the two Brits working for Klaas 'The Preacher' Bruinsma in Amsterdam.

One of the most senior drugs investigators within UK Customs during the 1980s revealed in November 2003 that the organisation was working hard on Brian Wright in the '80s and that Charlie Wilson kept 'popping up' in Spain and sometimes the UK, as well as on trips to Colombia. 'We could see what was happening with Charlie,' he said, 'but until we had some concrete evidence it was difficult to even contemplate an arrest. You can't nick someone for guilt by association.'

After reading the extensive US and UK surveillance reports on Charlie, he also commented that Charlie 'was up to his neck in drug dealing throughout this period'. He goes on: 'We mapped his movements across the world. He only went to Spain in the first place because he thought there would be less heat on him from the law. I was on four different drugs seizures in Pakistan at the time and during one of them we nicked two Brits – a minder and a drugs courier – well known to Charlie and many of the dodgy characters down on the Costa del Sol. Neither of them said much, but when I traced back their movements to a hotel in Rawalpindi, Pakistan, I found that a man whom I believe now to have been Charlie Wilson was also staying there at the same time. The funny thing is that I wasn't even after him myself. I just knew his name was linked with another Customs investigation and then up he pops like a bad penny.'

The Customs source further explained: 'This was much more likely to be heroin than cannabis because Rawalpindi is the jumping-off point for all heroin in the region. Charlie's appearance in Pakistan fitted in perfectly with his movements and activities at that time. He'd definitely stepped up a gear in Spain and was trying to be one of the big boys. The DEA had a man inside the Medellín cartel at the time and he was listening to everything that was said, and Wilson's name came up regularly.'

Despite the surveillance operation on Charlie and others on the Costa del Crime, law enforcement agencies failed to uncover Charlie's own contacts inside the ultra-secret and hugely important NCIS – the National Criminal Intelligence Service – a UK police organisation set up in the late 1980s with a staff of 500 and an annual budget of £25 million. The unit's job was to gather intelligence on serious organised British criminals like Charlie and to also coordinate work between Customs and police agencies. Anyone working at NCIS also had access to reports from Interpol and sometimes even MI5. Charlie claimed to one criminal associate in Spain that he had a tame NCIS detective prepared to give him the nod on any relevant inquiries that might have targeted him. Unfortunately for Charlie, the DEA and UK Customs had chosen not to reveal the full extent of their surveillance operation to either the British or Spanish police, so he never realised just how closely he was being watched.

So, for the moment, Charlie and his powerful criminal pals continued to thrive in Spain. The government in Madrid was still under pressure to clean up the Costa del Crime fraternity, whose presence gave the impression Spain provided a no-questions-asked safe haven for wealthy crooks on the run. Spanish laws, however, were complicated and open to abuse. In theory, a foreigner could be expelled if he'd served more than a year's imprisonment in another country or if his presence was an embarrassment to a nation considered friendly, but in reality the Spanish only really required foreigners living in their country to have a genuine up-to-date passport to remain there.

There were incidents on the Costa del Sol which should have served as a warning to Charlie that Spain was no longer the easy-going place it once was. The authorities were fed up with the area's image as a haven for British criminals and they didn't like the way many of them were openly laundering their money in Gibraltar either.

A new Spanish police crackdown in late 1987 led to the dismantling of two British drug firms in less than a week. That coincided with the arrival of 20 senior detectives to boost the Spanish crime squad on the coast. These raids were small fry, though, compared to what Charlie and his friends were up to.

The authorities' number one priority was to break up the big syndicates handling the tens of millions of pounds worth of hashish and cocaine which were arriving by sea and air before being transferred by road to Britain and the rest of Europe. Up to that point in 1987, an anti-drug offensive codenamed Operation South had netted nearly 35 tonnes of resin and some top-grade cocaine, but police openly admitted this was less than one-tenth of the drugs being smuggled through Spain.

Charlie learnt from a tame Spanish policeman that local officers had been ordered to step up the surveillance of various British criminals, including himself. They'd been told to pounce on the slightest infringement of the regulations. Charlie also knew that two-man teams of British policemen continued to turn up on the Costa del Crime with specific targets, one of which would undoubtedly have been him.

One member of Charlie's smuggling gang who was interviewed in November 2003 said: 'Then we started to hear about the Sceptics [Yanks] being down here. It wasn't just the DEA either. There was a CIA presence on the Costa del Crime because they were watching the IRA and ETA. There were a lot of Libyans around as well. I heard the CIA and maybe even MI6 were allowing things to happen, killings and stuff, if it suited them. Those spooks are more evil than any crims or normal coppers. The governments involved must have known what was happening but did nothing to stop it because they didn't care if a terrorist or a drug dealer got killed. We were just vermin to them. Charlie was getting himself sucked into something much bigger than he realised.

'Then, some heavy faces came knocking on his door after hearing how well he was doing and wanting to invest in his operation. That was the last thing Charlie wanted, but what could he do? So he takes their money and gives them a fat return two or three weeks later. Then he prays they won't come back for a while. I dunno what happened after that.'

Charlie's only place of refuge from the big, bad world of organised crime was Chequers, his now fully modernised hacienda, overshadowed by those vast mountains. Pat was always so relieved to see Charlie home in one piece. She had begged him to slow down and start enjoying a more simple life with her and their dogs. Their daughters were settled back in the UK with their own families, by now; Charlie was a grandfather in his mid-50s, not a young hood out on the streets of south London. Pat knew that he still constantly worried about money, but surely they didn't need that much to live on now it was just the two of them?

Charlie Wilson remained a driven man, however. Before, he had a big family he felt obliged to provide for; now, it was mainly about pride and greed. He loved the freedom that money gave him and he didn't want to give up that lifestyle; the women, the booze, even the drugs. He loved ducking and diving, buying and selling shipments, landing a big property deal. All of it gave him that buzz he still desperately needed. It would never match that feeling of grabbing those sacks of money from inside the train, but Charlie was hooked on it all the same.

For the first time in his life, he was starting to really feel his age, thanks to the emphysema that was creeping up on him. By early 1988, Charlie's breathing difficulties had become so accute he was losing his breath climbing the stairs at Chequers. Pat was so concerned she persuaded Charlie to see a specialist in London on his next trip to the UK. Charlie was told there was no cure, although he was prescribed an inhaler similar to those given to asthma sufferers. Charlie hated the contraption and rarely used it, except when no one was looking. He found it difficult to accept that here he was, a well-toned man in his 50s, struggling like an 80 year old to get up a few stairs.

His illness became a catalyst for his work aspirations. He started to fear that his days might be numbered so he tried to earn even more money before it was too late. One of his oldest friends later commented that he had become 'reckless . . . as if he didn't care any more'.

In 1988, Charlie's close friend Brian Wright was named at the Old Bailey as having offered a £20,000 bribe to a jockey to throw a race at Cheltenham. In court, gentleman jockey Jamie Osborne said he assumed Wright was behind it because 'he was somebody who had been connected with things . . . that were corrupt'. Osbourne later insisted he did not take the money. By this time, Wright was betting between £50,000 and £100,000 on fixed races. In Spain, Charlie met a number of jockeys who regularly visited Wright at his house in Sotogrande, just a few miles up the coast from Marbella, often with their airfares paid and an £18,000 Rolex as a gift from the grateful Wright. Others were supplied with drugs and women, plus the occasional brown envelope stuffed with cash.

In the racing world, Wright – now nicknamed 'The Milkman' because he 'always delivered on time' – was known as a man of enormous charm, wit and generosity, with connections everywhere. Then again, he could afford to be kind with a personal fortune estimated at more than £20 million and numerous luxury properties across the world, including one in London in the Chelsea Harbour complex overlooking the Thames.

* * *

In the autumn of 1988, Charlie was out driving along the Marbella seafront with his North African girlfriend when he spotted an attractive British-looking blonde woman in her mid-30s walking along the promenade. 'Cheeky Charlie' slowed down alongside the woman, even though his lover was sitting next to him, and introduced himself. Her name was Georgie and she said she was on a get-away-from-it-all holiday having just fled from her lover in England.

Georgie later recalled: 'Charlie did a straight pick-up on me and at first I didn't want to know. I thought, "What the hell is this? Please go away!" but he was so charismatic, with a terrific personality, I weakened and we all met for a drink together. I even gleaned from him that he was running drugs from coast to coast across the Mediterranean, although I had no idea who he was at first. He had a very strange girlfriend who was a drugs runner from Marbella, but they were good fun, amusing and friendly and, in a nutshell, just what the doctor ordered.'

Georgie was the daughter of Ruth Ellis, the last woman to be hanged in Britain, and she was very different from most of the women Charlie had encountered over the years. Georgie had been just three years old when her mother had been hanged in 1955 after being found guilty of the murder of her racing driver lover David Blakely. Georgie's former lovers included film idol Richard Harris and soccer star George Best.

The day after that first meeting, Charlie and Georgie embarked on an affair. She later summed up her relationship with men like Charlie by saying, 'Unfortunately, my satisfactory relationships have always been with other women's husbands. Just like my mum, I find these sort of men hard to resist. Money and success is sexually attractive to women and gangsters certainly fit the bill. Charlie took me to Marbella, to gangland paradise, and introduced me to lots of people.'

And the relationship didn't just involve sexual attraction. Georgie later recalled 'taking thousands of Irish punts stuffed under my daughter's buggy to a bank in Marbella for him'.

Georgie explained: 'The people who are supposedly evil gangsters are actually the more gentle ones. The so-called hard men aren't hard at all — they're soft as butter . . . I was 37 and he was nearly 60, but we just clicked. Everywhere we went he was so protective about me. He wasn't ludicrously possessive, but if anything had gone wrong he would have been the first one there to protect me and I liked that. Charlie was a nice, happy-go-lucky rogue with a winning smile and a great wit.' Talking about her attraction to criminals in general she added: 'I just think it's less boring than a guy who sells insurance. It's also power and sex, but it's not as simple as that. It's that you think those men will really protect you. But being with a gangster also means you have to accept certain rules. You go through the hoop. You do what you're told. Marriage to a normal man, living in suburbia with 2.3 children, would never do.'

One night in Puerto Banus, Georgie was surprised to find that Charlie had also invited his North African lover along with them. Georgie later explained that they were 'in [a bar called] Sinatra's, having drinks before we had dinner at Silks, when Chas and the girl, well oiled with alcohol, engaged in the mother and father of a row, during which he promised revenge with the loss of her beauty'. According to Georgie, the other woman 'went crazy' and threatened to go to the police and tell them about some money Charlie had hidden in his flat in Marbella. She then stormed off. Later that night, Charlie and Georgie were approaching his apartment when they spotted three police cars outside the building. Charlie told her to go off alone and that was the last time she saw him.

Georgie Ellis did later admit she was deeply frustrated by Charlie's carefree attitude towards her. She explained: 'Because a gangster's work has to be secretive you can never gain their trust or the closeness you need to keep a relationship alive. There is a price to pay for getting involved with rich and dangerous men. I was just a trophy blonde and that can have a limited appeal after a time.'

Charlie never exposed Pat to his 'other life' on the Costa del Sol, but her relatives back in London had their suspicions. In January 2004, one family member commented: 'None of us really knew what Charlie was up to. That was just the way it was back then. But Charlie didn't harm anyone who didn't deserve it. We all knew Charlie was a lady's man, there was no doubt about it, but what could we do? He loved Pat with all his heart and that's all that really mattered.'

Another relative who visited Charlie in Spain said: 'I know he kept some secrets from Pat, but that was Charlie's way. He just didn't want to hurt her.' Charlie even managed to explain away his secret apartment in Puerto Banus by telling Pat it was one of a number of properties he'd bought as investments, which, strictly speaking, was quite true.

At the same time, Charlie's emphysema was deteriorating. As Freddie Foreman explained: 'Charlie was starting to look a lot more haggard. He'd always seemed so fit and young for his age and then I heard he was struggling even to dig a flowerbed in the garden at Chequers. We were all worried about him and some of the chaps even wondered if he had cancer.'

Foreman was therefore delighted when he persuaded Charlie to attend the fully fledged world boxing-title fight he had organised on behalf of his Marbella Boxing Club. Every important face on the Costa del Crime looked set to make an appearance at the bout between Lloyd Honeyghan and Gene Hatcher for the World Welterweight title to be held on 29 August 1987. Also on the bill were the UK's finest heavyweight Frank Bruno against a relatively unknown American called Reggie Gross and another contest featuring lesser-known British heavyweight Gary Mason.

Freddie Foreman was openly hosting the bill even though he was still under investigation by police in Britain over his alleged role in the Security Express robbery of 1983. Others due at the ringside included Ronnie Knight and Clifford Saxe, plus Jimmy Hussey, Ronnie Everett and John Mason. Everett had been acquitted of murdering underworld figure Ginger Marks while Mason had been cleared of his involvement in the £8 million Bank of America raid in the late '70s.

The big night out turned into a disaster when the coast was hit by torrential rain and the main fight had to postponed until the following evening. It ended up being fought in front of a half-full stadium with Honeyghan knocking out Hatcher in the first round. Bruno won his fight with embarrassing ease and, afterwards, Charlie, Freddie and all the rest of the chaps retired to Silks in Puerto Banus to drown their sorrows.

7

Back at Chequers, Charlie generally maintained a lower profile than most other British criminals by resisting the temptation to drive around in an expensive car – always a big giveaway. One Marbella associate commented that they all wondered what Charlie did with his money, assuming he probably kept it in the safe in his secret basement.

Charlie either drove his white Toyota Corolla, which was perfect for attracting the ladies, or a beaten-up, old, red Datsun estate he called his 'workhorse', which he used to pick up building material during the reconstruction of Chequers and to take the couple's two dogs out for their daily walk.

Businessman Bernie Finch and his wife Liz moved into the house next to Chequers just a year after Charlie had bought the property. Bernie soon noticed that whenever Charlie was grafting away in the garden, he'd be dressed in shorts and a T-shirt, but at night he'd often drive off for business meetings looking like a different person in smart clothes.

Charlie also usually left the house once a day to walk the couple's dogs, either in the mountains up behind the development or down at the beach at Las Dunas between Marbella and Estepona. 'He said he could clear his brain when he was out with just the dogs,' recalled one close friend. 'He'd be out for hours, sometimes going through everything in his mind. Charlie was quite a worrier and was still obsessed with planning every deal down to the last detail.'

The Finches became close to the Wilsons through their dogs, who used to regularly jump over Charlie's beloved wall. The two couples went out for dinner several times together.

During their dinner dates, Charlie would drink wine and beer followed by a huge Spanish measure of local brandy at the end of the meal. Bernie said they were always virtually the last to leave but that that was just typical of Charlie. He was well known wherever they went, Bernie noted, recalling one instance in Marbella when Charlie bumped into a very nasty-looking American, but thankfully didn't introduce everyone.

However, there was one subject Bernie Finch quickly learned not to mention in front of Charlie – his secret basement. 'I'd heard about it from another neighbour, but when I mentioned it he went silent so I never made any jokes about it again. I was fascinated by the little window it had. Many times, I noticed the light on late at night. God knows what he was up to down there.'

Bernie also commented that Charlie seemed to do all the gardening and most of the cooking in the Wilson household, mowing the lawn and clipping everything himself, even though most people in the neighbourhood had a gardener.

Charlie also let slip that he'd travelled to a number of exotic locations around the world since moving to Spain. 'I remember Charlie going on about the aloe vera in our garden and taking a cutting of it and keeping it in his fridge. He said it had great healing powers and might help his emphysema. I asked him how he knew that, and he said he was told about it on a trip to South America. I didn't like to ask what he'd been doing there,' said Bernie.

Charlie once agreed to run Liz Finch and her elderly mother to Malaga Airport when Bernie was away, waiting happily at the airport while she said goodbye to her mother. As Liz later explained: 'Charlie didn't seem to mind at all. Most men wouldn't have wanted to just sit and wait there, but he knew I was upset because my mum was going home.'

Liz insisted on buying Charlie lunch as a thank you for taking her to the airport and cancelling a business appointment arranged for that afternoon, but at the end of the meal Charlie insisted on paying. 'Put that money away, girl, look at all these men here, they'd hang me if they saw a woman payin' for lunch,' said Charlie. Years later Liz reflected that his actions were just about kindness that day. 'There was nothing in it for Charlie. He knew I was feeling down. I think in some ways he felt more comfortable with women in general because he was so used to an all-female household,' she said.

A few months later, the Finches witnessed another example of the kind and considerate side of Charlie when their dog Toby went missing. The couple ended up sleeping on a local beach while out looking for the dog. When Charlie heard about the missing animal the next day, he insisted on driving Liz around all the places where he believed the dog might have gone. She explained: 'We even went to a local gypsy encampment which he seemed to know well. I didn't ask why. He knew all sorts of strange places. Again, there was nothing in it for him. He was just being a kind person.'

While driving around looking for the dog, Charlie turned to Liz and asked if she was afraid of him. She responded by asking why she should feel afraid of him, but then Charlie just changed the subject. Liz later said it was as if he'd wanted to tell her something, but had changed his mind at the last moment.

Later, Liz described the Costa del Sol as 'a strange place filled with all these criminals' when she was talking to Charlie, to which he replied, 'Yeah, Liz, I know exactly what you mean.'

It wasn't until months later that the Finches heard about Charlie's background at another neighbours' drinks party. Bernie explained: 'But it didn't make any difference in our attitude towards him. Charlie was a good bloke in my book. He was certainly a very good neighbour.'

Despite his problems with emphysema, Charlie still kept himself trim. 'His breathing sounded bad sometimes, but he still looked like he could handle himself,' added Bernie.

The only hint from Charlie of his own criminal connections came when the Finches went round to Chequers for a glass of wine one evening. Bernie mentioned he'd had a problem with a man in a local bar the previous evening who'd been rude to him. 'Charlie told me I should break his fuckin' legs,' recalled Finch. Just then Pat appeared at her husband's shoulder and said, 'Oh Charlie, you and yer' jokes.' That's when Bernie Finch noticed Charlie pat his nose with the tip of his finger and look right at Pat as he did it. 'I realised afterwards that was their sign to each other to be careful what they were saying,' recalled Bernie.

The dynamics between Charlie and Pat fascinated the Finches. Charlie continued to do virtually all the shopping and Pat rarely went out, even into the garden. Charlie even bought his wife most of her clothes. Bernie recalled: 'He was often popping out on his own. We wondered if Pat had agoraphobia. Then we thought it might all be a control thing. Pat was like one of those wives in the gangster films; she didn't really seem to want to know what her criminal husband was really up to.'

Charlie often used his friendly wisecracking side as a convenient shield to protect himself from the real world. Bernie never forgot the day he found a snapped-off doll's hand in the garden as he was talking over the wall to Charlie. 'I waved the hand over to Charlie in the garden and said, "Here Charlie, d'you want a hand in the garden?" and threw it at him. He loved that joke so much he never stopped going on about it for months afterwards. And he even kept the hand in a flowerbed and would wave it at me every time I passed.' Another time, Bernie spotted the now infamous hand sticking out of a flowerbed and said, 'Now look what Charlie's done with Pat – he's buried her in the garden.' Charlie doubled up with laughter.

The only other significant clue about Charlie's criminal connections came when Liz knocked on the Wilsons' front door and asked to borrow a lawn mower. A seriously overweight man in his mid-30s answered and abruptly asked her who she was, Liz recalled. An uncomfortable silence followed, which was only broken by the sound of Charlie's voice from inside the house telling him to let her in, before he appeared at the door with a huge smile on his face.

Another of Charlie's neighbours said he was introduced to that same man, who Charlie called 'Twiggy'. Charlie said he lived in a newly built block of flats nearby. 'I got the impression Twiggy worked for Charlie . . . the two men often drove off from Chequers in Charlie's Toyota,' explained the neighbour. The criminal aspect of Charlie's character also came to the surface on one occasion when he was on the phone in the garden and neighbours heard Charlie's angry voice swearing and shouting down the receiver.

There were also other days when Charlie was up at dawn, painting on an easel in his garden. One neighbour recalled: 'I watched him from our bedroom window and he seemed totally at peace with himself. He'd stand there for hours concentrating on the particular flower or bush which he was painting.'

In 1988, Charlie encountered another neighbour, an Argentinian called Fernando, leaving his home with a dog basket full of Alaskan/German Shepherd mix puppies. Fernando gave Charlie one of them. 'I knew he'd give it a good home,' he recalled. 'He was soon feeding her too much food and getting her fat, but he really loved that dog.' Charlie christened the dog Boo-Boo and the two became virtually inseparable when they were at home together.

Fernando occasionally bumped into Charlie in the nearby supermarket when he was doing his weekly shopping. Fernando also saw Charlie in Puerto Banus and heard he had business interests in Gibraltar, as well as dealing in hash and coke. But Fernando was more impressed by the little wooden house Charlie built for the dogs. Fernando also commented however that he could see in Charlie's eyes and face that he'd been in prison. 'He did not have an earring like many criminals, or tattoos. I guess that made him a professional in every sense of the word,' recalled Fernando.

8

In May 1988, three hardened south London criminals covered in tattoos and scars went on the run after beating up their guards and hijacking a prison bus en route from jail on the Isle of Wight to Blundeston Prison in Suffolk. The convicts handcuffed the prison officers together, then drove the bus to Gants Hill Tube station, situated on the edge of London's East End, before fleeing. Scotland Yard immediately issued a warning to the public to avoid them at all costs and call the police if anyone matching their descriptions was seen.

Danny 'Scarface' Roff and Billy 'Porky' Edmunds, both notorious for the violent nature of their crimes, were two of the escaped prisoners. Roff was inside for armed robbery while Edmunds had been convicted for supplying drugs and wounding. Both men eventually turned up in Holland, where they looked up fellow south Londoner Roy 'The Lump' Adkins to see if he had any work for them.

One retired Flying Squad detective, who met both Edmunds and Roff at the start of their criminal careers, recalled: 'Danny was a bad, mad bastard. A lunatic. I nicked Porky after some idiot started loosing off a fuckin' loaded .45 next to a coffee stall in Elephant and Castle. He didn't shoot anyone, but we had a look at him and he was up to all sorts of mischief. He even threatened to kill a policeman at one stage.'

Towards the end of 1988, Charlie, accompanied by two other men, flew to London and visited two banks in the West End with suitcases containing money that was later transferred to Spain. Scotland Yard were so concerned by Charlie's movements in the UK they completed complicated formalities to get a new Commission Rogatoire, a legal document signed and sealed by the Home Office, giving detectives authority to operate overseas. The document was essential because without it, no formal investigation could go ahead in Spain. Even after it had been granted, British police would still have to work under the supervision of the local force.

The objective of the Commission Rogatoire was to aid the gathering of further evidence against Charlie Wilson, Mickey Green, Tony White and others, which would mean visiting Costa del Sol banks with Spanish police. There were further claims Charlie had spent a lot of money buying at least six apartments on the Costa del Sol as 'investments'. Detectives also intended to take a look at Charlie's villa to see what he was up to.

According to one UK Customs source, while he was in London Charlie held meetings with South Americans who represented the British end of the Medellín cartel. Charlie spent one evening in the company of beautiful Colombian 'La Patrona' – Lady Boss – Luisa Bolivar, who lived in a £500-a-week apartment overlooking the Thames, complete with a driver and limo to take her to £100-a-head restaurants and all the most exclusive designer clothes stores. Luisa, at the time only in her late 20s, later brought murder and mayhem to the streets of London after another South American showed disrepect to her handsome drug baron lover. Bolivar's transformation from a prim, naive teenager, who arrived in London in 1978, to a manicured, sophisticated drug baroness was remarkable. Bolivar – who stood just a shade over five feet without her favourite strappy platforms on – rose through the ranks to become an important member of the Medellín cartel in Europe. She'd begun her career working as a mule for one of the cartel's cocaine gangs back in Colombia.

The Medellín cartel were in London primarily to act as intermediaries between drug gangs in the UK and suppliers back in Colombia, but La Patrona's work also included providing safe houses for other employees of the cartel. She remained one step ahead of the Law by moving her henchmen and teams of couriers to different addresses in the capital on virtually a weekly basis. These were the sorts of people Charlie was doing business with. It was a lot different from the good old days, but Charlie had become increasingly philosophical about the changes. 'If this is what it takes, then so be it,' he told one old friend back on the Costa del Sol.

By the end of 1988, Charlie was 56 years old and life certainly wasn't as much fun as it used to be. Many of the old familiar faces had been hounded out of Spain since the change to the extradition treaty and Charlie's initial enthusiasm about living in a sunny climate had been dampened by difficulties impinging on his business activities. He'd cleverly managed to avoid the constant media attention that followed associates like Ronnie Knight and Freddie Foreman, but the unmarked cars with men who looked like detectives still regularly turned up at the end of his street.

The British red tops projected 'Gangster Wars on the Costa del Crime' every time there was an incident in Spain. It had got so bad that Charlie – who usually read *The Sun* on weekdays – stopped reading a newspaper for the first time in his life. He even feared that press photographers at Malaga Airport might snap him as he departed and arrived back in Spain from his regular trips abroad. Yet, somehow, Charlie kept below the press radar. One friend later explained: 'Charlie was as quiet and careful as ever. Few outside his close circle of friends even recognised him because the photos used by the press were from before he was nicked for the Great Train Robbery more than 20 years earlier.'

The other reason Charlie liked to keep a low public profile was because of the constant threat of kidnappings on the Costa del Sol. One old criminal hand in Spain explained: 'There were a lot of lower end villains desperate to make a few bob and, at that time, there was a lucrative sideline in kidnapping. Most of these cases never even got to the police. What usually happened was that a rich villain got pulled by a bunch of desperadoes, a ransom of at least a hundred grand would be paid within hours and then the victim would be handed back to his family.'

Another form of 'kidnapping' took place in July 1989 when Charlie's old mate, Security Express suspect Freddie 'The Mean Machine' Foreman was asked by Spanish police to help them with their enquiries on the southern coast. He agreed to meet them in a hotel in Marbella, accompanied by his Spanish lawyer, but when Foreman's passport was found to be false it was enough to get him on a plane back to London. Foreman had been declared a *persona non grata* – an undesirable alien. Foreman and others considered his extradition nothing short of kidnap by Spanish police. Hours later, the former Krays' henchman was escorted back to London by two burly Marbella detectives to stand trial for his part in the Security Express robbery. The Spanish were sick of being derided for harbouring UK criminals and felt restricted by the strict terms of their own extradition treaty. Many of the chaps in Spain accused the police of outrageously bending the rules to get Foreman home.

However, there were other, far more cold-blooded, characters waiting to take the place of the Freddie Foremans of this world. Decades after the first British chants of *'Viva Espana'* and early-morning German sorties to bag a sun-lounger, the Costa del Sol was being invaded by the Soviet Union and other Eastern Bloc nations. The murders of a Muscovite couple and their two young children in Marbella in 1989 heightened fears amongst the old British faces that the traditional rules of engagement were about to be thrown out of the window. Gangsters from countries that many British villains couldn't even find on a map were making southern Spain their home. Interpol issued warnings that these characters were about to change the face of organised crime in Europe. Their specialities were drugs, prostitution and money laundering. One old timer on the Costa del Crime recalled: 'These people were cold, hard, ruthless bastards. They didn't care about reputations. One Russian I met said to me once: "We like to spend all our money quickly because we never know how long we're going to live."'

British criminals along the coast from Estepona to Torremolinos tried to steer clear of these villains, but they were united by their common aim – to make money from drugs. The Soviets and their Eastern European rivals were building up contacts in North Africa and South America. It was the hope within the British criminal fraternity on the Costa del Crime that they'd all shoot one another in the back.

A few small-time crooks even began turning up dead after getting too big for their boots. Take Hugh Lomax, a 31-year-old odd-job man, working for a number of British villains. He was pulled in by Spanish police on a couple of occasions before someone decided he might start blabbing, so he was taken to a field near Torremolinos and stabbed so many times it took police several days to identify his scarred and bloody body. The rules on the Costa del Crime were different from back home. Here, in the sunshine, the local police weren't that interested in the criminals' internal feuds. Their only priority was to make sure they didn't affect the lucrative tourist trade.

In the summer of 1989, Charlie's old friend master smuggler Jimmy Rose and five members of his gang, known as The Rose Organisation, were arrested by police in a massive operation codenamed Diplomat. They were caught after a container, which had been tracked from Afghanistan via the Soviet Union, was found by police following a tip-off. Hidden in sacks of liquorice was Afghan Black cannabis resin with a street value of £135 million. It was the first-ever joint operation between British Customs and their Soviet counterparts. Jimmy Rose was put under enormous pressure from authorities to name his paymasters, but, as a Bermondsey boy of the old school, Rose knew that unless he wanted to prematurely shorten his life expectancy, his lips must remain sealed.

However, over in Holland, Charlie's old prisonmate Roy 'The Lump' Adkins and his boss, the psychotic 'Preacher' Bruinsma – who even owned a £2 million yacht called the *Neeltje Jacoba* – were bitterly upset because the hash had belonged to them. Adkins was already wanted by British police over previous offences and his addiction to cocaine had turned him into, in the words of one Dutch associate, 'almost as big a monster as The Preacher'. One of Bruinsma's chief rivals had recently been found upside down in a barrel of cement, having had his penis and legs cut off while he was still alive.

Bruinsma and Adkins even suspected each other of being a grass. This bad feeling boiled over when the two men had a vicious argument in Amsterdam's most notorious sex club, Yab Yum. Shots were fired, but nobody was injured. When the police arrived at the scene, witnesses refused to say what had happened.

Refused bail and with his trial back in Britain not due until the following January, Jimmy Rose had plenty of time to think about how to reduce his sentence without risking his life in the process. There was no way he could name Adkins in open court, but maybe he could throw his name into the ring? What harm could that do? Adkins was already on the run over other incidents and details of his involvement with the drugs shipment were well known to many criminals and policemen.

But, for the moment, Jimmy Rose decided it wasn't worth upsetting the highly strung Adkins.

★ ★ ★

Back in Britain in August 1989, Charlie's old Great Train Robbery pals Tommy Wisbey and Jimmy Hussey went back to prison after being sentenced for their part in trafficking cocaine with a street value of more than £500,000. Hussey had put down a cash investment in a shipment without ever getting directly involved, but the judge effectively told him the result would have been the same.

When Charlie heard the news about Wisbey and Hussey, he thanked his lucky stars he was in Spain, where things still seemed more relaxed. He'd had enough hassles in the UK during those difficult years after he'd got out of jail. Charlie sent the two men handwritten notes, telling them to keep their spirits up, but he feared a similar term in prison would have been too much for him to handle. When former south London gang boss Charlie Richardson was arrested for allegedly trying to bring 339 lb of cocaine, plus two tonnes of cannabis worth £6 million into Southampton docks in a balsawood container, it was further proof that drugs were now the main source of income for members of the underworld in the UK.

There were other, more serious criminal developments in Spain in late 1989 when ETA announced the end of their ceasefire with the Spanish government, and the alliance between the terrorists and drug barons began to look very rocky. Explained one of Charlie's oldest friends: 'Many London villains were locked into drug deals that had to come through ETA, who then decided they wanted a bigger cut of the profits to buy even more weapons.'

When a Spanish gangster with strong links to a number of British criminals on the Costa del Sol was blown up by a car bomb in Marbella, it was seen as a deadly warning to all criminals to watch their backs when dealing with ETA. The bomb had been planted in a stolen Fiat Tipo and despite receiving on-the-spot medical attention, the victim died 30 minutes later.

In the United States, the DEA's war on drugs had persuaded a US Presidential Organised Crime Drug Enforcement Task Force to instruct the law enforcement agencies of several countries to step up their probe into a number of 'heavyweight' druglords, including Charlie and certain other British criminals on the Costa del Sol. On the basis of those findings, the Assistant United States Attorney,

Bob O'Neill, hoped there would be sufficient evidence against characters such as Tony White, Brian Wright, Micky Green and Charlie to put them before a grand jury in Florida. The next stage was to get Spanish and British police to agree to raid homes and confiscate anything that might suggest these characters had been dealing in drugs. The DEA intended to prove at least a dozen charges against the suspects, including conspiracy and money laundering as well as drug dealing.

The DEA had arrested a Colombian in Miami who was linked to 'El Doctor' Pablo Escobar and his Medellín cartel about this time. He'd thrown three British names, including Charlie's, into the ring when he was being interrogated. It was a classic move; offer up a few people *not* from your own home country and the authorities might give you a break. The DEA's prisoner stated that Charlie and the others were financing massive cocaine shipments from Colombia. The organisation had suspected there might be a Green/Wright/White/Wilson cartel, financing a group of criminals, smugglers and financiers who organised fortnightly drug deals.

In late 1989, a criminal called Michael Michael – whom Charlie met through his armed robber-turned-drug baron friend Mickey 'The Pimpernel' Green – became a Scotland Yard police informant. Michael was working as an accountant and helping to run a string of massage parlours in Britain with his common-law wife Lynn when he was arrested for a £3 million mortgage fraud. In exchange for a light eight-month prison sentence, he became a registered informant. Michael was given the pseudonym Andrew Ridgeley, after George Michael's singing partner in the pop duo Wham! Michael passed information about members of various criminal families and their activities in the UK and Spain to his handler, Detective Constable Craig Allum. Copies of Michael Michael's contact sheets (forms filed by his police handler) named Charlie Wilson, Mickey Green, Brian Wright, Tony White and numerous other UK criminals as dealing in drugs in Spain. Michael also claimed Charlie was then laundering large sums of money through a system used by Mickey Green, which included fake money exchanges in certain areas of London.

Michael himself supervised the UK distribution of massive amounts of cannabis and cocaine, much of it smuggled into the UK from a transit point in southern Spain. Cannabis resin was hidden in drums suspended inside tankers, while cocaine tended to be hidden in cars because the quantities transported were much smaller. Some drugs were even regularly hidden inside a secret compartment on a tourist coach, nicknamed the 'Magic Bus' after the song made famous by The Who.

Michael met with Charlie, Green and White on numerous occasions in Spain and at expensive hotels in London's West End. He also laundered vast sums of cash for them through a currency exchange bureau specially set up in west London. Women were usually hired as couriers to fly cash and drugs between Heathrow or Gatwick and Spain using two-week return tickets. Instead of staying, they usually returned the following day.

Michael Michael claimed he paid tens of thousands of pounds to corrupt police officers on behalf of Charlie and Mickey Green in exchange for information about other criminals and ongoing police investigations. Detectives known to have gambling or drug problems were prime targets for Charlie and Green. A bit of blackmail always worked a treat if past secrets could be exploited. Once they'd reeled in a bent detective, there was no way back for them. Like many others before and since, Charlie and Green kept asking for more information, knowing that whatever came their way could also be sold on to the highest bidder within the criminal underworld if it was of no use to them personally. With Michael Michael now working for the other side, characters like Charlie and Mickey Green needed to watch their backs.

9

In late 1989, Charlie received a call from Patty Rose, the wife of his old friend, jailed smuggler Jimmy Rose. The Roses knew Charlie well and had been to stay at Chequers. Patty wanted permission for her husband to name Roy 'The Lump' Adkins to police in the hope that he might get a lighter sentence at his trial. Charlie's initial response was not to get involved. However, when Patty explained that it wouldn't really harm Adkins because he was already on the run from British and Dutch police for other offences, Charlie promised to think it over. Charlie had a soft spot for Jimmy and Patty, and dearly wanted to help them. Rose had done him a lot of favours down the years.

Associates have always insisted Charlie would never have given Patty permission to name Adkins, especially not over the phone, since he suspected it was being tapped. But Charlie did leave a message for a well-known criminal called Eamon Evans, who was connected to Adkins on the Costa del Crime, along the lines of 'What harm could it do?' As another of Charlie's criminal associates later explained: 'It wasn't really grassing up in the true sense of the word because Adkins' activities were already well known to the police and Charlie hoped he'd understand the reasoning behind the Roses' request.'

It's alleged that a few days later, Jimmy Rose told detectives to 'talk to Roy Adkins'. Soon after that, Dutch police – acting on information from UK Customs – raided Adkins' hideout in Holland. This infuriated Adkins even though he'd fled before they turned up. He immediately connected the police raid to Charlie because of that earlier phone call to Eamon Evans.

Then, in early January 1990, Charlie got a furious call from Roy Adkins. Charlie tried to explain why Jimmy Rose had named him. 'But Adkins wouldn't have any of it. He accused Charlie of grassing him up,' one of Charlie's oldest friends on the Costa del Sol explained. The fact that Charlie and Rose were such close friends fuelled Adkins' paranoia. Charlie even tried to warn Adkins to be careful what he said in case others were listening.

A couple of days later, Jimmy Rose, his son Richard and three other men were jailed for a total of 47 years at Chelmsford Crown Court. The gang was also ordered to pay back nearly £3 million of their £7.5 million in illegal assets. It was the biggest seizure of investments, bank accounts, homes and businesses made under the fairly recently introduced Drug Trafficking Offences Act. The court heard that Jimmy Rose had set up at least six bogus companies and masterminded further plans to import cannabis resin from Afghanistan and India in cargoes of acid, bleaching powder, mango chutney and liquorice root.

Rose, by now 53, was described in court by his counsel as a 'company director', although the judge simply called him a drug baron. He was given 12 months to comply with the confiscation order or face a further 10 years in jail. It was predicted, however, that the sentence would be cut considerably on appeal because Rose had helped police by naming Adkins.

A few days after the Rose trial ended, Eamon Evans delivered a message from Adkins to Charlie saying, 'You should not have given that permission to Jimmy Rose.' 'The Lump' Adkins – sniffing grams of coke up his nose – and Klaas Bruinsma had lost a fortune when Rose and his gang were arrested with all their hash. In any case, having threatened Charlie, Adkins couldn't back down without losing the respect of the underworld. Reputations were at stake.

Law enforcement agencies from the US, UK and Spain monitored phone calls during which Adkins' threats were made to Charlie, but they chose not to step in. They had no intention of blowing their own cover until they had enough evidence to make substantial arrests.

At the end of January 1990, Charlie flew to London for another medical check-up relating to his emphysema, which had become even worse over the Christmas period, not helped by the stress Adkins was causing. Shortly after arriving in London, Charlie was contacted by Evans, who repeated the earlier threat. Charlie responded by calmly asking Evans to a lunch he was having the following day with Jimmy Rose's wife 'so you can find out what really happened'. Neither Adkins nor Evans took up Charlie's lunch invitation.

A couple of days later, Charlie was crossing Harley Street, in central London, when he noticed a man on a motorbike driving very slowly behind him. For the ten minutes which followed, the motorcyclist constantly stayed on his tail. 'Charlie didn't scare that easily, but he was pissed off with Adkins for making threats against him and reckoned the motorbike was part of it,' one friend later explained. Charlie met with one of his closest friends during that trip to London and asked him if he would have acted in the same way as he had, allowing Jimmy Rose to drop Adkins' name to police. Charlie's friend replied that he didn't think it had harmed anyone, since the law already knew what 'The Lump' was up to. Charlie told his close friend he believed Adkins would eventually calm down and the whole thing would blow over. Charlie's close friend later recalled: 'Charlie was more worried about his emphysema than Roy Adkins. Now that was *really* getting him down.'

Still in London, Charlie held a meeting with three major London criminals in a West End hotel to discuss a drug deal. Undercover police and Customs officers flooded the hotel with officers, eight at a time on round-the-clock duty, and followed the group's every move. Conversations were taped and all participants were photographed. By the end of the three-hour meeting, they concluded there was something big in the air.

The following day, Charlie was Brian 'The Milkman' Wright's guest at his private member's box at Windsor Racecourse. Wright had also persuaded his friend Roy Adkins – still wanted by British police – to attend the same meeting to sort out the problems between him and

Charlie. Rumour has it that the meeting was a disaster, Adkins and Charlie avoiding each other the whole afternoon. One source from the day at Windsor recalled: 'Adkins had wanted to have a go at Charlie there and then, but Brian Wright calmed him down. Charlie complained to Wright afterwards that Adkins' attitude was out of order. Charlie expected respect from characters like Adkins, not abuse, and he was outraged that Adkins thought he was a grass.' Adkins travelled overland to Suffolk that night where he caught a ferry to Holland, still brimming with hatred for Charlie.

The law enforcement agencies involved knew they could no longer adopt a scorched-earth policy. Taking out a few soldiers in the drug war wouldn't help them get the big players. They needed to lay the bait for Charlie and his friends in the hope they'd start making some serious mistakes, and this feud with Adkins looked like the perfect catalyst. The surveillance team on the Costa del Sol had established that Charlie was by this time using a warehouse on a brand new *poligio* (industrial estate) near Marbella as his unofficial office. They picked up simple 'overhears', snippets of information, as Charlie walked past members of the surveillance team in the street. They also followed Charlie to his house in the Urbanization Montana. They still lacked enough concrete evidence to issue arrest warrants, though.

In mid-February 1990, eavesdropping investigators established clear plans that Charlie was to import 40 kilos of cocaine and 200 kilos of cannabis resin into Spain, then move it on to Britain at high speed. One of the key figures at both ends of the deal was Brian Wright.

Then, on a warm night in late February, Charlie was seen leaving his Marbella house at four in the morning and was shadowed by two undercover policemen. They followed Charlie to the Atalaya Park Hotel on the road towards Estepona, where Charlie met Brian 'The Professor' Doran and three other South American-looking men. An anonymous couple then drove up to the same hotel and waited in their car until one of the South Americans came out. Later checks established that the couple had driven through the night from Madrid after flying in from Bogota, the Colombian capital.

The following day, someone inside Marbella Police Station told a well-known British criminal that Charlie was definitely under 24-hour round-the-clock surveillance. Alarm bells went off everywhere from Madrid to Colombia. The last thing anyone wanted was to deal with a man who was being shadowed by the authorities. The surveillance team even pulled back from Charlie and left him alone in the hope that the Colombians would still agree to deal with him.

Charlie himself was hopping mad when he was told he was under constant surveillance. In Holland, the paranoid Roy 'The Lump' Adkins believed Charlie was trying to set everyone up for a fall. He convinced himself that Charlie was deliberately exposing himself to prevent Adkins carrying out his threat to kill him and he remained convinced that Charlie was a grass.

Back at Chequers, the stress of the previous few weeks had led to a considerable deterioration in Charlie's health. He'd stopped taking cocaine a few months earlier after being warned that it would make his lungs even worse. Neighbour Bernie Finch recalled: 'I remember seeing Charlie struggling to lift a barrow because he was so short of breath. He definitely hadn't been like that when we first moved in. He said he'd been back to the UK, but there wasn't much they could do to make it any better. I could see it in his eyes that he didn't really believe any treatment was helping. Charlie even tried a herbal tea cure. But we all knew he was clutching at straws. After January, there was a definite deterioration. He lost a lot of weight very quickly. He was coughing all the time and seemed very short of breath.'

The Finches noticed that Charlie and Pat rarely ventured out anywhere together after Christmas 1989. Bernie said: 'It was as if they were virtually trapped in that house. We tried to get them to come out for dinner, but they both looked exhausted at the very thought of it.'

On 26 February 1990, escaped convict Billy 'Porky' Edmunds was arrested in Amsterdam after a shoot-out with Dutch police, but managed to escape from his police cell a week later. Within days, Edmunds met up again with Danny 'Scarface' Roff, whom he'd escaped from a prison van with in England in 1988. In early March, the pair were summoned to a meeting with Roy 'The Lump' Adkins in Amsterdam. He had a 'very special job' for them and told Roff to book himself a holiday on the Costa del Sol with his wife and young child.

The net was closing in on Charlie Wilson, but he didn't really seem to care. Criminals and law enforcement agencies alike were after his blood. He was, in the words of one old Costa del Sol criminal, 'a walkin' fuckin' timebomb'.

PART 5

THE KILL:
23 APRIL–10 MAY 1990

Two thousand escudos of silver
They will give for his head alone
Many would win the prize
But nobody can succeed
Only a comrade could.

Old South American Proverb

1

23 April 1990. No one took much notice of the young man with badly dyed, spiky blond hair sunning himself on a mini-roundabout close to the Urbanization Montana. A yellow mountain bike lay beside him as he sat on the grass verge. At midday, Charlie's cousin Norman Radford and his wife, who were staying at Chequers, were driving down to the shops in Marbella when they spotted the youth. Norman didn't give the man a moment's thought until much later, when he drove past a second time on his way to Malaga Airport to fly back to the UK. Norman later recalled that the boy was still sitting on the verge and that he remembered him because they had made a joke about it, having previously thought he'd fallen off his bicycle.

In the garden at Chequers, spring sunshine was beating down on the lawn and the swimming pool as a warm breeze blew gently through the pine woods that backed onto the property. Charlie lit the barbeque and then crouched down to pick some mint from one of his favourite flowerbeds. He was preparing a very special dinner for himself and Pat to celebrate their 35th wedding anniversary.

Less than two miles away, a second stranger was beginning his journey up towards the urbanization in a white van, after calling his boss from a payphone on the N340 coastal road, known locally as the 'Road of Death' because it had claimed the lives of so many motorists and pedestrians over the years. The white van took a right up the hill through the middle of two recently constructed blocks of flats. After passing the Europa Health Club, the driver came across many larger detached houses. Some of the properties must have seemed like virtual palaces to the driver, who was more used to the crumbling white tower blocks and grey, drab terraces of Vauxhall and Bermondsey. He passed another block of apartments before negotiating a roundabout where he ignored the signpost north to Nageles and instead took a smaller turning west on Avenida Nerja towards Charlie's urbanization.

The white-van driver passed a ten-bedroom hacienda on the left before reaching the mini-roundabout where his friend was waiting with his mountain bike under the shade of a big eucalyptus tree. The youth nodded as his friend parked the van up just beyond the roundabout and got out. Then, separately, they began walking up a quiet side street dotted with ornate street lamps, expensive houses on one side and a huge, empty plot of land on the other. They walked past number seven, a white house, then to number nine, then number eleven. There was no number thirteen on the next house, just the name Chequers. They'd been here three times over the previous few days, so they knew which was Charlie's house. Bougainvillea and carefully cultivated shrubbery covered much of the front of the property. They'd earlier checked out the garden wall at the rear and concluded that it was better to knock on the front door and then leave over the back.

Contrary to some newspaper articles written at the time, Charlie was in the garden preparing that special meal when the doorbell rang. Pat answered it and a pale-faced young man stood on the doorstep in a grey tracksuit. A baseball cap hid his eyes. He seemed to have just arrived on a yellow mountain bike. With a distinct south London accent, he told Pat he had a message for Charlie from someone called Eamon. Pat told the young man to come in and put his bike in the porch. The youth placed the bike between the front door and Charlie's beloved garden wall.

Pat later recalled what happened next: 'Charlie was busy outside, cutting up tomatoes and cucumbers for the salad, so I called to him and he came in. Charlie seemed to recognise the name Eamon and immediately showed him out to the patio area next to the pool.'

For some inexplicable reason, the legendary sixth sense which had helped keep Charlie Wilson one step ahead of his enemies for a lifetime failed to trigger any alarm bells. The men walked to the patio, then Pat heard raised voices. She later revealed: 'I remained inside. Charlie and this man must have been talking for at least five minutes. Perhaps he was telling Charlie about someone he knew back in London, giving him a message or something. He must have told Charlie something which caught his attention, otherwise they wouldn't have been together so long.'

Evidence suggests that once the visitor had finished delivering Roy Adkins' message of contempt, he kicked Charlie in the testicles. As Charlie doubled over, struggling for breath, his nose was broken by a powerful follow-up karate chop. The messenger then took a Smith & Wesson 9mm revolver out from under his tracksuit top and fired at point-blank range. The first bullet pierced the carotid artery of

Charlie's neck. The second entered Charlie's mouth and exited out of the back of his head.

Boo-Boo, leaping to his master's aid, received a vicious kick in the chest, which snapped his front leg and shoulder bone like a twig. Charlie's cousin Norman Radford said later that Boo-Boo must have been trying to defend his master, Charlie unable to fight back because of the poor state of his lungs.

Back in the kitchen, Pat heard the two loud bangs. At first, she thought they'd come from some builders on a site behind the house. She then heard Boo-Boo screaming and came out to see Charlie.

Charlie was staggering towards the pool, blood spurting from his neck, his faithful dog lying wounded on the ground. There was blood everywhere and Charlie was desperately trying to stand up. 'He stared at me,' she said, 'but could not talk. Then he just pointed his finger to his open mouth; blood was streaming from it.' In fact, Charlie was most probably trying to point to the back wall, over which the gunman had escaped. 'As I looked at him struggling, everything went into slow motion,' said Pat. 'I couldn't do anything.'

Suddenly, that slow motion snapped back to real time. Pat screamed over the wall to the Finches to try and raise the alarm. When no one responded, Pat rushed in and telephoned Marti Franco, who later recalled: 'She just said, "Shot Charlie. You come!"'

The man who had taken the shot could easily have waited and turned the gun on Pat when she came running out into the garden, but he went straight over the back wall instead. The escape had been well planned because the killer knew precisely which part to climb over. Along most of the length of the wall there was a 20-foot drop into a dry riverbed, tangled with thorny scrub and strewn with litter, but at the point he had chosen, just to the left of the barbeque, the earth was banked up on the other side to reduce the distance to just 6 feet or so.

After jumping down from the wall, the shooter ran around to the front of the house and snatched the yellow mountain bike, which he then freewheeled down the hill to the mini-roundabout where his accomplice was waiting in the white van. They put the bike in the back of the van and drove off at a modest speed so as not to attract any attention.

Had this been a fully fledged Mafia-style execution, Pat would almost certainly have been killed as well, since she was the only person who could identify the killer. It was evident the shooter had strict orders that the argument was with Charlie, and to leave Pat out of it.

The two men drove back to the big roundabout and headed down towards Old Marbella and Avenida Cascada Samojan. Approximately six minutes after shooting dead one of Britain's most famous criminals, the two men parked their van next to a petrol station opposite the Hotel Don Pepe, took out the yellow mountain bike and went their separate ways. It has since been revealed this happened about 5.45 p.m.

Marti Franco got to Chequers 15 minutes after Pat's call. She recalled: 'When I saw Charles, he looked already dead. But what surprised me most was that there seemed to be no bullet wounds and Pat had told me she heard a gun. There was a swelling on the side of Charles' neck, so tiny it seemed like it was made by a small blade or scalpel.'

Other neighbours alerted by Pat's shrieks quickly arrived at the house. They saw a 20-foot trail of blood where Charlie had clawed his way across the grey marble patio. One of the first policemen at the scene later recalled: 'There was so much blood around his neck, it was impossible to say whether it came from a nosebleed, the dog or the bullet wound.' Paramedics arrived and attempted to revive Charlie, even though it was obviously already too late. Marti Franco recalled: 'I couldn't take my eyes off Charles. Everyone was rushing around the house, but my eyes were on Charles.' Just then, Pat asked Marti to go to the hospital with Charlie.

Marti had no choice but to agree and it was only later she realised that Pat didn't want to leave the house because it was swarming with police and she was worried they might find incriminating evidence that could link Charlie to crimes. Marti later recalled: 'What could I say? "No"?' Pat didn't want to leave them alone in the house.'

In the ambulance – which was the size of a standard estate car – Marta had to sit right next to Charlie's corpse. His legs were up in the air because his body was too long to fit in the back of the vehicle. 'It was awful. There I was sitting next to the dead body of a friend. It was the most traumatic thing I've ever had to do in my life.' Marti returned to Chequers by taxi within minutes of arriving at the Marbella Clinic, five kilometres away.

The Finches had just driven back from a shopping trip to find their street buzzing with police and paramedics. Bernie Finch recalled: 'I saw the Guardia Civil and said "I'm going up to see what's happened. There must have been a break-in." My wife said not to get involved, but I ignored her.' He added: 'By the time I got to the house, Charlie had already been taken away, but the dog was still lying in the garden. He was alive, so I phoned the vet to come and put him down. It was a terrible scene. Pat was crying; there were police and neighbours everywhere.'

Liz Finch recalled: 'Just after we'd walked in and found out what had happened, Pat said to me, "Liz, I've got something to tell you. Did you know who Charlie was?" I said, "Yes, Pat, but it made no difference. You were just Charlie and Pat, our friends."'

A look of relief came over Pat Wilson's face. Then she turned to Liz and said, 'He always said you knew, but I always felt so embarrassed.'

'I told her it was nothing to be embarrassed about,' recalled Liz. 'Even as distraught as she was, I think she still felt she had to explain.'

The Finches stayed with Pat until late that night. Their dog Chico even leapt over Charlie's wall and spent the night with the Wilsons' surviving guard dog, Dino. The Finches eventually adopted Dino as their own rather than see him put down. 'It was strange to think that Charlie wouldn't be there anymore to cook those dogs a whole chicken and feed it to them like he did so often,' said Bernie Finch.

That evening, he walked out onto the blood-splattered patio area which hadn't yet been cordoned off by yellow tape. 'There was a big monkey wrench lying nearby on a flowerbed close to the barbeque, which no one seemed to have noticed. It might have been used by the killer to break the dog's leg or maybe even smash Charlie in the face,' said Bernie.

Back in the house, Pat was being consoled by Charlie's cousin Norman, who'd been contacted at the airport and had returned immediately to Chequers, and neighbour Liz Finch. Pat kept saying that Charlie had nothing to do with drugs, but Liz later said she hadn't believed that.

In the middle of all this death and destruction, Pat insisted on talking about Charlie's escape from Winson Green Prison. 'She kept saying he'd broken out against his will, that he didn't want to escape,' recalled Bernie Finch. 'It was as if Pat was on automatic pilot after being briefed time and time again by Charlie about how to react if the police ever came to the house.' 'Deny everything, love. You understand?' were probably his words.

2

To use a bright-yellow mountain bike was in itself an act of careless bravado. Bicycles were unusual in Spain, young people favouring mopeds. It would have been easier and safer to kill Charlie with a sniper's rifle from the cover of the new apartments being built on the other side of the small pine wood, from where there was an excellent view into the Wilsons' back garden. It seemed as if the killer had been ordered to deliver the message: 'I want Charlie to know he was out of order before you blow him away.'

Others on the Costa del Crime were asking questions: Why wasn't the killer worried that Charlie might fight back? Why was Charlie so relaxed when the youth appeared at his house? Did he know there was a threat? And if Charlie had been expecting trouble, surely he would never have invited the killer into his house? 'If you think there's going to be a "row", you deal with it outside on the street,' said one criminal shortly after Charlie's murder.

★ ★ ★

At the Marbella Clinic Hospital on the east side of town, Charlie's corpse was the subject of an immediate post-mortem examination which concluded he was killed by the first bullet, which entered the right side of his neck and lodged under his left shoulder blade. The coroners also intended to examine Charlie's beloved dog Boo-Boo afterwards. Norman Radford informed Spanish police Pat wanted Charlie's body brought back to south London and buried at the Wilson family plot in Wandsworth.

That evening, police began removing boxes, papers and plastic bags containing Charlie's belongings from the house. Neither Pat nor Norman mentioned there was a basement to the house. It was only entered by police after one detective asked them why there was a small window at ground level.

A senior Marbella magistrate was immediately appointed chief investigator in charge of the murder inquiry. He ordered police not to issue any official comments on the killing before they could establish a clear motive. Spanish authorities hoped the crime would disappear as fast as possible because it was bad for the tourist trade on the Costa del Sol. They also had no idea at this stage that a multinational force had been watching Charlie for some considerable time.

Back at Chequers, Marti Franco was now acting as interpreter for the policemen who were asking Pat preliminary questions about Charlie. Pat also helped a Spanish police artist to compile a photofit image of the man she said shot her husband. The picture was to be immediately published in newspapers and aired on Spanish TV.

Reporters who arrived at the scene noted the bars on every window and the six-foot-high wall which Charlie had spent so much time building. As dozens of Spanish and British reporters gathered outside the house, few doubted that the Costa del Crime lifestyle had finally caught up with Charlie Wilson. Unable to raise Pat, the journalists turned their attentions towards neighbour Bernie Finch. He told them: 'Charlie would do anything to help. He was always doing odd jobs and running errands for people. We knew who he was, but this is grotesque.'

Almost as grotesque was the behaviour of one small group of London tabloid journalists whom Bernie Finch later said tried to climb over their back wall to get into Charlie's house. 'I had to hosepipe them down in the end. They were like animals.'

Inside Chequers, a tearful Pat phoned her three daughters in London, who all pledged to fly over to Spain immediately. Pat then called Charlie's old train robber pal Gordon Goody, who immediately set off from his home in Mojacar, 250 km east of Malaga. There was little he could do apart from giving Pat's small terrier a nice home by the sea. Goody openly loathed reporters and refused to be interviewed when he turned up at the house five hours later. He was furious the following day when one newspaper wrongly reported that he was awaiting trial on a £70,000 marijuana smuggling ring.

Pat, chain-smoking and looking haggard, insisted to police that Charlie had left his life of crime behind long ago. She said: 'I can't think who would want to kill my Charlie. But I can tell you this, it is nothing to do with drugs. Charlie didn't like drugs of any description.'

Early next morning, Norman Radford invited a group of British reporters into Chequers and even helpfully retraced the killer's steps through the entrance gate and past the swimming pool. 'That's where they stood talking,' he said, pointing to the barbeque area. 'There was a handprint there. It trailed back to the pool where Charlie finally collapsed. I wouldn't allow anyone to clear up the congealed blood. I did it myself with a shovel. It was ghastly. I felt sick to my stomach.'

Radford also dismissed all talk of a drugs motive. 'When police searched the house they found no drugs. There was no shotgun, no weapons of any sort. Not even a pickaxe handle which, if Charlie had feared for his life, he would certainly have had at the ready.'

Then Radford floated the idea of two men being involved in the killing. 'I think the murderer jumped over the back wall after shooting Charlie,' he said. 'Then he removed the mountain bike and they met at the end of the road in a car.'

Radford also told reporters that Pat was going into hiding. He explained: 'Pat doesn't seem frightened – all she's concerned about is getting the killer – but we're worried for her safety.' Radford then added chillingly: 'The murderer must have had an ice-cool temperament to have carried out the killing with such precision. It's like something out of *The Godfather*.'

Spanish police had no doubt that an underworld feud lay behind Charlie's murder. Back in London, Fleet Street used his killing as the perfect excuse to drag up the sort of details about the Great Train Robbery that would have infuriated Charlie. Newspapers again made a point of saying how Charlie had been labelled 'the Silent One' after saying so little during his original trial.

Over in Rio, the only Great Train Robber still on the lam sent a message of condolence to Pat and the couple's three daughters. Ronnie Biggs commented that 'Charlie was a fun-loving kind of person, devil-may-care, good company.' Even the old enemy – the police – were saddened and surprised by Charlie's demise. Jack Slipper, the man who'd spent years tracking Biggs, said 'Wilson had a strong character and physique. No one deserves to go like this.'

Rumours were soon flying around about who'd ordered the killing. Freddie Foreman – then serving time for his role in the Security Express heist – was named by *The Sun* as the man behind the murder after claims that Charlie had grassed him up and then got him kicked out of Spain. Foreman was furious when he read the report. 'I was spitting blood about these lies. I was inside for the Security Express job and the last thing I wanted was to be connected to Charlie's death. It was outrageous.'

The following day, *The Sun* ran an apology for trying to connect Foreman to Charlie's death. Pat told the paper how Foreman's wife

Maureen had called to say her husband had nothing to do with Charlie's murder. Pat stated: 'As far as I am concerned, Mr Foreman and his wife have always been friendly with myself and Charlie. To say that Freddie had anything to do with the death of my husband is absolutely ridiculous.'

Foreman was genuinely shocked by the death of his friend Charlie. He later recalled: 'I don't think Charlie believed Adkins would do him for such a stupid reason. I was told Charlie believed that Adkins had given permission for his name to be used anyway because the law already knew all about him. If anyone was going to cop it, I would have thought it'd be Jimmy Rose.'

News of the World veteran reporter Trevor Kempson had known Pat for 20 years, ever since Charlie had allowed her to sell her story to the paper for £30,000 after his recapture in Canada. Pat told Kempson she believed a London underworld boss with a long-time grudge had hired the hit man who blasted her Charlie to death. Clutching Kempson's hand, she sobbed uncontrollably and said: 'I'm absolutely sure this murder has something to do with Charlie's past back home. I'm convinced the killing was ordered by a person he upset many years ago. The murderer was about 22 years old, far too young to have known Charlie in those days. He must have been paid to do the killing by an older man, possibly one of Charlie's old associates from his criminal days.'

Many of Charlie's pals in Spain remained baffled by certain aspects of the killing which simply didn't add up. One of Charlie's smuggling team on the Costa del Sol explained: 'This karate business was a classic Russian calling card because all their killers are trained in martial arts in the military. They have the balls to do it. They don't come behind you, they don't shoot you in the back, they want you to see it coming. That's how they think. It's cruel. And it just doesn't make sense for someone to come to the door and say "I'm a friend of Eamon", and then his wife tells Charlie and sends the bloke through. Maybe he was expecting this guy and it was a set-up. But then surely Charlie would have been on his guard? None of it adds up.'

It was hardly surprising that Spanish detectives encountered a wall of silence when they tried to interview some of the ex-pat criminal fraternity on the Costa del Sol. As one unnamed British detective told the *Daily Mail*: 'This is a British Mafia killing. The British Mafia here know who did it, but they're not going to help the police.'

★ ★ ★

Inspector Juan Lorenzo of Marbella's International Delinquency Squad was appointed chief detective in charge of the investigation and he had no doubt Charlie's death was linked to drugs, despite Pat's denials. Lorenzo, a stocky, quietly spoken, neatly dressed character in his mid-30s, with a full head of thick, dark hair, soon heard about some of Charlie's visits across the Mediterranean to Tangier and the Atlantic to Colombia. There was also talk of trips to the Far East.

Less than 48 hours after Charlie's death, Lorenzo admitted to reporters: 'We are under no illusions that the British underworld is just as keen to find Wilson's murderer as we are and they may get to him before us.' The file on the Wilson case was held in a small bare room on the first floor of Marbella Police Station, the shabby, overcrowded two-storey building tucked away in the dusty backstreets behind the city's Moorish castle and a world away from the ritzy piano bars, nightclubs and pricey restaurants of tourist Marbella. It was a building designed to deal with the sort of petty crime that only seemed to occur around Marbella, until British gangsters turned the area into the Costa del Crime. Outside the police station were rows of cars impounded from drug dealers, every one vandalised, every window smashed. One was a brand new Mercedes, recently set on fire by street urchins.

Lorenzo's office contained just two desks, an old typewriter, a single telephone, which worked erratically, and a battered filing cabinet. On the brown-painted walls were a couple of plaques from visiting police forces. To call it shabby would be a gross understatement. A faded map of the town, the street names just legible, covered half of one peeling wall. The squad, comprising the inspector and two sergeants, was responsible for investigating all crimes involving foreigners, from bag-snatching to murder.

Lorenzo was quick to note that Charlie had no visible source of income, yet had spent considerable sums of money renovating and rebuilding his house, transforming it from a poky little bungalow into a garish hacienda complete with that two-foot-thick, six-foot-high stone wall, which Charlie had manically built around the property. Inspector Lorenzo already had a full caseload because Charlie wasn't the only foreigner to have recently had his life cut short in the locality. A few months earlier, the body of an American drugs trafficker had been found dead, shot twice in the head, like Charlie, in a burnt-out car that bore traces of cocaine. The corpse of a French man, tortured then killed, had also recently been discovered in a chalet in nearby San Pedro. A man out walking his dog in Marbella centre then spotted the arm of a corpse, the rest of which had been covered in quick lime to prevent identification. Only a couple of days before Charlie's murder, police arrested 14 Turks and seized 210 kilos of heroin. Two foreigners carrying 175 kilos of cocaine were also arrested later that same day in a separate police raid.

Two days after Charlie's death, neighbour Bernie Finch went to Inspector Lorenzo's office at the National Police Headquarters in Marbella to be interviewed. He later recalled: 'There were two Scotland Yard officers there. They turned round to me and said, "Charlie was one of the good old boys. The younger ones wouldn't think twice about shooting their own mother."' British police and Customs had already revealed to the inspector their suspicions about Charlie's drugs empire in Spain.

On 27 April 1990, a Spanish judge prevented Charlie's body being flown to Britain and called in a second pathologist to carry out a new port-mortem as a precaution because of the immense public interest in the case. At Chequers, Norman Radford told reporters: 'Pat's in a dreadful state. She'd hoped to be taking Charlie home this weekend and the unexpected delay is causing further anguish. We have no idea what is going on.' At this stage, Pat was refusing to leave the house at all, although she'd told her family she'd quit Spain permanently once she got Charlie home.

Also that day, the British newspapers carried reports that Scotland Yard and the British National Drugs Intelligence Unit had extensive dossiers containing Charlie's contacts and criminal dealings over the previous couple of years. One Yard source told journalists: 'The criminal community here knows who is behind this and we have our own very strong suspicions. The type of people who did this stick to the old-fashioned ideals of not hurting women. How else can you explain the fact that Wilson's wife was not killed?' Speculation that Colombian drug barons, angry about an unpaid shipment of cocaine, had killed Charlie was dismissed for that very same reason. 'They wouldn't have left Pat standing,' said one of Charlie's friends.

One of Charlie's smuggling team, who still resides on the Costa del Sol, said: 'There were lots of theories flying around at first. Some people said a delivery of cocaine was due to take place, but for some reason it didn't show up. And when that happens, everyone's in trouble. That could have made Charlie vulnerable.

'Then there was ETA. Some of us wondered if Charlie had upset them. There was a story going round at the time that a British crim had double-crossed them over a drugs deal. We all started to wonder whether that "crim" was Charlie.' But any suggestions that Charlie was a grass were dismissed out of hand. 'No way. Charlie was from the old school and they never told tales,' said a source in Spain.

In London, many of Charlie's hardest criminal associates were deeply upset by his death. Long-time pal Joey Pyle said: 'I was stunned. I knew Charlie didn't work well with people – he was a loner – but that didn't mean he deserved this for Christ's sake. I'd heard he was depressed that all his train robbery cash had gone and he'd had to keep on working to keep things going. Charlie was a hero with 90 per cent of south London. No one wanted it to come to this.'

Ronnie Knight, whose wedding Charlie had attended just three years earlier, said: 'Charlie's death just made no sense. We all wondered what he could have been up to to get shot like that. Charlie and the boys used to go down to the port [Puerto Banus] now and again, but he never mentioned anything about these sorts of heavy characters. But most of the time, him and Pat kept themselves to themselves. I didn't even know Charlie was up to anything.' Other faces, who contacted Pat to pass on their condolences, even dropped broad hints about how they'd like to have first refusal on Chequers when it was sold.

Charlie's murder put a lot of other criminals' backs up because his death implied that the old guard was losing its touch. It seemed as if the up-and-coming younger gangsters were sharpening their weapons and gaining a stronger grip on the Costa del Crime. There were genuine fears that Charlie's death could spark a deadly cycle of violence. Scotland Yard had known for some time that Charlie was up to his neck in drugs, along with Mickey Green, Tony White and others, but was a bloodbath now looming on the horizon?

Charlie's architect friend Marti Franco was so terrified her own life might be in danger that she denied all knowledge of Charlie's criminal activities when interviewed by reporters in the days following his slaying. 'I was in their house nearly every day for years and I never heard or saw anything funny happen. Never, never, never! No cars going in and out, no money, no strange people visiting, no neighbours watching. You understand what I am saying? I tell you this on my life. Charlie and Pat were beautiful, beautiful people. All 20 neighbours will say the same thing. They were like Mummy and Daddy to me. They had very high morals; very faithful, very concerned for their family. I never felt when I was with Charlie that I was with a crook, no way.'

Back in England, Charlie's friend Georgie Ellis read with shock about his death in the newspapers. She'd heard nothing from Charlie since their last date together, except for a Christmas card a few months earlier with the simple message, 'From Charlie'. Georgie Ellis later recalled: 'I took a deep breath when I saw the story in the paper and looked at Charlie's smiling face, staring at me from a photograph. I just hoped he was as happy where he was then as when I'd met him.'

At Scotland Yard, supergrass Michael Michael was, as they say, singing like a canary. Just days after Charlie was killed, he told his handlers that two young hoods called Danny 'Scarface' Roff and Billy 'Porky' Edmunds had carried out the hit on behalf of Roy 'The Lump' Adkins. The Yard were initially sceptical, but passed the names on to Spanish police.

A few days after Charlie's death, Bernie Finch was helping dismantle the dog house Charlie had so carefully built out of plywood for Boo-Boo and Dino when he noticed the doll's hand, which Charlie had found so amusing, still sticking out of a nearby flowerbed. Bernie recalled: 'I looked down at it, smiled and wondered what sort of crazy joke Charlie would crack if he was there. Then I bent down to remove the hand, but stopped in mid-flow and left it exactly where it was just in case Charlie was watching over me.'

3

Difficulties in getting Charlie's body released added to Pat's distress over the shooting. She still insisted to family and friends she'd never set foot in Spain again once she'd accompanied him home to London. She also asked the staff at Wandsworth Cemetery to leave room for her to follow her dear departed husband one day.

The second post-mortem on Charlie's body was completed on 29 April and no extra injuries were uncovered, so Charlie's body was released for embalming and laid in a zinc coffin at a Marbella mortuary. However, Charlie's funeral was then further delayed because legal papers dealing with his death had to be translated into English before his body could be shipped back to the UK. Also, Westminster Coroner Dr Paul Knapman had decided that the violent nature of Charlie's death qualified for an inquest to be held in London. The funeral could not go ahead until that inquest had been opened.

It wasn't until 1 May that Charlie's body was finally released by Spanish authorities. Pat gave the Chequers house keys to a neighbour and asked them to keep an eye on the place. Pat 'forgot' to include the key to Charlie's secret basement. Bernie Finch drove Pat to Malaga Airport in Charlie's Toyota behind a hearse carrying the casket. Norman Radford followed in a rental car. Bernie later recalled: 'It was a nightmare journey because the paparazzi followed us on motorbikes. It was disgusting. They were chasing us up the motorway and then overtaking and firing off shots with their cameras. I nearly crashed Charlie's car, it was so chaotic.'

Bernie had forbidden his wife Liz to accompany them to the airport because there were fears Pat might still be the killer's next target because she was the only witness to her husband's murder. 'The police protection was pathetic. One squad car accompanied us to the airport and they did nothing to even stop the journalists stalking us,' Bernie recalled.

At Malaga Airport's departure terminal, two armed Guardia Civil officers accompanied Pat and Norman on an electric buggy that was waved through the check-in desk and passport control. Out on the sizzling hot tarmac, the casket containing Charlie's corpse was wrapped in a plain green tarpaulin with a red airline label unceremoniously stuck on the side as it was pushed by four airport workers into the cargo hold of a British Airways Boeing 737. Shortly afterwards, Pat and Norman boarded the jet, filled with holidaymakers bound for London's Heathrow Airport. Pat said virtually nothing during the two-and-a-half-hour flight and refused all offers of food and drink. On arrival at Heathrow's Terminal One building, Pat and Norman had to fight their way through a mob of hysterical girl pop fans waiting for the American group New Kids on the Block. Pat covered her face as photographers swarmed around her and refused to talk to reporters before heading straight to a waiting car, which set off at high speed. Back on the tarmac, there were no flowers to put on Charlie's coffin as it was checked through Customs before being driven away in a hearse.

The following day, Charlie's coffin was laid out in the front room of Norman Radford's three-bedroom council house on Lidiard Road, just off Wandsworth Common, south London, less than half a mile from where Charlie was to be buried. Pat had accepted Norman's invitation to stay at the house until after the funeral.

A whole procession of Charlie's old associates came to the house to pay their respects over the following few days. Then on 5 May, three well-known members of the London underworld visited the house and asked Pat about rumours that Charlie had whispered the name of the man behind his shooting as he lay dying. No one knows what Pat said to those criminals, but they went away muttering about 'taking measures' on behalf of Pat and her daughters.

Even Charlie's traditional enemies at Scotland Yard were keen to help solve the murder. Pat let it be known she was comforted by their efforts while others wondered whether it really was in anyone's interests for his killer to be found. No one seriously expected Pat to still be a target since Charlie's killing had all the hallmarks of an old-fashioned hit in which only the legitimate target was the victim.

On 9 May 1990, an inquest at Westminster Coroner's Court into Charlie's death was opened and adjourned until 6 June, so that formal identification and the funeral could go ahead the following day. After attending the brief hearing, Pat returned to Norman's semi on Lidiard Road to prepare for the following day's service.

Detective Inspector Alec Edwards was appointed by Coroner Dr Paul Knapman to carry out investigations into Charlie's death on his behalf. Edwards worked for SO1, Special Operations 1, otherwise known as the Organised Crime Group. Its offices were on the 15th floor at New Scotland Yard and the team consisted of six superintendents, ten inspectors, twenty sergeants and forty constables. Edwards explained: 'What happened was, like so many cases we pick up, the body was returned to the UK so the local coroner could hold an inquest. The coroner asked us to look into the case on his behalf and report back to him for the eventual inquest. But the matter would still have to go back to Spain for a trial – they had the jurisdiction over the case.'

Back at Norman's home on the eve of the funeral, wreaths and bunches of flowers filled the triangular-shaped garden at the front of the white-painted semi, as the last of the visitors paid their respects.

The following morning – 10 May 1990 – Charlie's coffin was carefully removed from the front room and placed in a hearse which would lead a funeral cortège of eight cars. Behind the glass sides of the hearse was a flower wreath spelling 'Chas'. Other floral tributes alongside the coffin included a small white dog, a chair and miniature archways.

Five limousines had roof racks awash with huge flower baskets. 'A two-grand affair,' somebody connected with the cemetery guessed. Pat was in the first car, rocking with sobs. Her daughters, Cheryl, Tracey and Leander, held onto their mother. Teardrops chased one another down their cheeks.

A few minutes later, train robber Bruce Reynolds watched Pat struggling from the undertaker's Daimler at Wandsworth Cemetery, and turned to one of the other robbers standing next to him and said, 'Charlie was a good family man, can't you see? A good friend and it's just tragic what happened to him. But I'm not going down memory lane. Charlie was a quiet man, a loyal man and a family man. I will miss him.'

Spritely Reynolds, at fifty-nine just one year older than Charlie would have been, looked a million dollars in a navy-blue mohair suit, slim and distinguished like someone running a City bank. Just then, Roy James was approached by a reporter and denied his own identity. 'I'm not Roy James,' he said. 'You've made a mistake; you've got the wrong guy.' Then he whispered, 'OK, Charlie was one of the best.' Minutes later, James, Reynolds and two more Great Train Robbers, Bobby Welch and Buster Edwards, joined Pat and her daughters behind the coffin as it was carried towards the chapel of remembrance in the grounds of the cemetery.

Cousin Norman helpfully explained to the dozens of assembled reporters that some of the characters attending might not appreciate having their photos taken. 'They're coming for the funeral,' he said, 'and may be in the background because, let's face it, a lot will be from Charlie's profession.'

Train robber Buster Edwards, his hair all snow white, had left his flower stall under Waterloo Station to attend. Bruce Reynolds was next to him alongside Bobby Welch, struggling on crutches after a cartilage operation had gone wrong in prison, Reynold's arm ready to stop him falling. Roy 'The Weasel' James – who looked much heavier than in the 'good old days' – was bringing up the rear, his hands clasped in front of him and his head low in mourning. As cameras prodded through the crowd, the train robbers turned away once again.

The coffin had the big family wreath on it as it was carried into the chapel behind the minister, the Reverend Kevin Parkes, from St Anne's Church, just down the road in Tooting. His hair was in a ponytail with a blue ribbon. 'The family liked the way he handled Charlie's Aunt Nellie's funeral so they asked for him again,' undertaker Roger Gillman explained afterwards. As the coffin was carried past the mourners, Kevin Parkes chanted, 'I am the Resurrection . . .'

The service began with Charlie's favourite song, 'My Way' by Frank Sinatra:

> *And now, the end is near*
> *And so I face the final curtain . . .*

At the end of the service Pat's choice, 'When Your Old Wedding Ring Was New', came crackling over the speaker system. Then the crowd parted to let her and her daughters through to follow the coffin out to the graveside. Pat was supported by the arm of Charlie's cousin Norman.

Three women, who'd been weeding around the grave next to Charlie's, left when they saw the crowd emerge from the chapel. 'I think we'd better move fast,' one of them said.

Charlie was to be put in the ground in the same place as his father Bill, with flowers strewn around him and cards signed by people from the history of crime. 'Charlie from Reg and Ron' was on a ticket taped to a wreath of red and white carnations from the Krays. There had been a rumour one of the twins might turn up, but it wasn't likely since they were both still in prison.

The wreaths were then spread out. One was of a large dog, sculpted in white chrysanthemums to resemble Charlie's beloved Boo-Boo, with the message: 'I'll make you proud of me. I will always love and remember you – David, grandson.'

Several other ageing criminals were unable to attend in person, but also sent flowers, including Ronnie Knight, still fighting extradition from Spain on those Security Express robbery charges, and Tommy Wisbey, another Great Train Robber in jail for cocaine trafficking.

Pat, Tracey, Cheryl and Leander looked down as the mahogany coffin, polished like a mirror, was lowered into the ground. Pat stood by the grave, squeezing a single red rose in her hand as still more tears shone on her face. 'We have entrusted our brother Charlie to His keeping,' Mr Parkes said, Bible in hand. Then Pat kissed the rose and let it fall on the coffin. Her daughters followed suit.

As Pat was led from the graveside, the train robbers stood aside while Welch wobbled alongside the grave, reached down for some earth and let it trickle through his hand onto the wooden casket below. Only Bruce Reynolds was seen to look down. Then he quietly muttered his own epitaph to Charlie: 'He never left anyone behind.'

Everyone gazed in admiration at Pat. She'd been married to Charlie for 35 difficult years, including the Great Train Robbery era, their chaotic life on the run in Canada after his audacious escape and those last few years out in Spain.

Half a dozen men, with thick-set necks and white socks flashing under the bottoms of black trousers, dragged themselves past the grave. A few minutes later, as the limousines began slipping away, a man plucked the cards off the wreaths before they went for souvenirs.

It was left to Charlie's friend Nosher Powell to sum up how high emotions were running: 'The murder was all so unnecessary and whoever did it is now the walking dead. Someone will get him.' Just then, another man chipped in: 'They'll get somebody for doing this to Charlie. They'll have him, you watch.'

The old men who'd robbed the train and spent scores of years in jail soon vanished from the cemetery, leaving only a couple of police detectives with raincoats folded over their arms. Pat was grateful for them because she remained the only person who could identify the man who had killed her husband. Detectives had already given her the name of the assassins, following a statement by supergrass Michael Michael, although they weren't making anything official at that time. Cousin Norman informed one reporter at Charlie's funeral that it had given Pat a lift to know police had identified who did it. Four men with shovels then slowly started filling in the sandy grave.

The story of who murdered Charlie Wilson – and why – was about to take a very strange twist.

PART 6

AFTERMATH:
1990–2004

Maybe one day a *fiambre** will turn up and we
will put two and two together and discover it
was the man who killed Wilson.

Inspector Juan Lorenzo, Marbella police

(*fiambre literally means cold meat)

1

Three days after the funeral, on 13 May 1990, the *News of the World* blasted a banner headline across their front page: 'WE NAME TRAIN ROBBER MURDER SUSPECT.'

The *News of the World*'s sensational crime scoop claimed that jailbreak fugitive Danny 'Scarface' Roff was the police's prime suspect. The paper said that after a number of leads from 'crime intelligence sources', one of their reporters had obtained photos of Roff from their own library and showed them to Charlie's cousin Norman. After carefully studying the photos, he picked Roff out and said: 'It looks like the man I saw sitting on the grassy bank with his bicycyle near Charlie's villa. The man I saw had spiky bleached-blond hair and was thinner in the face, but everything else looks identical.'

Radford and Pat both spoke to the *News of the World* at Charlie's cousin's house in Wandsworth, where she'd been staying since flying back with Charlie's body the previous week. Pat was also able to pick out the face of a second man from another set of photographs as the man who shot her husband dead. That man was not identified by the newspaper at the time, but it was Billy 'Porky' Edmunds, from Vauxhall, south London, who'd gone on the run with Scarface back in 1988 after hijacking the prison van in Norfolk.

The *News of the World* article reported that: 'Tears welled in Patricia's eyes as she studied the photo: "That's him. I'm 99 per cent sure of it. The lips are pursed and bow-shaped. The nose is the same — so too is the jawline and bone structure."' Earlier, the paper had shown Pat a photofit sketch of the killer wearing a baseball hat. She said the artist had drawn a perfect likeness, apart from the eyes. But when she saw the photograph of Edmunds she said: 'Fit those eyes on the sketch and that's him. I'll never forget the way they stared at me.'

Pat and Norman claimed in the *News of the World* that just one hour before they'd met the paper's reporters, they'd received a separate tip-off from an underworld figure also alleging Roff was one of the men involved. All this conveniently ignored the fact the police had actually already told her the identity of both men after getting that tip from supergrass Michael Michael. The tabloid also claimed in its exclusive that it had received further information alleging that Roff was part of a drug-smuggling team in Spain. The paper then claimed that Charlie had been killed because he double-crossed a gang over a lorryload of cannabis. Pat again insisted her beloved husband was not involved in drug trafficking. 'My Charlie hated drugs,' she said.

Back on the Costa del Sol, Spanish police informants told detectives that ETA and Charlie had at one stage teamed up to invest in a network of villains trafficking sex slaves, bringing women into Spain for sexual exploitation. The gang 'imported' women from South America, West Africa and Eastern Europe. On their arrival in Spain, they were installed at brothels in the Marbella area. 'The women were forced to pay two million pesetas [£8,000] for bringing them into Spain and once this amount of money was paid off, the women were forced to continue working as prostitutes, handing over 50 per cent of their earnings to the owners of the clubs,' one Spanish police spokesman later said. There's never been any clear evidence that Charlie really was involved in prostitution and many on the Costa del Crime believed Charlie was being deliberately 'smeared' to the Spanish police.

A few days after Charlie's funeral, police in Spain released the body of Charlie's beloved dog Boo-Boo and his ashes were scattered on Charlie's grave in south London.

2

In early June 1990, Inspector Juan Lorenzo and one of his detectives flew to the UK to interview a British businessman suspected of involvement in Charlie's death. The tycoon, who lived in a luxurious house in Kent, was linked to an international drugs ring believed to have smuggled tens of millions of pounds worth of narcotics into Britain. His name has never been disclosed by Spanish police, but the suspect denied all knowledge of Charlie's killers even though Scotland Yard had strong evidence linking him to the two alleged hit men, Roff and Edmunds.

While in the UK, Inspector Lorenzo also interviewed Charlie's family and associates as they rooted around in south London for any more clues as to why Charlie was killed. With assistance from Scotland Yard, but little or no intelligence from the other agencies who'd been watching Charlie, the two Spanish detectives believed that their five-day trip to England had been worthwhile. Besides Roff and Edmunds, they now had a suspect in Holland, Roy 'The Lump' Adkins, whom they believed had ordered the hit on Charlie. They also established the chain of events which seemed to lead to his death.

British police, however, were not overly impressed by their Spanish counterparts. One of the officers who investigated Charlie's death on behalf of the Westminster Coroner later recalled: 'Juan Lorenzo is a very nice chap, but somewhat laid-back. They didn't even have a proper layout of where the body of Charlie Wilson was positioned when he was killed. Their file was about a quarter of an inch thick when we looked at it. Their attitude seemed to be that it was just another British villain and they weren't really all that bothered. They were given a few names and seemed to think that was it. There was nothing more to do.'

When two Scotland Yard officers flew out to Spain a few weeks later they energetically tried to cover all aspects of the case. The British detectives visited Chequers, examined the location of the actual shooting, but weren't allowed inside the house itself because of a problem with the locks which seemed to have been changed. One detective recalled: 'We spent a lot of time with Juan Lorenzo and his team in Marbella. We built up a good rapport with him, although you must remember we were not actually investigating. We were just reporting back to the coroner. We had no powers of arrest.'

In London, Pat Wilson was interviewed by a detective a further three times. He recalled: 'She was a very nice lady, but she insisted she knew nothing of what her husband was up to. She'd stayed on the top deck, so to speak. God knows how she missed it all!'

Detectives knew Charlie was up to no good and – like many other London police officers – they believed the sympathetic treatment of the train robbers by the public was undeserved. One explained: 'As far as we were concerned, all the train robbers were scum. They'd been treated as heroes, but they were far from it. They'd all dipped into some pretty serious crimes over the years, so it was important to show what really led up to Charlie Wilson's death.'

British detectives working on behalf of Wesminster Coroner Dr Knapman investigated the details behind Charlie's murder through the classic point-of-the-circle system, which police often adopted in apparently motiveless killings. As one detective explained: 'You start from the point of the circle and move outwards, beginning with immediate family, then spreading out to friends, followed by business associates and so on.' One of the lead detectives explained: 'There were two points of the circles we examined. One was the circle of Wilson's close friends and family, the other was the criminal fraternity. The reason why they killed him wasn't that important. It was how they did it and who did it. We all knew drugs were involved.'

Meanwhile British newspapers published stories naming other criminals besides Roff and Edmunds as suspects in Charlie's killing. In July 1990, *The Sun* named a man known as 'Scots Willy' and claimed that Pat had identified him from photos shown to her by the paper. The 26-year-old, 6-foot-2-inch-tall Willy Grant certainly fitted the bill in some ways, but when the tabloid revealed that Grant's name had been put forward by an anonymous underworld tipster, one of Charlie's oldest mates said the story was 'a load of fuckin' lies'. 'Either that, or Pat was fingering any old photo that was put in front of her,' he said.

★ ★ ★

In the aftermath of Charlie's death many criminal associates put their own spin on his murder. Gordon Goody summed it up: 'Charlie was a lovely guy, you know. A really lovely guy. Everyone'll tell you the same thing. He'd do anything for you. Everyone liked him . . . Well, I suppose someone didn't like him. That's obvious, innit?' Goody, like all the other gang members, felt a deep loss at Charlie's death and still couldn't understand why anyone would want to kill him. 'How did Charlie let it happen? He hadn't been well of late, got a spongy lung I heard, but he could still handle a row. Why did he let the bloke into the house? Why did he let him get so close? I've no idea who did it, but I can tell you I'd bloody well like to know.'

On 15 August 1990, Danny 'Scarface' Roff – one of the two men suspected of killing Charlie – and his wife Tina were arrested by Dutch police, who swooped on a flat in the small town of Naarden. Roff was still wanted in Britain for the prison-van getaway in 1988, having served less than 12 months of his original 13-year sentence. The Dutch police had been tipped off by Flying Squad officers in London, who'd tracked Roff to the Continent. Roff was held in a Dutch jail, pending his extradition to Britain, after which Spanish police were expected to apply for permission to interview him in connection with Charlie's murder. The other prime suspect, Billy 'Porky' Edmunds, remained on the run.

★ ★ ★

By the late summer of 1990, it was rumoured that a bunch of Charlie's closest associates were tracking Roy 'The Lump' Adkins across Europe, so when 42-year-old Adkins was gunned down by two men at the fashionable Nightwatch bar in the American Hotel in Amsterdam on 28 September 1990, it came as no real surprise. Adkins' killers – who hit him in the head five times – escaped on foot and two men drinking with the victim, thought to be his minders, also disappeared. Detectives presumed that Adkins' death was an act of revenge for the killing of Charlie.

Within hours of Adkins' murder, his terrified girlfriend was barricaded inside the couple's fortress home surrounded by barbed wire and floodlights, and constantly watched by closed circuit TV. But just like Pat before her, she would never be under any real threat. This feud was about men from the old school of criminality.

A few days after the Adkins' slaying, Spanish police seized 1,200 kilos of cocaine, the largest single amount of the drug ever found in the country, and worth at least £300 million on the black market. The cocaine was found hidden in a van parked in the north of Madrid. As the driver, a Colombian called Juan Carlos Morales, started the engine detectives swooped. At the same time, in the northern region of Galicia, five more people were arrested. The ripple effect of this police success could be felt as far afield as South America and London. These drugs were part of a consignment Charlie Wilson might well have invested in if he'd still been alive.

On 14 December 1990, the Madrid-based daily newspaper *ABC* published an extensive investigation into the Charlie Wilson murder in which they revealed that Danny 'Scarface' Roff had taken his wife and child to Spain with him as cover for the hit. The paper talked of a drugs vendetta and questioned Pat's ability to identify either Roff or Edmunds because she was short-sighted. *ABC* also claimed to have been told by a criminal informant on the Costa del Sol that Roy Adkins only paid £5,000 for the hit on Charlie (most criminals had presumed a fee of at least four times that amount had been involved). There were also rumours that Charlie had told a few friends he was worried about 'that nutter Adkins' although if he was taking the threat seriously, why didn't he take any extra security precautions in the months leading up to his death?

By the end of 1990, neither the murder weapon, the bicycle nor the getaway van had been recovered and no arrests had been made. Pat also still hadn't sold Chequers for the asking price of just over £200,000.

Many believed that Charlie's murder had scared people off. Pat hadn't set foot in Spain since accompanying Charlie's body back to London. June Hackett, a local neighbour, was handling inquiries on her behalf. She told reporters: 'It's a lovely house. They spent a lot of money doing it up. Mrs Wilson is leaving things to me because it causes her a lot of bother coming back here.'

In February 1991, British and Spanish newspapers claimed that the investigation into Charlie's murder had been wound down by authorities because of a lack of evidence. Inspector Juan Lorenzo later explained: 'We'd tried everything and could not find enough evidence to prove that Roff and Edmunds did it. In any case, the man who commissioned the hit, Adkins, was dead. It was difficult to know what to do next.'

Scotland Yard were 'somewhat surprised' by the Spanish police attitude. 'We had Roff back in the UK serving his time for that earlier offence and we were expecting the Spanish to ask for his extradition but it never happened,' said one Flying Squad detective.

3

In June 1991, Roy 'The Lump' Adkins' boss Klaas Bruinsma was assassinated by two hit men in front of Amsterdam's Hilton Hotel. The criminal known as 'The Preacher' had been under intense police surveillance and become such a liability within his own organisation that many suspected he was eliminated by one of his own people, but later it was a former Dutch policeman who was convicted of the hit. Meanwhile, the flow of drugs through Holland continued unabated as two of Bruinsma's former lieutenants took over his empire.

Chequers was finally sold for 32 million pesetas (£200,000) in September 1991. A Danish gentleman called Previn Anderson bought it on behalf of a wealthy client after seeing the private 'For Sale' sign outside the property. Hours after completing the sale, Previn Anderson went to visit Chequers. 'It had been stripped bare, even the toilet paper rolls had been removed. Wall lights had been taken and bare wires left hanging. I had never seen anything like it before.' Anderson dealt with a local lawyer and never saw or heard from Pat. 'They'd removed everything before the sale was completed.' He added: 'It didn't matter because their taste was dreadful, but we were a bit surprised.'

It was only when a surveyor inspected the house after Pat had shipped her belongings back to England that Previn and his client even realised there was a basement. He explained: 'That was very funny because at the end of the living room there was a whole mirror covering an entire back wall behind this really vulgar bar. Well, Mrs Wilson's friends had taken the bar, but, strangely, they left the mirror . . . then we found the safe still in the basement.' Anderson went on to quickly re-sell Chequers for 37 million pesetas, giving his client a 5-million-peseta (£20,000) profit.

The death of Charlie's one-time prisonmate 'Mad Mickey' Blackmore in October 1991 had a bizarre connection to the cycle of violence sparked by Charlie's murder. Blackmore had only just come out of Maidstone Prison after serving a sentence for arms offences and attempted murder. He claimed he was owed £250,000 by Adkins for going to prison without squealing on Roy 'The Lump' and believed he could still collect on the debt even though Adkins was dead. Word was that Mad Mickey was so furious he was threatening the men behind Adkins' death, even though the debt was not their problem.

Freddie Foreman explained: 'Blackmore was ranting and raving about it and decided to go to Holland to collect his money, but they wouldn't stand for that.' Hard man robber and drug dealer Blackmore was eventually gunned down and dumped in an Amsterdam canal. One story on the grapevine was that he was first shot in Marseilles, then his body was dumped in Holland. Another rumour had him shooting it out with a man in a bullet-proof vest who, in Hollywood style, feigned death before killing Blackmore. The day after the death of Mad Mickey, newspapers named him as having been involved in Charlie's murder, which wasn't, strictly speaking, true.

Blackmore's family made a public appeal denying his involvement in Charlie's death. A number of newspapers were suggesting he played a role in the murder. As one villain explained recently: 'They'd missed the point. Mickey had to go because he was threatening to bring down the fellas who'd avenged Charlie's death by gettin' Adkins topped.'

* * *

In November 1991, Charlie's death was dragged up for public consumption all over again when the inquest into his murder was finally heard at Westminster Coroner's Court. Dr Paul Knapman opened the case by pointing out: 'It's ironic that Charles Wilson should end his days being gunned down in the barbeque area of his retirement home.' Ironic was perhaps not the word Pat would have chosen.

Detective Inspector Alec Edwards told the inquest there was clear circumstantial evidence linking Charlie to some major drug deals. He said: 'Mr Wilson is thought to have been connected in some way with drug dealing and he upset a member of a rival gang and an execution was ordered against him.' Edwards also told the inquest: 'We know of him meeting British criminals who are known drug dealers and who have since been convicted of drug dealing, and with one who has also been executed in a gangland killing.'

Alec Edwards told the court Charlie was alleged to have given permission for Jimmy Rose to name Adkins to police, 'which upset Adkins enormously'. Edwards did not name Roff and Edmunds in case it prejudiced any subsequent criminal proceedings.

A few minutes later, Pat broke down in the witness box as she described how she found Charlie bleeding from the mouth on the patio after letting that stranger into their Spanish villa. Home Office pathologist Dr Rufus Crompton said that the first bullet which hit Charlie went in through the side of the neck and the bullet had lodged inside him. As the shot passed through his larynx, it would have caused heavy bleeding and as he inhaled blood, he would have been unable to speak or cry out which seemed to contradict earlier claims that Charlie had muttered the name of the man responsible for the shooting as he lay dying in his garden. A verdict that Charlie had been shot by persons unknown was recorded. Outside the court, the Wilson family solicitor insisted: 'The drug allegations are strongly denied.' Pat was determined not to let Charlie down.

On that same day over at the Old Bailey, a jury was listening to an account of the final minutes of Kenny Baker, an old-school armed robber who'd met Charlie many times in Spain. Baker was wearing a Ronald Reagan rubber mask when he was shot and killed by members of Scotland Yard's PT17 blue-bereted sharpshooters. He'd been on a robbery with two brothers from one of south-east London's most notorious families, the Arifs, who'd known Charlie from when he was serving time for the Great Train Robbery. Baker should have retired to do VAT fiddles, flogging fake Rolexes or handling a bit of puff on the side; instead, he ended up on a mortuary slab just like Charlie.

AFTERMATH

The following morning, 21 November 1991, Pat was back at Westminster Coroner's Court listening to the details of the last moments of Roy 'The Lump' Adkins, the man everyone was saying had commissioned the hit on her husband. Connections between Charlie's assassination and the death of Adkins were made public during the opening to Adkins' inquest. Detective Alec Edwards told the court: 'There was much speculation and some evidence' to suggest the link between the two high-profile deaths. The connection with the killing of Wilson is Adkins.' The inquest was told Adkins had ordered the killing because he believed Charlie had given permission for him (Adkins) to be named as boss of the drug gang behind the shipment The Rose Organisation were carrying when they were busted.

Scotland Yard detectives later admitted they were 'baffled' by the failure of Spanish police to interview people clearly connected to Charlie's death. 'I don't know why the Spanish police didn't go to see the Rose trial defendants, for example, but that was up to them,' said one detective.

Shortly after the two inquests, it was announced that Sir Peter Imbert, the Metropolitan Police Commissioner, was to receive a cheque for £1.5 million from the grateful US Drug Enforcement Agency administration. It was said to be Britain's share of more than £200 million worth of assets seized following that joint Anglo-American operation, which had rolled up a worldwide web of crooked deals uncovered by detectives investigating the Brinks Mat gold bullion robbery and 'other crimes'. However, one of Charlie's oldest criminal associates said: 'I'd call it bounty money for Charlie being killed: £1.5 million is peanuts, so why else would they bother paying that? It's a bloody disgrace.' But the cash award was the only public hint that a massive surveillance operation had been under way on the Costa del Sol for years.

Eventually, legislation had to be passed in the US to enable the British authorities to get their reward money. All the relevant law enforcement agencies claimed that 'international agreements' were starting to mesh and that would spell even bigger problems for major criminals. The reality was that the drugs business, then estimated to be worth £70 billion a year throughout the world, was still making huge fortunes for certain individuals and with the stakes so high, murder had become virtually a daily occurrence. As one senior Scotland Yard detective explained at the time: 'Ten, or even five, years ago they simply didn't have the bottle to kill in the way they do now.'

On 2 January 1993, another hit-man victim was linked to the Charlie

Wilson case. Scotland Yard detectives believed that businessman and property developer Donald Urquart might have invested in some of the same drug deals as Charlie. Urquart was shot dead in broad daylight in London's West End by a man on a motorcycle. The description of the man who murdered Charlie matched that of the shooter who blasted Urquart to death and there was soon press speculation that Billy 'Porky' Edmunds was responsible, although this was ludicrous since Edmunds was in prison for a number of offences at the time. Others on the Costa del Crime claimed that Urquart might have been killed in revenge for Charlie's death. Urquart himself was considered something of a criminal eccentric because most of his business deals were carried out in the back of his stretched chauffeur-driven Rover, which contained several phones and a fax machine.

In early 1995, Charlie's old pal Mickey 'The Pimpernel' Green ran a red light at a busy Dublin city junction in his Bentley and killed a taxi driver. Green was fined and banned from driving, but there was uproar in Ireland because he was not given a custodial sentence, despite the death of an innocent man. Under mounting pressure, Eire police said they intended to confiscate all of Green's assets, so the Londoner disappeared. Later, it was claimed during another trial that Green had bribed two witnesses in the death-crash court case to keep himself out of jail. Green then turned up once again on the Costa del Sol, using yet another of his numerous forged passports. 'He was still wanted in France and the UK, so he kept a bit of a low profile, but he was around,' explained one old face out in Spain. Green was closely associated with many of the criminals involved on both sides of the hit on Charlie Wilson.

In a surprise move in early May 1995, Inspector Juan Lorenzo returned to the UK and tried to interview Billy 'Porky' Edmunds, by now thirty-four years old and serving a nine-year sentence in Durham Jail for wounding, assault and possession of drugs. One of the Scotland Yard detectives, who accompanied Juan Lorenzo on his trip to the north of England, said: 'Edmunds went crazy in the interview room, and turned the furniture over and insisted he had nothing to do with the Wilson hit. Juan was shocked by his response and Edmunds then refused to answer any questions.'

The police believed that Edmunds' behaviour implied he was guilty of killing Charlie. Yet Juan Lorenzo still failed to get either Edmunds or Roff extradited from the UK. Scotland Yard remained baffled by their failure to bring the two men to justice. One London detective said: 'They had to make a request and they never did. You'll have to ask them why.' During that trip to London, Pat Wilson was asked to re-identify Billy 'Porky' Edmunds from a piece of video footage filmed around that time. Pat now said she was only 70 per cent certain he was the man who killed her husband; earlier, she'd been 90 per cent certain. Why was she backtracking? Billy 'Porky' Edmunds' parents – when interviewed at their south London home in October 2003 – claimed Pat Wilson deliberately identified their son to take the attention away from those really responsible for her husband's death. 'He didn't do it, I swear,' said Edmunds' father.

While still in London, Inspector Lorenzo also questioned Jimmy Rose's wife Patty, and Eamon Evans, the man whose name was given by the killer after he knocked on Charlie's front door. Patty Rose admitted to Lorenzo she knew the Wilson family, but insisted she had no recollection of phoning or seeing Charlie in January 1990. Evans, who still owned a house on the Costa del Sol, told the Spanish detectives through an interpreter that he could not remember where he'd first met Charlie Wilson or when he had last seen him. Evans also denied knowledge of any connections between Charlie, Jimmy Rose and Roy Adkins. Evans was surly and uncooperative, but became even more agitated when the Spanish detective asked why the killer had mentioned Evans' first name at the door to the Wilson's villa. The interview was terminated shortly afterwards.

Billy 'Porky' Edmunds was transferred to Whitemoor Prison, in Cambridgeshire, shortly after Inspector Lorenzo's visit to Durham. He told his family he still feared for his life because of his alleged link to the Charlie Wilson hit. 'He knew Charlie had a lot more mates in Whitemoor and we were really worried,' explained his father. Edmunds had good reason to be afraid because many in Whitemoor were hardened old crims who knew the Great Train Robbers. They included Charlie's old friend Joey Pyle, who'd run the illegal gambling club, The Charterhouse, with Charlie in the early 1960s.

Pyle had been sent to Whitemoor in 1995 after being found guilty on drugs charges he insisted were 'a fit up'. He soon heard that the man rumoured to have 'done' his friend Charlie was housed in a cell in a neighbouring wing. Pyle recalled: 'I said to another inmate I didn't want him coming anywhere near me 'cause of what he'd done to Charlie, but then this geezer went and told Edmunds I had the hump with him and he insisted on coming to meet me. I thought he was mad, but gave him the benefit of the doubt and agreed to see him. He swore on his grandmother's grave that someone had wrongly picked him out of a photo album and he really didn't do it.'

Pyle added: 'He seemed a nice enough kid and nothing more than an old-fashioned thief from what I could see, and I couldn't really see a bloke like that coming to see me if he had done Charlie.' Pyle then added: 'Look, I don't know who shot Charlie. They said it was Edmunds but Edmunds told me he didn't do it. I don't know what happened. I certainly don't believe that Charlie named someone. This was a man known as 'the silent one'. He doesn't just tell another villain to name someone. That's not Charlie's style. I know Charlie didn't deserve it and he certainly didn't expect it either. All that karate chop stuff. It was strange then they did the legs of the dog. Doesn't make no sense.'

Joey Pyle confirmed Charlie's meeting with Brian Wright and Roy Adkins at Windsor Racecourse in the January before his death. 'Look, Charlie had certainly drifted into doing a bit of stuff and I know all three were at the races together, but that's it.' Pyle described Jimmy Rose as 'a nice fellow'. He went on: 'Brian Wright worked for me as a croupier at The Charterhouse, which Charlie and I ran, but Wright's not the kind of bloke to get Charlie killed. As far as Adkins is concerned, he was certainly well known in his little circle. I've no idea if it was him who got Charlie done. It's not my business to say who it might have been. I simply don't have a fuckin' clue.'

Charlie's old friend Freddie Foreman says today that Charlie's murder 'will never be forgotten'. He said: 'Edmunds will have to watch his back for the rest of his life if he did do it. These sorts of jobs are never cancelled. They're never forgotten. It doesn't matter how long ago it was. Payback can come at any time. He could be in his 70s before they get him, but it'll happen.'

4

And so the spiral of violence continued: At 3 a.m. on 10 February 1996, Danny 'Scarface' Roff, recently released from prison at the age of 35, was in an upstairs bar at the Passport Club in New Cross, south-east London, when a gunman walked in and sprayed the crowded bar with bullets, smashing Roff's spine and hitting a girl of 16 in the arm.

Miraculously, Scarface survived, but the incident raised serious questions about why the Spanish police had never charged him with Charlie's murder. Scotland Yard had no doubt Roff was targeted to avenge Charlie's killing. One detective said after the attack that Roff knew who shot him, but was too terrified to tell them.

A few weeks later, the now crippled and wheelchair-bound Roff and his family moved into a £300,000 five-bedroom house in Wanstead Road, Bromley, Kent, and promptly tried to turn it into a virtual fortress. Workmen installed ten-foot-high lattice fencing. One man whose garden backed onto Roff's property said that the family were so terrified of something that 'they wouldn't talk to anyone and they were determined to be left alone'. The neighbour's wife once tried to talk to Roff in the garden one day, but he had told her to get lost.

Roff's £20,000 Mercedes was specially adapted for him to drive because of his injuries, although as the months passed he left the house less and less frequently. Then neighbours noticed he stopped going in the garden with his two young sons. 'He looked terrible, pale and shaking and hardly able to stand because of his injuries. He looked like a dead man walking, even then,' said one neighbour.

On a quiet Monday morning in March 1997, Roff – released from jail after being inside for three months on remand – pulled into his driveway. The front garden was littered with toys belonging to his two young sons. Scarface was about to heave his crippled frame over onto his wheelchair when a dirty, white Ford Escort van pulled up outside the house and two masked gunmen opened fire, shooting him in the head and chest, and leaving him sprawled on the driveway. They sped off down the neat, tree-lined residential road in the van with its back doors flapping open. It was later found abandoned half a mile away.

Roff's wife Tina rushed out of the house on hearing the gunshots and dialled 999 on her mobile phone. Within minutes, police had sealed off the area. An air ambulance landed on nearby parkland and took Scarface to the Royal London Hospital in east London, where surgeons fought for, but ultimately failed to save, his life.

Back in Bromley, one neighbour told a local newspaper reporter: 'When I heard the shots I knew it came from their house. They didn't fit in here and they were the only people I could imagine this happening to.' Detectives quickly announced that Scarface's death was linked to the feud started by Charlie's murder, which had already cost at least three other people their lives. Drugs were obviously the main motivation behind the killings. After all, Roff had lived in a pricey suburban house and drove an expensive car with no visible source of income. Police hoped his wife might shed some light on the murder, but it was more likely she'd take the same attitude as Pat Wilson. One south-London face pointed out that it only took them so long to ice Scarface because he'd only just got out of prison again.

★ ★ ★

In October 2003, Detective Inspector Juan Lorenzo – now a neat, tidy, even-stockier man with greying hair and in his late 40s – got out Charlie's case notes and began talking about the killing in detail in his tiny office at the newly built Marbella Police Station. It was still an extremely thin file, considering the serious nature of the case.

Lorenzo said: 'Yes, I interviewed Edmunds in jail. I also interviewed Eamon Evans. I think he was involved, but I was never able to charge him. But Roff and Edmunds were not extradited because the extradition was not sought by the court, which means that the court decided there was not enough evidence to guarantee a prosecution. The trouble was we had no actual evidence that Roff was in Spain at that time. There was other evidence, but it wasn't enough.' Lorenzo added: 'I have to be honest about this, I don't think we will ever see anyone go to court and be prosecuted now. It is too long ago.' Lorenzo did admit, however, that it was strange that Edmunds had never suffered the same fate as Roff. 'Maybe that means he is innocent. Who knows?'

Lorenzo believes the killer was delivering a clear message to Charlie and his friends and that was why he suffered the indignity of being kicked in the balls as well as being struck before being shot dead. 'This was a crime built out of hate,' said Lorenzo.

Charlie's murder had kicked off one of the deadliest feuds in British underworld history. At the centre of the struggle was the control of the drug routes from North Africa and South America to London. Police in the UK and Spain were watching the spread of cold-blooded violence with apprehension, but seemed unwilling to do anything to prevent it. The experts at Scotland Yard's elite SO-11, the criminal intelligence branch, said they couldn't even predict who'd be the next victim.

Gordon Goody was far from convinced by the Spanish Police's version of the events leading to his friend Charlie's death. He was also acquainted with Jimmy Rose, although he hadn't seen him for years. 'None of it makes much sense, none of it,' he said. 'Charlie would never have given no one no names. Never. And definitely not on the telephone. Christ, he thought his phone was hooked up [bugged]. Any case, you don't get chopped for giving out a name. You might get a good hiding, but that's about it.'

Goody even denied the existence of professional hit men who could have carried out the job. 'I don't know if there are any professional hit men. I've certainly never met one. I've done most things for money in my life, but I don't understand how anyone could kill for money. Although you never know with the young villains of today. For a couple of grand and a few lines of coke, they'll get a gun and use it. It's not like it was in my day – we just didn't do things like that.'

5

Some criminals on the Costa del Sol believe to this day that intelligence on Charlie was leaked by the DEA and other law enforcement agencies to rival criminals, which may have convinced Roy Adkins to have him killed. Many in Spain were eager to get rid of Charlie because he was threatening to take over one of the most profitable cocaine supply routes in the world. 'The law doesn't care if we live or die. It's another one out of the way whenever we get popped,' explained one of Charlie's closest friends.

This author has been told by a UK Customs source that copies of UK and Spanish surveillance reports did fall into the hands of criminals close to Klaas 'The Preacher' Bruinsma and Roy Adkins in Amsterdam. These reports were forwarded to Bruinsma's people by a unit of crooked Dutch policemen who'd been in his pocket for years and one of whom was eventually imprisoned for the hit-man murder of Bruinsma himself.

Freddie Foreman, once a full-time Costa del Crime resident and long-time friend of Charlie, is convinced Charlie's loyalty to master smuggler Jimmy Rose probably cost him his life. In an interview in Spain in April 2004, Foreman explained: 'Jimmy Rose sees himself as a master smuggler, not a criminal. He's been around a bit and this was all about Charlie protecting one of his mates. That's how we saw it at the time. Jimmy had a problem and Charlie thought he was helping.

Adkins overreacted. It's as simple as that. In the case of Mickey Blackmore, Adkins owed him money. He was another link in the chain so when he got out of Maidstone Prison, he went after his money. He was screamin' about wanting his money and then got thrown off a bridge. You can draw your own conclusions from that. But poor old Charlie just didn't see his end coming.'

One particular aspect of Charlie's life in the months before his death has always haunted Foreman. He explained: 'The word back then was that Charlie had cancer. But there's no way he would have got himself killed to help Pat. What would be the sense in that? That's a mad, crazy idea, but there's so many things about his death that just don't make no sense.'

In south London, Edmunds' parents still insist their son did not kill Charlie. His father said: 'Billy was interviewed in prison and they didn't charge him. Billy's even built up his own file that's with his solicitor. It's filled with evidence that proves he couldn't have killed Charlie Wilson. He was more than a thousand miles away at the time of the murder. We know where he was.'

Mr and Mrs Edmunds believe Charlie might have been murdered on the orders of a jealous lover. 'It could have been one of his girlfriends. There were enough of them.' At the time of this interview with the Edmunds family, Billy was once again on the run after failing to keep to his bail conditions. Mr Edmunds explained: 'Yes, it's true, he's on his toes again, but he's determined to prove his innocence over the Wilson killing. You gotta understand Billy has never even been involved in drugs. OK, he's smoked a bit of pot, but that's it.'

Edmunds' own wife and children are said to be desperately worried about him. His father explained: 'We know Billy flipped out when the Spanish police went to see him about Charlie Wilson, but they were trying to suggest that just because he got upset at the mention of Charlie's name that meant he was trying to hide something, but my Billy's no killer. He just wouldn't do that to another human being. He's not that kind of boy.'

Edmunds' father even went to a south London police station to plead his son's innocence after his name was connected to the later hit on Donald Urquart in 1993. Mr Edmunds made the following point: 'You have to ask yourself why wasn't Billy or Roff extradited if they were so guilty? Everyone who matters knows our Billy did not murder Charlie Wilson. That's why he's alive today. If he'd done it, he would be dead by now.'

Mr and Mrs Edmunds say it's 'outrageous' that there was a four-year gap between Pat's original identification of their son and her later identification of him when the Spanish police visited the UK in 1995, explaining that during the intervening time Billy's photo had been in countless newspapers so she could simply have recognised him from that publicity.'

Over in another part of south London, relatives of the late Danny Roff, the other man alleged to be one of Charlie's killers, also insisted he was innocent. His cousin Patsy said in an interview on 29 October 2003: 'He didn't do it. A lot of unfair things were said about him. They weren't charged with it or extradited. That says it all. We all know he didn't do it. My cousin and Edmunds were convenient red herrings.' Patsy Roff didn't return any more of my calls, nor did I hear from Scarface's widow Tina.

One of Charlie's oldest friends, now retired and living near the Costa del Sol, also knew both Roff and Edmunds. He explained: 'Look, Danny and Porky worked together as a team and I've heard that Porky is still looking for the people who did Danny and, of course, other people are after him. This thing's not over yet.'

Master smuggler Jimmy Rose, perhaps the key figure in this entire real-life drama, invited me into his £500,000 detached home in Kent on 6 November 2003. Rose, now in his late 60s, began by talking to me about himself. What it was like coming out of prison after that long stretch inside for the Operation Diplomat bust, finding himself an old man. How squash courts have disappeared and been replaced by golf courses. Rose – a very anxious, nervy, yet fit-looking character for his age – literally sat on the edge of his seat throughout our 30-minute interview. 'I'm not a criminal. Smuggling's my game. I'm the fella who just takes the orders and gets on with the work. I'm not a heavy at all.'

Rose told how he first met Charlie when they were in jail together in the '50s. 'We became lifelong mates. Charlie was a wonderful man.' Then he slipped into the conversation, 'I've known Kenny Noye [M25 roadrage killer and Brinks Mat fence] for just as long and he's a decent fella as well. These blokes are just professionals. They're not bad people.'

When I asked Rose why he thought Charlie had been killed, he mentioned that he had heard it was about a woman *not* because of a drug deal. Then he shrugged, obviously embarrassed by talking about his close friend in such personal terms, but also keen to try and change the emphasis of the book. 'Maybe that's why the Spanish police didn't pursue it? Maybe they thought if it was because of a woman then . . . who knows?' He shrugged his shoulders again.

Rose then talked about Charlie Wilson the man. 'He didn't suffer fools gladly. He took the same attitude inside and outside. Get yer bird done. Get in, then get out, then get on with the business. Our families knocked around together. I visited Charlie in Spain and went down the clubs in Puerto Banus with him. He knew everyone. He seemed to have the perfect life.'

Jimmy Rose's voice lowered and he looked at the ground as he started talking about Charlie's murder. 'I was shocked when it happened. I was inside and felt really down when I heard. I can't talk about all these names said to be involved. But I only smuggle puff. I don't touch the white stuff.'

Rose naturally denied passing on Adkins' name to police. 'I think the police made it all up. It was a shame and it cost Charlie his life,' he said. Then Rose stopped talking for a few moments before adding: 'I could never talk about any of the boys. It's more than my life's worth.'

The Scotland Yard detective who visited Holland and found evidence of Charlie's dealings with Roy Adkins and his boss Klaas 'The Preacher' Bruinsma stumbled upon this information while he was investigating the hit-man killing of businessman Donald Urquart in London in 1993. The detective also confirmed that Billy Edmunds' father and sister visited him at a police station to insist Edmunds wasn't involved in Urquart's death, as well as Charlie's earlier killing. 'They were fed up with him getting mentioned for every killing that was going on, but I told them he wasn't being blamed for that one. Mind you, it's highly likely that Roff and Edmunds did do Charlie Wilson together. They stayed in partnership after escaping even though you'd expect anyone sensible to go their own way, but they didn't do that. We know they were in Holland together. I went to Holland to look into the Urquart job and to find out more about Adkins. I saw evidence in Holland that Wilson visited Amsterdam many times between 1987 and 1990 on drug meets with Adkins and Klaas Bruinsma.'

Back in Marbella, Charlie's architect friend Marti Franco still fears for her life. She explained: 'I am angry because of what I experienced. For a criminal, everything that happened that day might seem normal, but for me it was terrifying. It was a bad experience. Something you only usually see in the movies. I saw it all with my own eyes and it was scary. I don't want to talk about it any more.'

In London, Charlie's relatives all said that Pat would not help with the writing of this book. One of Charlie's closest relatives in south London commented when asked that 'the past is the past'. 'Good luck with your book,' he continued. 'He's dead and you can write what you like. But Pat's getting on now and she won't want to help.'

However, that same family member had a message from Pat to the Edmunds family: 'She wasn't 100 per cent certain he was one of Charlie's killers. Maybe it was another bloke. Who knows? But you gotta understand Pat has tried to put all this behind her. We feel sorry for the Edmunds family. We really do. It seems wrong that they are living their lives in fear, it really does.'

In a very frank interview, another of Charlie's relatives noted, 'If you live by the sword you die by the sword.' Continuing: 'I don't know who did it, but maybe a woman was involved in it? So many people just want to blame his criminal activities, but maybe it wasn't that after all.'

Another of Charlie's family members agreed to speak to this author on the morning of 29 October 2003 after hearing about my inquiries. 'We all loved Charlie, we really did. He had his job, but the rest of the family are all straight. His daughters now all have families of their own and they are leading respectable lives. Pat is getting on now. We've all moved on, but we'll never forget Charlie. He was a one-off.'

Charlie's relative then switched the conversation to the subject of Charlie's failing health. 'Look, Charlie had emphysema even though he wasn't a smoker. The guy who blew him away did him a favour in the end because that was going to kill him anyway. He was very ill. He called it his spongy lung.'

One of the detectives who investigated Charlie's murder on behalf of the Westminster Coroner remains puzzled about why Billy Edmunds was never charged with Charlie's murder. In an interview in the autumn of 2003 he said: 'The Spanish police had enough to bring Edmunds back, but they didn't. I'm surprised they haven't done it, but you'll have to ask Juan Lorenzo why.'

In February 2000, Charlie's pal Mickey Green's Irish lawyer was shadowed to a hotel in the Spanish city of Barcelona by UK Customs agents who'd been investigating Green's links to the Mafia and Colombian drug cartels for years. When Green turned up, he was arrested by Spanish police and immediately transported to the nation's most secure jail in Madrid. An extradition hearing was set for Green and it seemed just a formality before he'd be heading home to London and a long stretch inside. Newspapers at the time estimated Green's personal fortune to be at least £50 million. Green also still faced a long prison sentence back in France for earlier drug offences. Mickey Green isn't known as The Pimpernel for nothing, though; shortly after his dramatic arrest in Barcelona, a Spanish court refused to extradite him after insisting UK Customs did not have enough concrete evidence to mount a prosecution.

At supergrass Michael Michael's trial at the Old Bailey in 2001, prosecutor Nicholas Loraine-Smith named Mickey Green as a major drugs baron. He said of Green: 'He was and continues to be involved in importing large amounts of drugs into this country.' It was also said in court that Green had organised the murders of at least two other criminals. These days, Mickey Green spends much of his time either on the Costa del Crime or in Costa Rica, where he owns another luxury home. He's also been rumoured to be planning a property purchase in Thailand.

As someone involved in his Barcelona arrest says: 'Mickey's a survivor, but you can be sure he's watching his back very carefully.'

No one in the underworld does something for nothing: a thief only obeys the stick of violence or the carrot of cash.

6

Crime booms in recessions. There will always be young men out there happy enough to pull triggers for money or grudges. It's as flash as playing for Chelsea or being a big-time fighter. It's showbiz. And as Legs Diamond says in the musical named after him: 'I'm in showbiz, only a critic can kill me.'

So where does all this bloodletting leave us? There'll always be a gangland; the police know that and merely wonder how to stop its boundaries spreading. These days they are more reluctant to get in amongst the criminals, like they did in Charlie's day. The chances of planting an undercover cop in the most potent gangs are very slim. Budgets, politics and ethics have all played their role in changing the rules of the game.

For at least the last 100 years, the emphasis has been on trying to read the soul of the criminal and that is what, to a certain extent, I've tried to do with the story of Charlie Wilson. Was he really a born criminal or did he develop those instincts from the circumstances in which he was brought up as a child? Many have attempted to prove that criminal characteristics are inherited. Others will argue, on almost Marxist terms, that society has the criminals it deserves. In other words, society causes crime. In Charlie Wilson's case, there do seem to be a few clues which point in that direction. A difficult relationship with his father, an uncontrolled juvenile life on the streets, and a brutal fight for survival from a young age.

Crime is undoubtedly a mental activity. Criminals like Charlie Wilson made a choice, which doesn't necessarily mean he could do anything to stop it. Those early days of abject hunger sparked within him a need to get out of control and led to antisocial behaviour, which manifested itself in many different forms from sexual to financial. In my opinion, Charlie's most significant role was the hunger for recognition, for admiration, to be respected. All of us have this innate need, but in a criminal like Charlie Wilson it loomed abnormally large.

That hunger for recognition was a psychic need. Fromm, in his *The Anatomy of Human Destructiveness*, called it 'the need to make a dent'. Charlie wanted to let the world know he existed. That demand for more life was all consuming and often at other people's expense. Charlie once said that he could never match the buzz he felt as the train robbers were throwing those mailbags containing £2.6 million into their lorry. This is that very mechanism of hunger at work. It is a fact of human psychology which cannot either be condemned or approved. It is a simple fact of life. The problem is that it can manifest itself in either a positive or negative fashion. In its positive form, it leads to entrepreneurs, captains of industry. But in Charlie, it resulted in the ultimate risk-taking enterprise – crime.

Charlie was very much a criminal in the traditional sense. In simple terms, he refused to accept life as he found it. He didn't just want to steal an apple from a tree, he wanted to burn the orchard down as well. Charlie was the archetypal scavenger, always on the lookout for an opportunity. He suffered badly from long bouts of boredom and depression that could often only be conquered by committing crime.

Friends and relatives say that Charlie often felt stifled and trapped, viewing crime and sometimes even violence as the only means of escaping from his metaphorical straitjacket. Charlie was the complete criminal – his existence a chain reaction which could only end in his imprisonment for life, or death.

Men like Charlie didn't need to stub their toes to react; he was continually on tenderhooks, prepared to hit back at society because he didn't feel he owed it anything. Like many other criminals, Charlie also never saw himself as being in the wrong; if he did say sorry, it was an unnatural response in a moment of weakness, which he would later regret. This can be illustrated in the case of train driver Jack Mills, attended to by Charlie after one of the gang coshed him.

Charlie truly was the stranger among us, never one of us. Many labels have been hung on him over the years, but they don't tell half the story. Yes, he was a rebel and psychopath; two shorthand symbols for a state of mind which is hate. Freud said that if a baby had power, it would destroy the world from the frustration of its infantile desires. In some ways, Charlie was the baby who quite simply never grew up. That's why he felt so superior to everyone around him.

At the height of his criminal prowess in the 1960s, the rules of the game were constantly being challenged. Yet young criminals like Charlie needed rules to ensure their lives had some meaning. Charlie's aggressive instincts were undoubtedly born out of sheer frustration with the world. It all seemed so meaningless to him. There was that feeling of hopeless drifting. As his crimes started to bring in previously unimagined wealth, he also committed some offences, like stealing cars, purely for the thrill. Even in this environment, there was a structure emerging. Codes and rank within his gang were obeyed to the letter. This was a classic example of youths seeking a purposeful group identity.

So the young Charlie, like many before and since, reacted partly against his own feelings of inadequacy. Many of his contemporaries say that if he'd had more self-knowledge when he was younger, then he would not have struck out for a life of crime with such determination. To me, Charlie Wilson was self-destructive basically because his life had no real purpose, despite loving his wife and children, and remaining married for his entire adult life. Charlie still felt alienated throughout.

Throwing him into prison did nothing to stem the problem. Charlie was a criminal who was intrinsically lacking in the normal psychological vitamins. His whole life was an act of hunger. To treat him properly would have required an examination of his psyche and hopefully that has now been achieved. Punishment was wasted on Charlie. It was no better than caging an animal demented by hunger and expecting it to reform. The kind of hunger from which Charlie Wilson suffered bred a terrible hatred that fed on itself.

★ ★ ★

AFTERMATH

It was typical of Charlie that he took with him to the grave the secret of his real role in the Great Train Robbery. While so many of the gang cashed in through films and books, he remained steadfastly quiet. In some ways, he relished his underworld nickname, 'the Silent One'. But then, this was a man who neither gave evidence nor called witnesses; he didn't even utter a word when he was sentenced. It was all part of a deeply rooted criminal philosophy Charlie had developed while a youth in south London: 'Never tell the police a thing. Never give an inch.'

When Pat sold her story to the *News of the World*, it was only because Charlie had given her permission from his prison cell and she was desperate for cash. Pat once said the Great Train Robbery was supposed to put them 'in clover' for the rest of their lives. Charlie was supposedly the only man who knew where the rest of the money was hidden and the size of each cut. Whatever the full extent of his power and influence over the other gang members, Charlie also revelled in his image as one of the brains behind the robbery. He wanted to prove that crime really did pay.

Charlie Wilson and the rest of the Great Train Robbers were a unique criminal team. In many ways, they worked like a business syndicate; they were young executives of crime. Yet, it mustn't be forgotten that most of them were perfectly willing to wield a cosh and use it if necessary. Charlie was their skilful organiser, sufficiently intelligent to think ahead and with enough insight into human nature to be part of a top-notch team. He knew how to use alibis, how to appear at ease in the dock or witness box.

The Great Train Robbery caught people's imagination because of its size and cunning. Charlie couldn't resist the buzz of robbing and felt, like many others, that the banks and post offices deserved to be punished for not protecting their money sufficiently. He also loved pitting his wits against Scotland Yard and its worldwide reputation for skill and dogged determination. Charlie always considered he had one big advantage over the long arm of the law: the police had to work within certain rules and regulations while he, on the other hand, could do anything he wanted.

For a giant of a man like Charlie, violence was his *raison d'être*. He'd grown up in gangs where a fight was the natural means to settle a dispute and he could never truly appreciate the middle class's abhorrence of violence. Charlie, and most of the others, shared a background in the subculture of working-class south London. Back then, there was an endemic poverty juxtaposed with a richer life just a few miles away, north of the river.

Charlie had been determined from a young age to pull himself out of the poverty trap and no one could help him apart from himself. He had a selfish drive to escape from the slums of Battersea. To call Charlie a Robin Hood-style villain would be a gross insult to the real star of Sherwood Forest. Charlie became an urban bandit who was probably given a little too much credit as an honourable human being.

There is an intriguing core of loyalty from many of Charlie's associates, however. Even virtual strangers came to him with information, often not even wanting money or a drink, but because they enjoyed helping the robber's battle against the Establishment. As E.J. Hobsbawm wrote in his book *Bandits*: 'The crucial fact about the bandit's social situation is its ambiguity. He is an outsider and a rebel, a poor man who refuses to accept the normal rules of poverty and establishes his freedom by means of the only resources within the reach of the poor: strength, bravery, cunning and determination. This draws him close to the poor; he is one of them. It sets him in opposition to the hierarchy of power, wealth and influence: he is not one of them.'

Since the Great Train Robbery in 1963, many Metropolitan Police officers have been thrown out of the force for corruption, having fabricated evidence or dropped charges in exchange for cash. A lot of this overt corruption convinced Charlie and many of the other train robbers that their crimes weren't so bad. Yet throughout his life Charlie showed total repugnance for the rules and formalities of the modern state – driving licences, permits, paying taxes, passports, even National Insurance Stamps. This was why he and the others appealed to the poor so much.

There was undoubtedly something seductive about the life Charlie and many of the other train robbers led. They seemed to be the last of a dying breed who despite their crimes still relied upon those old-fashioned virtues of courage and loyalty. Charlie's life stood and fell on the strength of friendships. He'd taken to crime in the first place to escape dire poverty and the sort of tedious, repetitive job his father had slaved over for such a long period of time.

Charlie's wife Pat responded throughout their marriage with undying loyalty; knowing all along that her beloved Charlie would never actually run off with another woman. This explains her refusal to find a man when Charlie was facing such a long stretch in prison. And in this domestic context, Charlie must be seen as a good family man despite his love affairs with other women.

In many ways, Charlie saw himself as one of the shock troops of the militant poor. That's why he fell out with his own father, who quite simply did not understand where his son was coming from. Of course, Charlie knew that, ultimately, crime did not pay, but he couldn't stay away from it because it was the main part of his life. He loved the buzz. He adored the planning. And most of all he was ecstatic about the smell and feel of cash. There was, he told one friend, nothing to match that feeling. But it was that quest for yet another roller-coaster ride that eventually led to his downfall.

Charlie clearly saw obedience to the law and collaboration with the police as a betrayal of his own people, which would mean losing all self-respect, but it was his love of gambling that was probably the most pertinent facet of his personality. There seems little doubt that even if he'd known before the train robbery that there was, at best, a one in five chance they'd escape with their loot, he and the others would still have taken a punt on the so-called crime of the century.

Charlie's obsession with money was fuelled by a desire for the better things in life: freedom, comfort, cleanliness, light, privacy and respect. But the good life that he so desperately craved was never going to be paved with gold. Charlie believed that the robbery which was supposed to justify the means was destroyed by those very same means. He knew the risks were high, but was one of the few robbers not to lose their friends (and, in some cases, wife) after the robbery.

Violence was explained away by Charlie and his boys as 'the name of the game' or 'what had to be done'. The evil that so many thought was endemic in the train robbers can be found in any of us and has little to do with the law of the land. There has always been a tendency to look back at a 'golden era' of crime, as if there was once a magical time when no one got hurt, crooks only attacked other crooks and a strict code of honour ruled. This theme of not hurting civilians was disproved by the attack on driver Jack Mills during the train robbery. And one must never forget the only true Robin Hoods in south London are the pubs.

Some look back with the sort of nostalgia one usually reserves for old people's homes. As one old-time crook said: 'We always wore suits, ties, collars. Today they're walking about with designer stubble and dirty old shoes, and you think – where's the pride gone?' Train robber Tommy Wisbey summed it up: 'Years ago, we could go out on blags, as you would call them, and you would be able to go home to sleep and you wouldn't worry about who you told because you were all united. There was more camaraderie than there is today. All the principals have gone by the wayside.' As for the underworld: 'There's no such thing as the underworld, they're just criminals, aren't they, known criminals.'

In the end, there was little respect left for the elder statesmen of crime like Charlie Wilson, shot dead in the sanctuary of his own home. As one of his oldest pals commented: 'What's the world fuckin' coming to when someone like Charlie is gunned down in front of his wife? There was things you did and did not do. Now it's just bang, bang you're dead. End of story.'

Postscript

RONNIE BIGGS lived in Rio de Janeiro, Brazil, until 2001 when he surrendered to British police and is currently languishing in a cell at Belmarsh Prison in south-east London, despite appalling ill health.

LUISA 'LA PATRONA' BOLIVAR is these days residing in a British prison after being found guilty of organising the killing of another South American, nicknamed 'Little Egg', who'd upset her lover, a drugs boss known as 'Snake Hips'.

CHEQUERS is today owned by a Polish princess who's trying to sell it for £1.5 million. It's no longer called Chequers but 'La Joya' although Charlie's beloved wall still stands to this day.

THE COSTA DEL CRIME continues to thrive even though many of the old familiar faces have been replaced by hardnosed Russians and Eastern Europeans, who are now said to be running more than 70 per cent of all the illegal activities on the coast.

BRIAN 'THE PROFESSOR' DORAN eventually returned to Britain from Colombia. In the late 1990s, he was sentenced to 25 years in a UK prison after being arrested in possession of millions of pounds worth of cocaine.

DRUGS have come tumbling down in price and many criminals have stopped handling them because the profits are so low. When Charlie was alive, cannabis sold for £675 a kilo. Today, it's down to an all-time low of £350 a kilo. A £50,000 investment in a shipment of cocaine will be lucky to earn an investor £10,000 profit. Says one UK drug smuggler in Spain: 'Your money's better off in the bank.'

BILLY 'PORKY' EDMUNDS is still alive despite his alleged connections to the hit on Charlie. He's currently on the run once again but continues to insist, through his family, that he is innocent of all involvement in Charlie's death.

RONALD 'BUSTER' EDWARDS hanged himself at the age of 63 on 29 November 1994 in a lock-up garage near the flower stall he had run at Waterloo Station for many years. He had a serious drinking problem and was suffering from depression.

GEORGIE ELLIS, picked up by Charlie on the seafront at Marbella, was exposed as a prostitute in a *News of the World* article in February 1995. It claimed the blonde made £300,000 a year running an international ring of 20 hookers. In late 2000, Georgie was diagnosed with cancer of the bladder and she died in December 2001, aged just 50.

PABLO 'EL DOCTOR' ESCOBAR was killed by Colombian security forces with the tacit approval of both the DEA and other law enforcement agencies in a bloody shoot-out in Medellín on 2 December 1993.

BERNIE FINCH kept the Wilsons' dog called Dino, which died in 2003. Charlie's neighbour moved to another house in Marbella after spending many years trying to sell his home next door to Chequers. He says Charlie's murder was the beginning of the end of his love affair with Spain and he'd dearly love to move back to the UK.

'FRENCHY' has never been unmasked and is said to have disappeared from London criminal haunts shortly after Charlie's recapture in Canada in 1968.

FREDDIE 'THE MEAN MACHINE' FOREMAN is enjoying a pleasant retirement following his release from prison after serving time for the Security Express heist. He regularly jets between homes in London and Spain with his partner Janice.

MICKEY 'THE PIMPERNEL' GREEN is still wanted in Britain and Ireland as the mastermind behind a drugs racket worth £130 million. He spends a lot of time on his toes, but frequently slips back onto the Costa del Crime to see some of the chaps.

ROY 'THE WEASEL' JAMES died of a heart attack on 21 August 1997 after a catalogue of problems in the 1990s, culminating in January 1994 when a court heard he'd shot his former father-in-law three times and pistol-whipped his ex-wife in a row over their divorce settlement. James was jailed for six years for the attacks.

INSPECTOR JUAN LORENZO still works from the police station in Marbella, but is looking forward to a long and healthy retirement. He openly admits he is unlikely ever to make any arrests for Charlie's murder.

NOSHER POWELL lives in a quiet suburb in the south of London, close to where he and Charlie used to meet so often. He sometimes pops into the graveyard where Charlie is buried, but says, 'It's gettin' a bit overgrown these days.'

NORMAN RADFORD, Charlie's cousin, now lives on the Costa del Sol. He loyally tried to sort out all Charlie's affairs after his death, but hasn't spoken to Pat since asking her about the identity of Charlie's killer some years ago.

JIMMY ROSE is now out of prison and back living in 'quiet retirement' in Kent trying to come to terms with all the death and destruction caused by the drugs industry.

BRUCE 'THE COLONEL' REYNOLDS wrote his autobiography, which was published in 1995, and he now lives in a modest flat in Croydon, south London.

TONY 'KING OF CATFORD' WHITE was seized at gunpoint by Spanish police at Madrid Airport in June 2003 over an alleged plot to smuggle £4 million worth of cocaine. Hours earlier, a Newmarket racehorse trainer was arrested in the same city with 60 kilos of the drug hidden in a horsebox.

PAT WILSON lives a very quiet life near to her beloved daughters in south London and has never recovered from the shock of her husband's brutal killing. She hasn't seen any of her husband's old associates since Charlie's funeral.

BRIAN 'THE MILKMAN' WRIGHT was in 2002 branded by a British court as one of the world's most powerful drug dealers after his son and 14 other gang members were jailed for more than 200 years following a 6-year investigation by law enforcement officers in the UK, Ireland, Spain and the US. Wright remains one of the UK's most-wanted men, alongside Mickey Green.

Bibliography

Biggs, Ronald (1994) *Odd Man Out: My Life on The Loose and The Truth About the Great Train Robbery*, Pan, London

Bowden, Mark (2002) *Killing Pablo: The Hunt for the World's Richest Outlaw*, Atlantic Books, New York

Campbell, Duncan (1996) *The Underworld: That Was Business, This Is Personal*, Penguin, London

Cater, Frank and Tullett, Tom (1990) *The Sharp End: Inside Scotland Yard's Flying Squad*, Grafton, London

Ellis, Georgie with Taylor, Rod (2000) *A Murder of Passion: A Daughter's Memoir of the Last Woman to Be Hanged*, John Blake Publishing, London

Knight, Ronnie, Knight, John, Wilton, Detective Superintendent Peter with Sawyer, Pete (2002) *Gotcha!: The Untold Story of Britain's Biggest Cash Robbery*, Pan, London

Lambrianou, Tony (1992) *Inside The Firm: The Untold Story of the Krays' Reign of Terror*, Pan Macmillan, London

MacLaughlin, Duncan with Hall, William (2002) *The Filth: The Explosive Inside Story of Scotland Yard's Top Undercover Cop*, Mainstream Publishing, Edinburgh

McLagan, Graeme (2003) *Bent Coppers: The Inside Story of Scotland Yard's Battle Against Police Corruption*, Orion, London

Marks, Howard (1998) *Mr Nice: An Autobiography*, Vintage, London

Paul Read, Piers (1978) *The Train Robbers*, W.H. Allen, London

Porter, Bruce (1993) *Blow: How a Smalltown Boy Made $100 Million With the Medellín Cocaine Cartel and Lost It All*, HarperCollins, New York

Pyle, Joey (2003) *Notorious: The Changing Face of Organised Crime*, Virgin, London

Reynolds, Bruce (2003) *Crossing The Line: The Autobiography of a Thief*, Virgin, London

Reynolds, Bruce, Reynolds, Nick and Parker, Alan (2000) *The Great Train Robbery Files*, Abstract Sounds Publishing, London

Williams, Mel (2000) *Nearly Famous*, self-published